John Mc

Sept. 2024

A LOVE
OF
MOUNTAINS

John Mackay

EARNSHAW
BOOKS

A Love of Mountains
By John Mackay

ISBN-13: 978-988-8843-40-4

BIOGRAPHY & AUTOBIOGRAPHY

EB207

Published in Hong Kong by Earnshaw Books Ltd.

CHAPTER ONE

Mountains have always been part of my life. I was born in a mountainous area of Scotland, spent some of my early years in the Indian Himalayas and worked for thirty years as a doctor in Hong Kong, where I climbed most of the hills and mountains.

Aged 50, I decided that when I retired from full-time work, I would climb the highest point of as many countries as I could.

When I did retire eight years later, in 1993, I started climbing in earnest. In the next 26 years I climbed 34 high points. I began with Scotland.

At 58, I was young enough and fit enough, weighing about 120lbs, to look forward to many years of climbing expeditions. I was never a 'rock spider' scaling cliffs, encumbered with ropes, a harness, helmet and carabiners, or venturing into the 'death zone' over 8,000m with oxygen cylinders. I enjoyed the achievement of reaching a summit and also the ascent itself, in my own time, drinking in the views as they widened with altitude, feeling free, often on my own. Where it was necessary, I was accompanied by a guide. A few times I trekked with a group of friends, a different dynamic—companionship.

I was fortunate in that I had the ability to climb, the motivation to do it, and the opportunity. I had time to spare, my wife, Judith, traveled to many interesting places as part of her work. Either I went with her, and we climbed together, or I went off on my own to climb while she was committed elsewhere.

My most memorable moment was when my guide and I were the first people of that day to reach the summit of Mount Kilimanjaro. Seventy people had set out of whom only twelve summited.

My first memories of mountains come not from Scotland where I was born, but from India, the country where I lived from the ages of four to nine. During the summer, to escape the heat of the planes, my mother, brother Donald and I left the capital Delhi for the mountains — Simla at 2,276 metres (7,467 feet) in the north or the military camp at Jutogh, a suburb of Simla. From both places, we looked out at the Himalayan mountains, snowcapped, which ringed the horizon, the highest, Ghoralantinu at 4,760m. One summer we spent in Kashmir, overlooked by the massive Nanga Parbat, the Naked Mountain, 8,126m (26,660 ft). We spent our last summer in India, in 1945, near Darjeeling, at 2,042 metres (7,100 feet) in West Bengal. There the northern horizon was dominated by Kanchenjunga at 8,586 metres (28,169 feet). I have an autographed copy of the account of the first climb of this mountain by an Indian army expedition; I obtained it through barter with a member of the expedition in exchange for a bottle of Black Label Scotch whisky.

After we returned to Scotland, we lived on the Moray coast. The nearest mountain, to the south, was Ben Rinnes, 841 m (2,759 ft); it is part of the Grampian range. I climbed the mountain — a gentle walk for a 20-year-old, on tracks bordered by heather.

In the summer of 1960, while I was still a student, I climbed to the highest point in Denmark — or so I was led to believe. It was called Yding Skovhoj, height 173 metres or 567 feet. Up until

1941, it was not considered the country's highest point; that was Ejer Bavnehø, which had been measured as such in the middle of the 19th century. Then, in 1941, new measurements established that the top of one of Yding Skovhøj's burial mounds was higher. This started an intense debate about whether man-made structures could be counted as part of Denmark's highest point. It finished with Professor N.E. Nørlund defining the highest point as being the highest natural point, without including the height of man-made piles of earth. As Ejer Bavnehøj was higher than the highest natural point of Yding Skovhøj, it was then regarded as Denmark's highest point until February 2005. In that month, researchers discovered that Møllehøj was slightly taller at 170.86 m (561 ft). It is in the Ejerbjerge hills in Skanderborg municipality, very close to Ejer Bavnehøj. The summit is marked with a millstone, a remnant of Ejer mill, situated on the hill from 1838 to 1917. In Denmark, as in many countries, modern measuring techniques have established more accurate altitudes.

What is the definition of a mountain? In the United Kingdom, a mountain is most commonly defined as landform that rises at least 610 metres (2,000 feet) above sea level. Most geologists classify a mountain as a landform that rises at least 1,000 feet (300 Metres) or more above its surrounding area. In Scotland, the Munros are mountains over 3000 feet, 914.4 m, all 282 of them.

ENGLAND
Scafell Pikes
Height: 3,208 feet, 978 metres
Date: June 1989

This climb was part of a summer holiday adventure. I was on my way to Elgin, driving up from Newquay in Cornwall where I had been staying with my brother Donald and his wife Jo. From Newquay, I drove to Buckfast in Devon where I had lunch with my cousin Alastair and his wife Barbie. Then I proceeded to supper with my sister Eleanore and her husband, Les, near Gloucester, and spent the night at a local hotel.

Next morning, I drove up to the Lake District on the west coast road, the A595, to Wasdale, then up that valley to Wasdale Head, a farm steading and the end of the road leading to Shap

Fell. Well-trodden paths led up a steadily steepening incline, over short grass, accompanied by sheep, and other hikers; higher up was largely over scree.

The direct route was very steep beside high cliffs; there teams of rock-climbers, roped up, were defying gravity and disaster. I took a gentler route up to the north ridge and on to the summit cairn of rocks. A photograph at the summit, taken by another climber, shows me wearing a blood-donor T-shirt. The day was cool, grey, and clear, perfect for climbing. I descended by the same route. After the climb, I drove north to Dumfries to spend the night with my aunt and uncle, Johanna and Irving Miller: thence to Ben Nevis.

SCOTLAND
Ben Nevis
Height: 4,406 feet, 978 metres
Date: June 1989

I climbed the highest mountain in Scotland, and Britain, with my son Richard. Nearly eighteen, he had a leave-out after the end-of-year exams at Trinity College, Glenalmond. I picked him up from school, near Perth, and drove to Fort William via Glencoe. It was a grey day, and the glen was forbidding. We stopped at a memorial centre there to learn again of the massacre of the Macdonald clan by the Campbell clan in 1692. We stayed that night at a B&B at Fort William.

The next morning, we picked up climbing route maps at the tourist office, as well as food and drinks. I drove to the north-west foot of the mountain. We walked up the clear footpath on an easy gradient, firstly up the River Nevis valley, then across onto the northern open slope; an old road wound its way to the top where there were the remains of a building, and snow drifts.

At the summit, we were in cloud and freezing cold. In trainers rather than climbing boots, Richard did very well to keep going. Ruins of a weather-station on the summit gave some protection from the wind.

We were down the mountain in a third of the time, weary but elated. I drove us on to Elgin to stay with my aunt Gwen Mackay at Old Mills. (We had to disappoint my aunt Gwen by saying we were too tired for a cocktail party that night.) Richard found it difficult to convince his schoolmates of his achievement when he met them back at school the next week; he had not been noted for his hill-climbing ardour.

IRELAND
Carrantuohill
Height: 1,039 meters. 3,407ft
Date: September 27th, 1994

This expedition started from the house of my brother Donald in Newquay, Cornwall. Up at 5.45 a.m. in time for Jo, Donald's wife, to drive Judith and me to St Mawgan airport of Newquay, Judith flying to London on BA; me flying to Dublin, Ireland on South West Airways on a Piper Mohawk Chief, the pilot, Dave, was also the ground staff, baggage handler. As the last person in the row of seats, I was responsible for passing forward the in-flight coffee and biscuits.

The Airline publicity posters boasting flights to New York, was very deceptive. The Mohawk had two propellers and could take only eight passengers, cruising altitude 6,500 ft. (There is no record of this 'airline' in Government aviation statistics.)

We arrived on time and had a clear view over Dublin and the flat surrounding countryside. The airport toilet dispensed condoms, which I thought surprising for a Catholic country. At Dublin Airport I hired a small Peugeot car. I bought petrol from a friendly attendant, a Scotsman from Ballachulish, Scotland, who warned me against Irish pick-pockets.

It took me an hour to get through Dublin then had a 200-mile drive across pleasant rolling countryside via Limerick to Killarney.

I booked in at the Gleneagle Hotel, a large place full of tour groups, but with excellent indoor sports facilities. I bought "The Reeks" Ordnance Survey map.

The next morning, the cloud was down to 2,500 ft, but with no rain. At 9.15 a.m., I set off from the hotel, took the B562 Killorglin road out of Killarney, first left and along country roads till the road-end at Kate Kearny's Cottage, Knocknafreaghalin, in the Gaddagh River valley. At 10.00 a.m., I started along a clear but wet trail up the valley, crossing the river twice on stepping stones, up Hag's Glen to Lakes Callee and Gouragh; still under the cloud cover, sunlit plains were visible away out of the end of the valley.

By now it was 11.00; the valley was narrowed by cliffs on both sides. The mild incline up peat moss and stony paths gave way to "The Devil's Staircase", a steep stream bed of scree and boulders, a scramble. A misty rain persisted. At midday, I had reached Christ's Saddle, a very muddy crest of the ridge and top of the "Staircase". No summit was in sight through the cloud but a row of about 30 stone cairns, leading up to the right, marked a narrow path.

12.30: at the summit, there stood a 20-foot-high metal cross, and a low stone-walled shelter. A cold wind was driving the rain. I met other climbers, in pairs, and had a photograph of me taken at the summit for the record.

As I was carefully coming down the steep "staircase", a sheep started baaing persistently from the other edge of the gully. I saw no lamb, but it seemed to be trying to tell me something, like the best way down. So I crossed over to the other side where it had been standing and followed it down what did seem a relatively easier route. I was back at the hotel at 4.30 p.m.

The next day I drove back across Ireland to Dublin and handed back the car. I took the train to Dun Laoghaire and the historic Royal Marine Hotel; its former guests included everyone from Queen Victoria to Laurel and Hardy. The hotel overlooked the harbour and the quay, from which I took the ferry next morning to Holyhead in Wales.

WALES
Snowdon (Yr Wyddfa)
Height: 1085m, (3,560 feet)
Date: September 30, 1994

I arrived in Wales from Ireland on the "Sea Lynx" a catamaran owned by Stena Line. It was 74 metres long, with space for 425 passengers and 88 cars.

At Holyhead, I hired a car and drove to "Base Camp" at the Royal Victoria Hotel in Llanberis. There I found the mountaineering supply shop of famous climber Joe Brown and bought "Chris Brasher" climbing boots and a route guide to the Llanberis Path. The boots are still in use thirty years later.

At 9 a.m. the next morning, I set off from the hotel, just across the road from the mountain railway and the start of the Llanberis

Path. The path was well-marked; clouds hid the summit all the way to the Half-Way House; it was derelict and being rebuilt. Now in the cloud itself, I was cold and wet and so put on my Gortex suit. I made steady progress in minimal visibility. I was passed by a train, the last part of the path being alongside the railway.

At 11.15 a.m., I reached the summit, after a final climb over rocks to the Trig Point at the very top. I had a train passenger take my photo at the summit. The railway station just below the summit had a restaurant, Post Office, and toilet. I did not linger; there was nothing to see through the cloud. On the way down, I saw a young man with a black and white sheep dog, just like the pair I had seen three days before on Carrantuohill.

At 12.45 p.m., I was back at the hotel. I changed into dry clothes and checked out. I left at 2.00 p.m. and drove 200 miles along the North Wales scenic route via Betws-y-Coed and Llangollen and across the English Midlands to Saltburn-by-the-Sea in Yorkshire; I arrived there at 7.00 p.m. to stay with Judith's parents.

This ascent completed my climbs of the four highest peaks in the British Isles and Ireland.

HONG KONG
Tai Mo Shan
Height: 957 m, (3,140 feet)
Date: Jan 3–April 5, 1994

My second home country has been Hong Kong. Many people who have never been to Hong Kong envisage it as the concrete jungle of the city district bordering on the harbour. They are astonished to find that about three quarters of the area of Hong Kong is country park, and there are many hill walks and rural barbecue sites. Stone-paved trails that have been in use by villagers for centuries, and more modern trails laid down by a government keen to open up the mountains for the good health of the population. The most famous is the Trail opened in 1979 by Governor Sir Murray Maclehose.

I started walking the 100-km Maclehose Trail on 3rd January, to celebrate the beginning of my retirement from Drs Anderson & Partners, with whom I had worked for 30 years. I completed the Trail, at intervals, stage by stage.

Having completed Stages 1 to 5 over the mountains in Sai Kung, on 5th April, I started walking Stage 6 from the point where the Maclehose Trail crosses the Old Tai Po Road, at Kowloon reservoir. I walked a distance of 4.6 km round Kowloon Reservoir—a haunt of Macaque monkeys—along Smugglers Ridge, past the World War II defensive line "Charing Cross", to the Jubilee reservoir dam, the start of Stage 7. This stage was 10.4 km over Needle Hill and Grassy Hill to a point overlooking Tai Po and Lead Mine Pass. Finally, I reached Stage 8, and walked nearly another 10 km almost up to the top of Tai Mo Shan. The Government, police and weather station at the very top blocked the summit. When I looked north, the ground fell away to the coastal plane and the Sek Kong airstrip; beyond that were the Mai Po bird sanctuary, fish ponds and the Deep Bay of the Pearl River estuary, China beyond. To the south was Tsuen Wan and Lantau Island.

It was a hard walk. I was cramping by the end, having carried adequate liquid but not enough food. It took me seven hours from the start till I began my way home on a bus on route TWISK.

That summer, back in the UK, I determined to climb the highest peaks in Ireland and Wales.

JAPAN
Mt Fuji
Height: 3,774 meters (12,738 feet)
Date: September 11, 1995

I had given myself one week to climb two more Asian summits, on my own, Judith being at meetings elsewhere.

Mount Fuji is the highest mountain in Japan. It is located 100 kilometers southwest of Tokyo on the main island of Honshu. On a clear day, residents of the capital can see it. This proximity and its remarkable symmetrical cone have made it a symbol of Japan, depicted in art, poetry and photographs. Since June 2013, it has been a UNESCO World Heritage Site. Every year thousands of Japanese climb to the summit — a mixture of mountaineering and pilgrimage.

I flew to Japan from Hong Kong, arriving in the early afternoon at Narita Airport. At 4:13 p.m. I boarded a JR (Japan Railways) train NEX (Narita Express) to Shinjuku, Tokyo; it was reserved seating, comfortable and clean, with a mobile display giving names of stations and graphics of the rail route and distance covered. For the first few minutes, we passed through pleasant countryside, rice fields, wooded knolls and small hamlets. This quickly gave way to interminable, unattractive suburbia. First stop was Tokyo station, then high-rise office and hotel blocks and a long tunnel, reaching Shinjuku station at 5:42 p.m.

Plan One had been to stay overnight near Shinjuku and catch an early train to Kawaguchiko next day, rather than to arrive at Kawaguchiko at night with no hotel reservation. Having seen Tokyo, I felt it much more preferable that the scenery of next part of the trip should be covered in darkness. So, at 6:30 p.m., I caught a JR LEX (limited express) train to Otsuki. It was an open carriage, clean, basic and worse than British Rail 2nd class. There was a large noisy holiday party with their own hampers of food, and a trolley selling snacks, ice cream and beer. The very 'limited express' did not stop at many stations but never reached a high speed and arrived ten minutes late.

At 7:46 p.m., I only just caught the connection to the Fuji Kyoko train across the platform; staff were blowing the departure whistle and ringing the bell. There were two open carriages and few passengers; the guard was running up and down to collect tickets and get back to his cabin in time to open the doors at the next station. The train rattled uphill to Fuji-Yoshida, then backed out for its final stop at Kawaguchiko.

I telephoned from the station to make sure there was a room available before taking a 10-minute taxi ride to the Fuji View Hotel. It was a good choice—a western-style hotel: small single room with bath, IDD phone, television choices of four Japanese stations but no CNN or BBC. I ate snacks from the fridge— dried meat, dried fish, sausage and nuts—and drank green tea.

I watched an excellent football cup-tie between two Japanese teams; their leading players were from Europe and America.

12 September
I slept badly despite a comfortable bed and a quiet room; I had drunk too much green tea and was certainly tense ahead of today's climb.

7;30 a.m. Western-style breakfast

9;45 a.m. Taxi to bus station

10:00 a.m. Bus to 5th Stage on Mount Fuji. It was the first bus of the day. During the Official Climbing Season from July 1 to 31 August 31, the bus runs every 39 minutes from 7:30 a.m. until the evening. There is a limited service outside these dates from September 1 to November 23. The bus was severely underpowered; it took fifty-five minutes to climb thirty kilometres through forest rising gently, then progressively more steeply to the 5th Stage at around 2,400 meters. There was a toll barrier at the entrance to the national park. The 5th Stage had large car and bus parks, four large buildings, tourist trinkets for sale, restaurants, hotels, a huddle of docile-looking ponies for hire to take people up to 7th Stage, and a temple, the Komitake Shrine.

On the 13th at 11:30 a.m., I started up Kawaguchi Trail having found an ideal walking stick, a branch of fir tree cut to just the right length; it only needed smoothing off the bark. I carried a light pack with sweaters, Gortex waterproof and wind-proof jacket, socks, thick gloves, thick hat with a plastic sun visor and two water bottles; I also had two cans of Pocari Sweat health drink, sweets, two cameras and spare film and sunscreen. I was wearing a t-shirt, long-sleeved Viyella shirt, jeans and climbing boots with extra-thick socks.

Initially, I walked on a wide road deep in larva dust, giving way to stone paving. I climbed up past the last of trees, birch, and pine, under a concrete bridge giving protection from a rockslide area to a 6th Stage mountain hut.

Then I climbed a zig-zag path, on dry cinders with retaining walls at intervals. I passed closed and shuttered mountain huts and reached the 7th Stage at 2,700 meters. About 20 other climbers were in groups; apart from one middle-aged couple, all were in their twenties. Each year 180,000 people are reported to climb Fuji, the vast majority in the official two months; there must be days when 3,000 climbers are struggling past each other to the top. The Kawaguchi-Yoshida route is the most popular, but there are alternatives; Subashi-guchi Trail and Gotemba-Guchi Trail from Gotemba in the East; and the Mishima-guchi Trail from Mishima or the Fujinomiya-guchi Trail from Fujinomiya from the south, which have a common track above the 5th Stage.

One hut was open at the 7th Stage. After a rest, I kept going up more difficult terrain over larva boulders; I passed more closed huts until I reached the Gansomuro hut, the only one open at the 8th Stage, at 3,360 meters. By now, despite the sunshine, there was a very cold wind, so I put on my warm clothing, left the back-pack at the hut and set off for the final 400 meters to the top. At 4:00 p.m., I reached the summit after a two-hour climb from the 8th Stage. My progress was slowed by the altitude effect –weakness in the legs rather than shortage of breath. About a dozen climbers were there at same time; those who were lightly clad suffered from severe wind-chill.

There was a Shinto gateway with guardian lions at the entrance to a Tibetan-style row of stone, single-story houses roofed with corrugated iron weighted down with boulders, all closed. I walked along the crater rim to the left to the highest point accessible to climbers; it was marked by another Shinto gate of wood studded with silver coins. Black larva rock at the rim was streaked with red further down in the crater. There was no lake. My Pentax camera was reacting badly to the cold but the Minox was working fine. As usual the view was hazy. I spent half an hour at the top before descending to the Gansomuro hut for the night. I could have made it back to the 5th Stage, but not before dark, nor before the last bus to Kawaguchiko at 5:00 p.m., nor without risk of an accident induced by fatigue.

The Gansomuro hut had a strong steel frame, wooden walls and roof covered with corrugated iron held down with boulders, a separate three-cubicle dunny, comprising a hole in wooden floor down to rock below, hosed down daily. The main living room was tatami-matted, no shoes permitted. A square hole in the wooden floor, lined with metal and half-filled with sand, was for a small charcoal fire. The walls were lined with curtained-off bunks in two tiers. To the right of the door was a sales area for drinks and food, a store area and kitchen. A dormitory led off from the main room, two tiers of sleeping platforms neatly laid out with plastic-covered pillows, a heavy blanket and an under-blanket. Supper consisted of a plastic bowl with compartments for rice, a very mild curry sauce with vegetables and green tea. There was a brilliant sunset, with thin clouds hiding the valley and distant peaks of southern alps clearly visible.

7:00 p.m. I went to bed—ten people in a room designed for sixty. I had little rest, with cramps in my legs possibly from salt deficiency, and a call at 3:00 a.m. for climbers aiming to watch the sunrise from the summit; then another call at 5:30 a.m. to watch the sunrise. I stayed in bed.

6:30 a.m. Breakfast was cold rice and a packet of spicy meat, totally unappetizing, with cold water to drink.

7:00 a.m. Started down. It was another perfect day, with light mist in the valley, clear sky and a few people climbing. I took my time, photographing, and was in no hurry, because the first bus down was at noon.

9:30 a.m. I reached the 5th Stage and drank a welcome cup of coffee. I bought picture postcards, wrote and posted them. I ate corn on the cob from a stall; spoilt by a soy sauce, it was less tasty than it could have been. A second course of lunch was pressed upon me at the Kawaguchiko taxi rank by a Japanese/American man, a portion of baked sweet potato. Did I look that hungry? A sweet potato seller rode his pickup truck with brazier in the back fuelled by a large log; he was blaring his wares on a tape-recorded message through a powerful loudspeaker.

During the official climbing season, a one-day ascent and descent is possible using public transport. Out of season, between April 1and November 23, the first bus arrives at the 5th Stage at 11:00 a.m. and the last bus leaves at 3:00 p.m. Alternatives are taxi or hire car. For accommodation, twenty-five mountain lodges are available on the Kawaguchiko trail during the season; the Gansomura hut at the 8th Stage and the Toyoken hut at the 7th Stage are available until late September and the Satogoya and Gogoen lodges are open at the 5th Stage until mid-December. The mountain is closed from late November until April.

It was 1:20 p.m. and I was back at the Fuji View Hotel where I enjoyed a much-needed bath. I walked round the beautiful lake-side grounds of the hotel. Two hundred fifty years before, it had been the estate of a nobleman and the original house was still there, wooden with a thatched roof. Now there are a nine-hole pitch, a putting golf course, tennis courts and woodland walks. At 3:00 p.m., I enjoyed tea and chocolate sponge cake in the lobby, looking out over lake and hills, with background music playing 'Summertime'. It was a good moment. From the sixth-floor observation lounge of the hotel, I watched the Mount

Fuji darken in the evening; it was as spectacular a sunset as it had been the night before. I was warmed by the knowledge that, whenever in the future I see Fujisan, I will be reminded that once I stood on that summit.

On the 14th, at Kawaguchiko bus station, I boarded a luxury coach to Shinjuku station. Seat 1A gave me a great view; it was a smooth ride, with speed consistently 100 kilometers an hour along a highway with a legal maximum of eighty kilometers. The first stop was the Highland Hotel in the middle of an amusement park—ugh.

The first half of the trip passed through a narrow valley, with the hillsides heavily forested and post-war plantations; on the valley floor were rice fields and villages and a few traditional-style houses. The second half was along the Tokyo coastal plain, with the most notable feature, golf driving ranges, towering structures of steel towers and netting; I counted nine.

The last few miles were along an elevated highway flanked by high-rise blocks, a hinterland of haphazard streets and poor housing. The Shinjuku area was a stark contrast—modern, imaginatively designed skyscrapers. Traffic was very heavy, we arrived at 10:45 a.m., half an hour late. I was willing to bet that the bus seldom arrived on time.

I had missed my planned connection with the JR NEX to Narita Airport leaving at 10:42 a.m. For the next one, at 11:42 a.m., all the seats had been sold, so I had to stand all the way with a few others. It seems I was lucky to get on at all. The train left ten minutes late and arrived at Narita Terminal at 1.10 p.m. I checked in with Korea Airlines just in time to catch the only flight of the day to Cheju in South Korea that did not require a change of planes. It was my lucky day.

Post Script
South China Morning Post, September 18, 1995
'Raging typhoon batters Tokyo'
TOKYO: The strongest typhoon to hit the Tokyo region since World War II swept along the eastern Japan coast yesterday, killing up to nine people, injuring scores and closing Airports."

I had been so very lucky.

SOUTH KOREA
HALLASAN
Height: 1,947 metres, (5,850 feet)
Date: September 14, 1995

I had just finished my climb of Mount Fuji the day before and was now on my way to climb another mountain, Hallasan on Jeju Island, South Korea. The flight from Narita Airport to Pusan lasted two hours. Pusan looked like Hong Kong—high-rise buildings crowding the coast and valleys, with hills rising abruptly in the background. We were on the ground half an hour, in an unattractive airport building.

I arrived at Jeju after a half-hour flight over myriad islands off the south coast of Korea. The pilot's idea of pre-landing "holding pattern" was not the usual gentle circles—much more exciting, straight spells connected by tight multiple-G-force turns. We enjoyed good views of the island though 45-degree angles.

Jeju is an egg-shaped island, 60 km long by 30 km wide, flat at the coast rising gently to the central cone of Hallasan, a long-dormant volcano. Scattered around it were subsidiary small volcanic cones. The island is green; in the plains are small fields of fruit trees protected by high fir tree hedges. Jeju City is on the north coast close to the airport and is the only substantial town; its satellite town is Shin Jeju.

At the airport, bad news. My suitcase had been unloaded at Pusan airport; I was given official apologies and assurances it would be delivered to my hotel the next day. This was a problem, because all my climbing gear was in the suitcase and I had hoped to make the climb the next day. At the tourist desk, I picked up maps and booked a room at the Green Hotel in Shin Jeju, close to airport; no better class hotel was available.

The taxi took ten minutes to reach the hotel, a newish building, Western style; the room was small with bath, telephone and television—three Korean channels only. The most attractive feature was a waterfall splashing down a four-storey high cliff at the back of the building. Staff were efficient and polite but only two of the front-desk staff spoke any English. Room-service produced a horrid hamburger on white bread and fruit salad out of a tin. I studied maps of the island; it appeared feasible to make the climb of Hallasan in eight hours, getting to and from the mountain by public transport.

September 15

7.30 a.m. Breakfast was lamentably slow—40 minutes to fry two eggs. But the coffee was good, with real cream, and refreshing iced green tea.

There was still no word of my suitcase but I decided to go anyway. I took a taxi to Jeju City central "Local" bus station, a 10- minute ride. I boarded a battered-looking bus that took 40 minutes to wind quickly through a shabby downtown area, then gently up through rural scenery and light forest to the crest of a ridge in the middle of the island; this was the Hallasan National Park Headquarters, at Seongpanak. On the way, I saw many large stone statues, *harbung*, regarded as protective gods; they looked like the statues on Easter Islands. Surprise, surprise — 29 large tour buses had already parked at Seongpanak, having disgorged passengers; they were presumably already on the trail up to Hallasan.

9.30 a.m. I started on Seongpanac Trail at 750 metres. My only worry was footwear — new leather formal shoes with thin soles; I also had a sweater, Gortex jacket, water bottles and sweets, and two cameras. The trail was 9.6 km, with an estimated climbing time of 4.5 hours up and 4 hours down. Much of the trail was pleasantly under cover of trees, with ground cover of short bamboo-type grass. The trail itself was roughly paved with boulders and large stones; without proper walking boots every step had to be watched to avoid a sprained ankle.

The gentle upward inclination was punctuated by flights of steps. I made good speed until I caught up with columns of earlier starters; there was often no room to pass on the single track. In the first hour, I covered 4.5 km before meeting the crowds — thank goodness Mount Fuji was not like this — and needed two more hours to reach the top. Good signposting along the trail indicated the distance covered and yet to cover, and altitudes. There were rest areas with chemical 'porta-loos' at mid-way and three-quarter way to top. There was no supply of drinking water.

At about 1,300 metres, early broadleaf forest gave way to firs and brilliant purple clumps of thistles. Near the summit, there were stunted firs on the north slope and bare grass and rocks to the south. I heard but did not see the resident wild game, such as pheasant and roe deer. The hunting season started 1st

November and finished at the end of February — not a good time to be walking!

At the summit, I found a wide crater with a lake at the bottom; the crest of the rim was rough with larval rocks. Access was only permitted to the crater on the east edge via the Seongpanak trail and the Gwaneumsa trail from the north. The Gwaneumsa trail starts close to Jeju city; it is shorter and more scenic, but steeper with long flights of steps; a National Park shelter provides shelter, food and toilet some way short of the summit. The western trails, Orimok and Yongsil, were closed to allow recovery from erosion and do not lead to the summit. The view was hazy.

The walk down was slightly slower because of my footwear; the soles were painfully thin and the inner sole on my right side wrinkling. I had to stop every so often to straighten it out. At 3.15 p.m., I was back at park headquarters; the area was littered with resting, footsore and weary climbers. I caught a local bus back to Jeju with a group of Korean students; I had not seen any Europeans all day. From the bus station, I took a taxi back to the hotel, arriving at 5 p.m. I called Korean Air; they said that they had recovered the suitcase and would deliver it at 7.30 p.m. The suitcase was delivered in person by Mr Moon, assistant manager of the Korean Air station in Jeju, with many apologies. Room service supper was a tasteless chicken "curry" and rice; dessert was part of my supply of "climbing" chocolate. I watched a game of baseball, but barely understood the rules. It compared badly with cricket for excitement.

September 16
After breakfast, I walked around Shin Jeju. I saw unprepossessing tightly packed hotels and tourist shops selling mostly cheap goods, as well as marvellous shells. I was surprised at the unexpected appearance of a steam locomotive half way up a hill

at Sammu Park. The best hotels and tourist development areas seemed to be on the south coast of the island, at Chungmun and Sogwipo.

11.45 a.m. I reached the airport confident that, with 24 flights on Korea Air alone, and many more on Asiana Airlines, I would have no problem in reaching Seoul in time to catch a Cathay flight to Hong Kong leaving 5.55 p.m. — but not so. There were hundreds and hundreds of school children sitting in groups or marching in columns, waiting to board planes. At that point, the cloud of the missing suitcase the day before developed a silver lining. I located the same Mr Moon at the airport, and he was able to find a seat for me on the next plane out, packed to the gills with school children on their way home. Seoul's Kimpo airport was enlivened by regular meetings with a friendly Christian missionary handing out pamphlets, and another game of baseball on television.

The return trip on Cathay, albeit economy class, was a celebration of good food, wine, and spoken English — none of which I had experienced during the previous week in Japan and Korea To be fair, the focus of the trip was not gourmet living nor social interaction, but mountain-climbing. In that respect it was a memorable success.

VIETNAM

FANSIPAN
Height: 3,140 metres (10,761ft)
Date: November 1995

I arranged this trip to north-west Vietnam to coincide with
a working visit Judith had been invited to make for the 3rd
National Workshop on Tobacco Control Strategy, and to assess
and advise the Vietnamese on anti-smoking policy. My plan was
that by the time I had returned from the climb, Judith would
have arrived at Hanoi from Hong Kong. My contact to organise
the climb of Vietnam's highest mountain was Justin Wheatcroft;
a British ex-army officer, who now managed Vietnam Veterans
Trekking Services (VVTS). He had made the climb himself, when
he learned that I wanted to make the climb.

November 3

I was up at 5.30 a.m. in Hong Kong to play "early-bird" nine holes of golf with a friend, Michel Arnulphy, at Clear Water Bay Golf and Country Club, situated at the end of the peninsula on which I live in Hong Kong. I played to my handicap.

At 2.15 p.m., I was on board a Vietnamese Airlines flight to Hanoi, with a French captain and Vietnamese co-pilot. The take-off was delayed for one hour to wait for a tour group. I was in business class; it had large uncomfortable seats, no film or music headphones but a magazine with an interesting article on endangered species. I had a hazy view of the China coast, then of the delta of the Red River, meandering through flood-plain of rice fields.

At 4.25 p.m, I arrived at Hanoi airport; it was basic, old and built of concrete. Staff were efficient. I was met by Bach Ngoc Chien, tourist guide and driver from VVTS, Vietnam Veterans Travel Service. He was short, of stocky build and with a big smile. He appeared happy to see me; he spoke good English and French. He later admitted he was surprised to see how old I was! I was 60. We took a car into Hanoi on a newish road and bridge built with Russian help, elevated above the flood plain; cyclists and motor-cyclists were all over the road, as well as their own cycle track. On the fringe of town, I saw poor single-storey shacks with shops at front and family accommodation at the back. Then came the Botanic Gardens leading to the old French quarter; it had large mansions run-down and needing paint. It was close to the Citadel area and VVTS office. I paid US$880 for my up-country trip.

A driver took Chien and me to a restaurant near the railway station; we ate local food, with handfuls of ingredients dropped into a bowl and covered by a ladle-full of chicken stock by an old woman; her husband, the owner, reclined on a settee watching television, a Brazilian costume-drama of a plantation in the days of slavery. It was reportedly a very popular show at that time. We walked half a kilometre to the station, an old, old building, where our train was waiting. There were no elevated platforms and people were sitting in circles on the ground drinking tea and chatting; vendors sold fruit, sweetmeats and cigarettes.

The train compartments were either "hard seat", "soft seat" or "hard bunk". We were in the expensive "hard bunk" class, with three bunks either side, plus room for a seventh sleeper in the luggage rack. Windows were of thick plastic with, in addition, a heavy metal grill and a wire-mesh screen — "to protect passengers from bandits, and stone-throwing by bored youngsters", Chien explained. At 8.20 p.m., the train left for Lao Cai on the border with China. It was north-west up the Red River valley, 11 hours to cover 300 km of ancient narrow-gauge track. It was a daunting prospect but less so than the trip south to Ho Chi Minh City, 36 hours to cover 1,000 km. The compartment filled up with jovial workers returning to their villages; all but one were smokers. Chien and I had been first in and had chosen the bottom bunks. So we were obliged to wait for everyone else to climb into their own bunks before we could lie down; I was warm enough in my sleeping-bag, with my valuables inside it.

November 4

My sleep was disturbed by frequent train stops. By 7 a.m., it was light enough to see that we were travelling along a winding track on the north bank of the Red River. The valley was flanked by low hills and vegetation not unlike Hong Kong's at that time — sugarcane, bananas, taro, sweet potato, corn, and rice on the valley floor. Half an hour later, we arrived at Lao Cai, the terminus. The Chinese railway across the border was only a short walk away — but no through trains had been allowed since the border war in the 1980s. Two mini-buses were waiting for passengers from the train on the way to Sapa, a market town popular with tourists; both buses were packed with luggage piled on the roof racks. It was a hard grind up the hills, with poor roads and several washed-out bridges under repair after the recently-ended summer rains. There was little traffic — only the occasional rickety bus or lorry, motorbikes and women and girls on foot carrying farm produce to the weekly market at Sapa. They were Zau hill tribe people, distinguishable by their red head-dresses, and the Hmong by their black ones.

An hour later, we reached Sapa, our base for the trek. Sapa was a favourite hill resort in French colonial times, like Dalat in the south, an escape from the summer heat. It is set on a plateau at 1,500 metres, with a Catholic church at the centre and a surrounding market; it has a few streets with substantial two- and three-storey houses looking north over a valley to the highlands. VVTS's original choice, the Sapa Hotel was full of backpackers, French, German, Americans and Australians. The French-speaking owner, a Vietnamese originally from Hanoi, was profuse in his apologies and directed us to a guesthouse, a large villa nearby; there Chien and I shared a large ground-floor room with four beds, mosquito nets, and bathroom off. It had originally been a drawing room as indicated by the bow windows overlooking the valley, and a fine wooden patterned ceiling.

Breakfast was French bread, butter, honey and tea, taken on the balcony of the Pang Trang hotel. It was a grey day with the peaks across the valley hidden in cloud, at the tail end of the rainy season. I rested in bed for an hour, had lunch of chow fan at the Chapa restaurant. Then I explored the town, while Chien went to organise the trip. There were many backpackers photographing the tribal people gathered in the market, colourful in bright clothing and heavy silver jewellery. The native houses had wattle and daub walls and thatch roofs. The centre of the town was a stone-flagged square in front of the church; people playing a simple gambling game that involved spinning a pointer over a board divided into four squares; people selling loose tobacco for smoking in rolled cigarettes or water pipes; vendors selling silver jewellery and trinkets, clothing and freshly killed meats. The atmosphere was very relaxed and friendly, the taking of photos was tolerated with a smile or giggle.

Chien and I had supper at the Chapa Restaurant on the main street — pork, cabbage, potato chips and rice, tea for me and beer for Chien. On the road outside was a gaggle of hawkers waiting to sell embroidered goods and silver. The owner's pride and joy was a large Suzuki motorcycle, worth US$3,000; it took pride of place in the centre of the restaurant. Most motorbikes in Vietnam were Russian-made Ochods, for a fraction of the cost. Chien had located a 30-year-old Hmong mountain guide named Chiu who had done the trip three times before. He had also contacted the policeman in charge of issuing climbing permits. At 8 p.m., he came to our guesthouse where Chien negotiated a fee after much discussion and inspection of my passport and visa. In the end, we got a permit for US$60 instead of US$80 — four days at US$20 a day. Chien had saved US$20 and the policeman had made US$60 for himself. We had a permit, albeit without an official chop — and I understood why there were no official figures for the number of climbers in the area.

Chien was in talkative mood. From him, I learned that the gauge of the railway was one metre, the fare from Lao Cai to Hanoi was US$12 for locals and US$19 for foreigners: 80 per cent of the population were farmers and only 20 per cent of the country was arable. The population of Hanoi was three million — one million were illegal, without house-cards that would give them permission to change where they live. Justin Wheatcroft had been in Hanoi for two years running the branch of VVTS; he was opening a restaurant in Hanoi that day.

November 5

I had a broken night's sleep, with Chien's watch alarm going off every hour.

6.30 a.m. We had breakfast at the Pang Trang Hotel. It was a beautiful sunny day, with the peaks to the north clearly visible.

7 a.m. The three of us were on the road — myself, Chien and mountain guide Chiu, a taller, serious, thin man, each with a rucksack. I was as old as the other two put together. Later I was to regret that I had turned down an offer by Chien to hire a porter. There was an easy walk down a farm track to the valley floor past a ruined mansion halfway down and a cold drinks stand nearby. We crossed the river at the bottom on a rickety suspension bridge and walked up to the shoulder of hill between farmsteads where Chiu's son, aged ten, was waiting with his herd of goats to greet us. Chiu had five children, of whom the youngest was three years old.

At the next river, we caught up with a party of five French climbers and three Hmong, one guide and two porters. They forded the river first while we had a rest. But we caught up and passed them, while they were resting at the top of the very steep, long, bank on the other side of the river. We did not see them again until we returned to Sapa. Then we found out that their guide had lost the trail, so they had to turn back after three days.

We climbed, leaving behind lowland cattle tracks, then on forest trails, crossing streams on fallen tree-trunks and squelching through boggy ground, where Chien picked up a couple of leaches much to his disgust. Like Chiu, he was wearing plastic sandals, while I had leather climbing boots. After four hours, we reached 1,600 metres, only just higher than Sapa! There we had a rest at a camp site, where hillmen come to trap butterflies in huge nets hung from the trees. At 2,400 metres, we reached the summit of Fansipoo, a lesser summit on the range, and rested again to admire the wonderful view — range after range of wooded mountains with afternoon cloud beginning to sweep up the valleys from the west. We were in the most attractive part of the rain-forest with azaleas, rhododendrons and bonsai trees. In his exhilaration at having reached the peak, Chiu climbed an ancient bonsai tree.

The next 100 metres was a tough climb up nearly vertical ladders of tree roots along a ridge to a roomy camp site at 2,500 metres, where we made camp at 4 p.m. Chien was tired and I even more so. But Chiu was still full of energy; he went off down the hill again to fetch water to cook supper. He harvested Bamboo-grass to make bedding, lopped branches off trees for firewood and strung a tarpaulin up between trees as a roof. Supper was rehydrated powdered soup, a ready-cooked curry pack, sweet biscuits and water; most of this food I had brought. Chien had brought high-energy dehydrated biscuits, possibly ex-army that tasted all right but required half a litre of water for me to get them down: and Chiu had a bag of rice. By 8 p.m., I was asleep, comfortably warm in a sleeping bag inside a windproof sleeve and on a waterproof mat.

November 6

6 a.m. Chiu was up first, to restart the fire. It was another fine morning, the full moon still visible. We had another steep climb out of camp, up more vertical root ladders, to above the tree-line into dense feathery bamboo four to six feet high.

9 a.m. We reached an outcrop of massive granite boulders, the summit of Pansipan, at 2,900 metres. At last, we had our first

view of Fansipan. It was at the western edge of the ridge, not so far away, but with a deep valley in between and an unbroken mass of jungle, bamboo at higher elevations and rainforest further down, below about 2,800 metres.

From this summit, we plunged down a steep streambed, stopping on the rocks for lunch, a large pan of rice and beef and vegetable stew. Then we climbed up again the other side, working our way along the south face of the ridge, descending some way to avoid the impenetrable bamboo, great stands 10 metres high; we had to edge our way round great outcrops of granite rock. At this point, Chiu became less assured in his trail-finding. We were clearly the first group to attempt the climb since the previous dry season in May. When he came to a stream at which he had expected to find water and our camping spot for the night, and found it dry, he began to look worried. We were already low on water. Chien and I waited while he tried to find the trail.

Sitting quietly there, I saw my first terrestrial animal, a large dark-coloured squirrel. Chiu had told me that there were monkeys in the rainforest, who had eaten all the snakes; and there were goats and bears in the uplands. After an hour, Chiu came back to say that he had located the trail higher up on the slope. At 4.30 p.m., we reached a camping spot after a scramble up and over large boulders and fallen tree trunks along the course of the stream. Chiu carefully marked the trail by slashing trees and bamboos for our return journey. By this time, it had started to rain, and a wind was roaring through the treetops. By 6 p.m., we had built a platform of bamboo on the sloping hillside on which to sleep, and had eaten a meal of hot soup, biscuits and chocolates.

November 7

6 a.m. It was a cold, grey, windy morning. For breakfast, I ate one

high-energy biscuit and drank water. Everything was damp and there was no fire.

6.30 a.m. We left camp carrying only biscuits, water, cameras and waterproof gear. The plan was to reach the summit in two-three hours and return to this camp for a meal before proceeding with the descent. The climb was on a fairly easy gradient along goat trails. Twice Chiu pointed out tree-trunks recently scarred by bears. When we reached the crest of the ridge, we met the full strength of a strong north-east wind. The others called this the winter monsoon wind; but, on returning to Hanoi, I learnt that a severe typhoon had crossed the South China Sea into Vietnam that same day. The most difficult walking was near the summit; the trail traversed a lattice of fallen bamboo — the thin, six-foot variety.

9.30 a.m. At the summit, I found a jumble of rocks surmounted by an aluminium cone, placed there by a Russian climbing party some years before. It was very cold, with driving rain, in the clouds and no view. We took photographs of each other, and beat a hasty retreat. Two hours later we were back in camp; I was still chilled to the bone and probably hypoglycaemic from lack of nourishment. However, after a bowl of hot soup, a rest in my sleeping bag and further protection afforded by my "Nomad" Sympatex Het Klimaatmembraan, I was ready to go on again. The other two seemed less affected by the cold and had been able to keep nibbling the high-energy biscuits. We set off at 1.30 p.m. and kept going till 4.30 p.m., when we reached our luncheon stop site from the day before.

This was not an ideal site, in the rocky bed of a stream with limited protection from the wind and rain; but it was getting dark and the next part of the trek involved a very steep climb back up to the summit of Pansifan.

We laid a mattress of branches down on the stones and

erected a tarpaulin canopy. Amazingly Chiu managed to light a fire despite the sodden wood, and cooked soup.

November 8

It was a miserable night for all of us, wet and cold. The others had less warm and waterproof gear than I. We were all glad to get up at first light, rebuild the fire to dry ourselves out, and cook a large meal—three bowls of thick soup each. I feel sure that I would have been better off the previous day if I had taken time to eat a big breakfast before heading for the summit.

Our plan was to try hard to get to Sapa by nightfall. At 7 a.m., we set off, uphill for the first 40 minutes to get back to the ridge line, a hard slog; then easier going down to our first camp site at 2,500 metres. The French party had been there the previous night, to judge by the still-smouldering fire and the mass of firewood chopped down since we had left. There is going to be a real problem of environmental degradation if this becomes a popular trek; the Vietnamese should learn from the Nepalis who insist that every party bring their own cooking fuel.

We came across a gang of hillmen illegally gathering seedlings of azalea and bonsai; further down the mountain, we saw evidence of small-scale logging, also illegal. At 1.30 p.m., we stopped for lunch at the 1,600 metres camp, again with a still smouldering fire under a vast tree-stump. I seemed to need much more fluid than the others, finding dry biscuits difficult to eat without copious amounts of water. Probably I was perspiring more than they were. My attempts to refill my water-bottle were often sabotaged by Chiu; leading the party, when he came to a stream, he would always carefully wash his feet in it.

The going was now much faster but more hazardous; the wet muddy paths were very slippery. Often Chien and I slid down the steeper slopes on logging shoots. Somehow Chiu managed to keep his footing. We crossed a stream on a tree-trunk bridge, leaving the rain forest behind. We walked onto a meadow carpeted in flowers, forded another stream and followed buffalo tracks down steep, dry, clay banks to reach, at last, the major river we had forded on the way up; it was a wonderful stream of clear water, rushing rapids and deep pools. We were now close to habitation, passing Hmong women with heavy loads of timber for firewood, and one man carrying a huge beam of hardwood; it was about 15 feet by 6 inches by 6 inches, a rafter for a house. I was unable to lift even one end of it.

We crossed the final bridge. The long climb up to Sapa remained, made harder when Chiu opted to take a short cut which entailed a series of giant steps up a flight of rice terraces; they were not easy to climb with tired legs. We made good time buoyed on by the thought of a very cold drink at the road-side stall. When we came to it, the Coca-Cola was as cold and as refreshing as could possibly be imagined.

At 5 p.m., we walked into Sapa, to the Pang Trang Hotel where the owner greeted us with surprise; he had not expected to see us for another two days. I sat down to a large pot of tea with much sugar to satisfy another craving that had developed on the trek. The hotel was still full, but a large double bedroom was available next door for Chien and me; we picked up our luggage left in the proprietor's care and headed over. Chiu was keen to get back to his farm in the valley before dark; so we said our thanks and farewells with parting gifts of all the spare food, a blanket, my battery-headlight with which he was particularly delighted, and a tip from VVTS.

He had been extremely valuable—finding the way, carrying the biggest load and lighting fires in the most unlikely circumstances.

I showered. It was wonderful to be clean again after wearing the same clothes for the last four days. I threw away the torn and mud-caked jeans and shirt. The bathroom was small and basic, a wash-basin without plug, waste water running out on the floor to a corner of the room, a flush toilet—but, if the toilet was running, there was no water pressure for the shower; and a shower without curtain or cubicle so wetting everything else, and water heated by a weak electric filament.

At 6 p.m., we were down at the Chapa restaurant enjoying our first decent meal for days. I had two fried eggs, a large plate of excellent potato chips, with tomato sauce, and copious quantities of hot tea. Warm at last. Chien had a pile of native dishes washed down by much beer. He then went down to the restaurant where the French party were having their meal, to crow about our success no doubt. I did not have the heart to join him.

After supper, we went to the Post Office which doubled as the booking office for the trains from Lao Cai. It turned out we were too late to make a reservation, but we decided to aim for the morning train anyway. Chien did manage to get through to his office in Hanoi to let them know we were on our way back, and to pass that message to Judith.

November 9
The great night's sleep I had been expecting did not happen. For the first hour, the young bloods of the town raced their motorbikes up and down the main road outside. At 4 a.m., a bus departed, with much revving of the engine and grinding of gears. At 5 a.m., there was screaming and screaming next door, as a pig was killed rather slowly for the morning market. Half an hour later we had to get up to pack.

We breakfasted at the Chapa restaurant, thinking the bus left from in front at 7 a.m. When it did not appear, Chien went off in search and was told it had just left. He jumped on the back of a bike; caught up the bus; persuaded it to wait for us; and raced back to alert me. Together we ran a quarter mile, weighed down by backpacks and suitcase, up the hill, through the market square—with bloody evidence of that morning's execution on sale—and caught the bus. The trip down the mountain was enlivened by backpacker talk of out-of-the-way destinations and low-cost accommodation; and by a stop for our driver to help repair a broken-down car.

8.15 a.m. Lao Cai station was built in heavy Russian style and faced across the street to a row of market matshed stalls selling farm produce. Its redeeming feature was a waiting area of rows of ornately carved long wooden seats. All bunks on the train were already booked, so we took the soft-seat alternative. To sustain us during the trip, Chien bought in the market oranges, bananas, nuts and "La Vie" bottled water.

9.40 a.m. The train left Lao Cai, winding its way slowly next to the river.

The Red River is indeed a muddy reddish brown. Even at low water, it is a major river, still over 400 kilometres from the sea, having travelled an equal distance from its source on the Yunnan plateau in China, at a point not more than 100 kilometres from the source of the Mekong. But the two rivers enter the sea more than 1,000 kilometres apart.

The rice harvest was under way; all the reaping, winnowing and stacking were done by hand. Farmhouses were thatch-roofed, with walls of split bamboo or wattle and daub. In the villages were more substantial dwellings with brick walls and slate roofs. The finest houses had two storeys and ornate French-style balconies. Chien pointed out that nearly all the houses faced south, towards the sun and away from the cold winter winds, whereas the graves faced East towards the rising sun, as ordained by the geomancers.

The first stop came after one hour of gentle progress. It lasted 20 minutes, time for more purchases from platform vendors of freshly steamed young corn cobs, pomelos, sugarcane, eggs and baguettes. There was also a trolley made of wood and chicken-wire that trundled down the compartment selling soft drinks, biscuits, tea, beer and cigarettes.

After the first five and a half hours we had travelled a third of the distance to Hanoi, down through the hills. From there on, we travelled on straighter tracks across the plains at twice the speed, 40 kilometres per hour. We rattled on through the afternoon and into the evening, pausing only for the regular, leisurely stops to refuel engine and passengers.

8.30 p.m. We reached Hanoi at last. Outside in the station square was waiting a milling, noisy throng of motorbike taxis, pedal trishaws, and car taxis. In response to a call from Chien on his mobile phone, the travel agent's car eventually arrived, to take us the last lap, to the Ministry of Health Guest House, 138A Giang Vo Street, and Judith. Our tired, dirty, but up-to-schedule train set off into the night to Vinh, a further 300 kilometres to the south.

Postscript 2016. In February, a Cable Car route was opened, taking 20 minutes from the base to near the top of Fansipan, and a stairway to the top, with the capacity to carry 2,000 people per hour. There are temples and kiosks at the cable stations. Trekking is still done, with permanent shelters at overnight stopping points. I had made my climb just in time.

LAOS
PHU BIA
Height: 2,819m (9,249ft)
Date: November 1995

Phu Bia mountain was reported, in 1995, to be in an area under military control because of continuing rebel activity, and therefore off limits to climbers.

Professor Bounthaphany Bounxouie Head of Surgery Department, Mahosoth Hospital, of Vientiane Medical School organised for me to be escorted by a colleague, Dr. Phoufai, on a climbing trip to Xienghuang Province in the north-east instead of climbing Phu Bia.

November 15
09.30 hrs I was picked up from the Belvedere Hotel, Vientiane, by

Dr Phoufai, a surgeon in the Vientiane government hospital and a native of Xienghuang, a small, ebullient character delighted with the idea of an expenses-paid trip to a home-town that he had not seen for years.

I checked in at the very basic grubby domestic terminal of Wattay airport. There was time for Dr Phoufai and the driver to have a meal in the upstairs restaurant, I had already eaten. The walls were adorned with posters. Just above us was one of 'The Cool Dane', a very buxom blonde drinking a Carlsberg; and close by, another buxom lady, a mother breast feeding her baby.

10.50 am We took off on a Yak aeroplane of Lao Airways for the half hour flight to Phousavanh. It was cloudy with no view on the way, and on arrival at the rattan shed that was the airport we found it windy and cold.

We were met by Dr Phoufai's brother, a doctor in the central provincial hospital at Phousavanh, and a Community Health pick-up truck and driver on loan from the local department. First stop was to pay respects to the Director of Community Health, by whose blessing we were to ride on the truck for the next two days as it made its monthly trip to a district hospital.

I was dropped off at the Phou Doi Hotel, a modern building on the main road, with upstairs two double bedrooms, and a couple of dormitory rooms; downstairs were a reception area, and dining room. This was the best in town apart from an establishment on the hill over-looking town run by a Frenchman.

One and a half hours later at 17.00 hrs Dr Phoufay rolled up again in the truck with his brother having visited various relatives, to start our journey to the hot springs resort near Muang Kham 30 kms away.

The road was terrible. Great potholes connected short stretches of tarmac. The summer rains had taken their toll, and heavy lorries were continuing to break up the thin surface. This road was part of the Ho Chi Minh trail, heavily bombed by the Americans during the Viet Nam war—and it looked it.

One and a half hours later, now in the dark, we reached a road junction graced by a couple of local transport cafes where we stopped to eat. The better of the two was a dingy single room which included the cooking area, and storage for crates of beer, rice, biscuits and sundry vegetables. A TV provided entertainment. The toilet facility was the open-air junk yard behind the kitchen.

The meal consisted of the standard sticky rice, a spicy green salad, soup, and several meat dishes, all washed down by beer or tea. I ate a small amount with extreme apprehension.

Another 15 kms later we turned off the road onto a dirt track which wound up a valley, forded a stream, and eventually arrived at our destination.

The hot springs resort, Baw Nam Hawn, consisted of half a dozen wooden chalets set around a garden, and a main building, also of wood, with a large verandah which was the restaurant.

Dr. Phoufay was greeted warmly by the host of a party in progress, a Dr. Gan, who ran a private clinic in Vientiane, and also the only night-club, The Blue Star.

Round the long table were his wife, the Thai ambassador, the guitarist from the Blue Star, and their wives.

Party Time. There was much singing of folk tunes, patriotic songs, and a type of song where singers took it in turn to invent a verse. The other great sport was to drink a toast with someone, both parties emptying their glass of whisky, Johnny Walker Red Label. I claimed an ulcer problem and stayed with beer. Even so by the time the party died, with the end of the second bottle of whisky, it was 23.00 hrs and I was happily exhausted from providing percussionist accompaniment to the guitarist.

November 16

I was up at 07.00 hrs after a good sleep on a vast double-bed under a mosquito net. Dr Phoufai and his brother had shared a double room in the same chalet and the driver had slept in a different cabin.

Together we walked through the grounds to the source of the hot spring water, from where pipes led to all the chalets and a separate bathhouse. Back at the restaurant we had a breakfast of soup and sweet tea.

09.15 hrs Accompanied by a local villager, Dr Phoufai, his brother and I set off on our 'mountain expedition' towards the high ridge bordering the valley to the east. We followed a Hmong hill tribal trail across the valley floor and up the first small slope. At this point Dr Phoufai turned around from his position at the front of the group to ask if I had gone far enough! Believing that he was just being politely considerate of my advancing years I urged him on.

A short while later he slowed down and started to breath heavily, clearly, he was not in good shape, indeed by the time we came to the crest of the first shoulder of hill he had developed an acute attack of asthma, was gasping at a Ventolin inhaler. He had reached his summit for the day.

While he recovered, we enjoyed a fine view over the valley as far as the Red Mountain, one of the higher ones in Lao but reported to be covered in bomb craters and possibly unexploded bombs—not a good prospect for a climb. Above us hung, invitingly, the lush green mountain ridge only another two to three hours of climbing away, but not today.

We were standing in a field of hill rice recently harvested. A villager was building stooks for the straw. The practice is for the villagers to burn off a plot of land each year for one crop of rice, edged with a fringe of corn, rotating annually through five hillside plots.

When Dr Phoufai was able to walk again, we set off down the hill, passing on the way Hmong women with green cotton headdresses coming back from the market, one with the most enormous goitre; and a party of men with .22 guns going hunting for birds.

By 11.00 we were back at the hotel enjoying deep baths of hot spring water, happily free of any sulphur smell.

Brunch was a major meal, paid for, like everything on this trip, by myself.

The lorry driver, who had joined the 'mountaineering' team, entered into the celebration of the expedition by downing at least four pints of beer, despite my protests bearing in mind the horrendous state of the road back to Phousavanh.

In the end I had to insist that we delay our departure to allow time for his recovery.

To fill in time the local medic, our mountain guide, took us a tour of his near-by clinic, newly built with Canadian money, where he was the masseur cum physical therapist. The equipment was simple but adequate and he seemed to know and take pride in his job.

He insisted we visit his bungalow next door where he introduced us to his wife and two children; his cotton weaving loom, chickens, ducks, the dam he had built last dry season, and the little fish that he netted that morning. They tasted delicious too, grilled by his wife as we talked, and served with the inevitable spicy salad.

13.00 hrs We were back on the road at last, the driver going very carefully. Village houses were of rattan with thatch or corrugated iron roofs, and on stilts. Uniquely, the stilts were more often than not made from bomb casings! At last something useful to come out of the Viet Nam war.

It was in this area that a whole community of villagers, reportedly about four hundred, were sheltering in a cave, Tham Piu, when they were killed by a rocket from an American plane in 1969.

In daylight the road was not quite so bad, maybe because of the load of vegetables we now had in the back of the van, or perhaps because I was distracted by the stunning scenery. Initially it was lush and green but as we climbed higher it became drier with fir forests on the hills contrasting with fields of brilliant yellow Mexican daisies by the roadside.

Two hours later we passed the site of the previous provincial capital, devastated in the war, just before re-entering Phousavanh which had been built as the replacement.

We checked into the Phou Doi hotel where I rested while Phoufai and his brother were driven to the cemetery to pay their respects at their fathers' grave. This was to have taken "half an hour", but true to form it was three times that before they came back to take me the planned trip to the Plain of Jars.

First, we had to call at the hospital to pay respects to the chief of the Community Health service, and a donation from myself to his department, namely himself.

The Plain of Jars was just out of town. On the dry brown-grass rolling plane were hundreds of great stone jars, the largest, about 6 tonnes, with a group of other large ones on a rise overlooking the others. Legend has it that they were constructed in the 6th century to commemorate a victory.

Near-by is a quarry where they are supposed to have been made.

It was in darkening evening light that we were there, the scene being dramatised by a grass fire sweeping past the more distant jars, flames and smoke in a line like an advancing army ready to do battle.

That night I stayed in the hotel grateful for an early night after the day's many activities. Dr Phoufai went off for a family reunion, with a donation of 10,000 kip (about US$10) from me to help celebrations. I had the impression that he had hoped that I would finance the entire evening.

November 17

Electricity was only on from sundown at 6pm for three hours, so there was only a cold wash available in the morning.

I was up at 6am and ready for the 'American breakfast' an hour later — green tea, half a small baguette, and two fried eggs — not quite typical but adequate for 1,200 kip.

It was a fine sunny morning, so I walked up the steep hill behind the town, to the French hotel beautifully situated overlooking Phousavanh and surrounding countryside. There were half a dozen wooden chalets set in gardens of bougainvillea, with the occasional bomb crater and a scattering of shell-cases as reminders of the war.

Tariff was USD35.0 single USD45.0 double. The main lounge-dining area was attractive with a huge open stone fireplace, and a collection of ancient hunting weapons hung on the walls.

On the way back to my hotel I was engaged in conversation by a middle-aged man who had alighted from his bicycle happy at the opportunity to practice his English. He was a school principal earning only 35,000 kip (35 US$) per month, hence the bicycle.

He had been burned by napalm during the war; and confirmed that there were still bandits in the hills who regularly robbed the buses.

At 09.30 I was picked up by Dr Phoufai in the truck to go to the airport. En route we stopped at the hospital to say farewell to the Director of Public Health and to hand over another 10,000 kip as a gesture of appreciation. The sum was equivalent to half a month's salary for a junior doctor.

Next stop was a shop on the main road owned by Dr Phoufai's family where I was introduced to his relatives, drank tea, and watched as they loaded more farm produce into the back of the truck.

Dr Phoufai managed to get 68 Kilos of produce onto the plane without paying any excess.

At the airport there was some time to wait, spent by Phoufai and yet more friends in the smoke-filled beer shack. I chose to spend the time in the fresh air photographing the brightly coloured jeepneys, and the airport buildings, the rattan-walled dunny, the well that supplied the water, and the huddle of tourists.

The flight back, in clear weather, gave a spectacular view of the vast Nam Ngam dam.

The Belvedere Hotel was a welcome oasis of comfort, in which I was happy to spend the rest of the day with my wife, Judith, declining an invitation from the indefatigable Dr Phoufai to go with him to the Blue Star night club owned by his friend Dr Gan, who, he reported, had been very impressed with my drumming skills.

Addendum. The mountain Phu Bia was still off limits for climbers in 2015. In 2021 there was an announcement that the mountain would be turned into a tourist site.

THAILAND

Doi Inthanon
Height: 8,000 ft. 2565 m.
Date: November 18, 1995

Base camp for this expedition was a large suite at the KPS hotel. The hotel was part of a vast shopping centre, situated just outside the north-west corner of the Chiang Mai old city wall, on Huay Kaew road.

Judith and I had arrived on a one-hour direct flight north-west from Vientiane, up the Mekong River valley and then over thickly wooded mountains until Chiang Mai came into view, spread out on the plains immediately to the south of the mountains.

It was founded in 1296 by King Mengrai who had conquered

the area from his mountain kingdom at Chiang Rai.

November 19

At 09.00 Judith and I set off in a mini-van with two other passengers, and a guide, for our ascent of Doi Inthenon, the highest peak in Thailand.

The roads were good, a contrast to those in Viet Nam and Laos, a sign of a much wealthier country which, unlike the others had been happily free of warfare this century, although occupied by Japanese in World War II.

The first hour was across the northern plains, heading south-west along the northern banks of the river Ping through heavily cultivated fields of rice and corn, bananas and palms.

The second hour was on a side road heading north and climbing up the mountain valleys, through forests of teak, then fir, and finally into evergreen rain-forest hung with mosses, ferns and orchids.

Our first stop was at a car park just 100 yards from the summit! Two military personnel were on guard to ensure that we did not take photographs of the communications station below the car park.

We walked through a light mist to the summit, marked by the tomb of the last king of Chiang Mai, King Inthawichyanon who died in 1897. Prior to his burial, the mountain was called Doi Angka Luang. The first recorded climb by a European was in 1905.

The journey back was more leisurely. We lunched in a restaurant at the site of the 55-meter high, brown, cheddi of King Rama 9, the reigning monarch, built when he was 60 years old; and the 50-meter high, purple one for his Queen, which was built five years later.

The cheddis were built on separate elevations connected by a long wide, flight of steps. The bases were tiled, with large panels depicting Buddhist religious scenes; wide esplanades allowed one to walk around to observe the monuments and to admire the views of lesser mountains and valleys.

A large group of novitiate monks wearing robes in various shades of saffron added colour. Inside the bases were shrines with large statues of the Royals, the Queen's a magnificent larger than life-size figure in white jade. The Thais revere their King and Queen in a way that our Royals must greatly envy.

Further down the mountain we stopped off at The King's Garden. This venture was started by the King to help the hill people of the area, (Blue Hmong, White Hmong in the uplands, and Karen lower down), to grow commercially saleable flowers instead of opium poppies. An attractive set-up, terraces of flowers mostly covered by high arched screens against the rain.

At the foot of the hill we stopped off for a look at the Mae Klang falls, not really impressive, at low water anyway.

Last stop was the market town of Chom Thong to see the Wat Phra That Si Chon Thong, a golden Burmese cheddi of exquisite design, built in 1451.

18.15 Back at the hotel for a well-earned rest after our day of mountaineering — another peak conquered.

EAST TIMOR
Ramelau
Height: 2,986 meters (9,501 feet)
Date: 2005

My next objective was to climb the highest mountains in East Timor and the Indonesian island of Bali.

Why East Timor? Judith and I had arranged to spend two weeks with Katie and Willie Houstoun in Perth, Australia, a repeat of a very pleasant holiday nearly two years before. Rather than fly directly there and back, I decided to stop off en route to visit the then world's most recently independent nation and climb its highest mountain. This was Mount Ramelau, 2,986 meters, 70 kilometers south of the capital Dili. It had been two years since I had climbed Toubcal in the Atlas Mountains of Morocco. After that, due to family commitments and the Bush/ Blair war against Iraq having put the Arab world off limits, I had been frustrated in my quest for more summits.

During the previous forty years, East Timor had endured one of the most tragic experiences of any country in Asia. In the early 16th century, Portuguese traders first arrived in Timor. In 1769, Portugal established the city of Dili and declared the colony of Portuguese Timor. The western half of Timor Island was part of the Dutch East Indies, which became the independent state of Indonesia in 1949. After the Portuguese revolution of 1974, the new government abandoned Timor, without preparing it for independence. Civil war broke out among rival political parties. Fearful of a communist state within its archipelago, Indonesia invaded East Timor in December 1975 and declared it as its 27th Province in July 1976. The next twenty-three years were marked by a vicious conflict between those fighting for independence and the Indonesian army and local militias armed by it. The Catholic Church estimated the death from this conflict to be as high as 200,000. Finally, in October 1999, the United Nations took over administration and organized elections. Timor-Leste (East Timor) was admitted as a member of the United Nations in September 2002. This conflict devastated the physical infrastructure of the country — as I was to witness — and divided families and communities.

November 3
To get to East Timor, I had to fly first to Bali, stay there overnight and fly on to Dili the next day. The flight to Bali was uneventful and comfortable in business class; the cabin attendant expressed disappointment that I did not drink alcohol — my abstinence was to last until after I had finished climbing. At Bali airport, a three-day entry visa cost $10. A taxi to my hotel cost $15 for a 30-minute ride; the driver told me how his earnings had dropped dramatically in the three years since the Bali bombing in October 2002. It had killed 202 people in the tourist district of

Kuta, including 88 Australians. My sympathy for the driver only lasted until the next day when I discovered he had charged me twice the normal fare.

I stayed overnight at the Sanur Beach Hotel, chosen for its situation on the quieter Sanur beach, away from the crowded Kuta beach. It was indeed peaceful; the guests were elderly German tourists lying round the pool like beached walruses, reading books. I swam for half an hour in a vast, deserted pool. On CNN, the news started to come in of the U.S. election, with a victory for George Bush Jr., which was deeply depressing. I switched to another channel to watch European football.

The following morning, I was up at 6.00 a.m. and the only passenger on the hotel bus to the airport at a cost of $5. I paid the departure fee of 100,000 Indonesian rupiah (about HK$100) and climbed aboard a new Boeing 737 of Mirpati Airlines for the two-hour flight to Dili. Immediately after take-off, I could see to the north Gurung Agung volcano (3,142 metres), and later great views of Mount Rinjani volcano (3,726 metres) on Lombok; it was an attractive trekking possibility with gentle slopes and a large crater lake. As we flew further east, we passed the Indonesian islands of Sambawa and Flores to our north, with long ridges of darkly forested land rising steeply out of the sea. Then we were skirting the northern coast of Timor, mountainous, sparsely treed with dry watercourses at intervals running down from the mountains, and through narrow coastal plains to the sea. The dry season runs from June to October.

Dili, the capital of East Timor, was situated on such a plain — dry and dusty before the rains due in a few weeks. The airport was west of the town, a single runway, an immigration hut where I paid a Class 1 Visa fee of $30, and a small terminal building. I looked around to see if anyone from Timor Megatours was there to meet me. There was not, so I took a taxi to the Hotel Turismo. To reach it, I was driven east just past the city centre, giving me a mini tour through the suburbs and along the waterfront. No building was higher than the palm trees and banyans that lined the roads.

The hotel was situated on the landward side of the main road, with a fifty-yard stretch of parkland between the road and the sea. It was a run-down, gray, concrete two-story building. L-shaped, it had an open veranda running round the side, overlooking a pleasantly treed garden restaurant, and connected by a bridge to the third side containing the reception area, kitchens and indoor restaurant. The fourth side of the garden was closed off by a wicker fence from the utility area. My room was on the second floor, large and clean but dark, lit by a single light bulb of minimal wattage. It had no carpet, twin beds, a good hardwood table and two chairs. It had marks on the white plaster-board ceiling from where hooks had held a mosquito net; there was also an air-conditioner, fridge and single wardrobe. At the back of the room was a washbasin with hot and cold water overhung by a large mirror and a strip of neon light. A door to the left of the wash basin led to a shower room, Spartan but functional.

From Hong Kong, I had contacted Rui Gonsalves from Timor Megatours to organize my stay in East Timor. He appeared shortly after my arrival and apologized for not having met me at the airport. We went through the planned schedule; the only disconcerting news was that I had to pay for everything in cash, US dollar. Credit cards could not be used. The currency in use was the US dollar, and very old ones at that; I was told that banks in the Australian city of Darwin, the nearest financial centre, had dumped them on East Timor.

Formalities over, I explored the waterfront park. In Portuguese days, it had no doubt been a delightful area of well-manicured lawns flanked on the inland side by banyan trees and on the other by the beach or further west by an esplanade.

After years of Indonesian occupation and the recent war of liberation, it was now much changed — it had reverted to village life. Fishing nets hung out to dry and to be mended. Fishermen sat at the roadside stalls, selling their newly caught fish to drive-by motorists. A herd of goats grazed happily on rough grass and weeds; their owner sat at a stall selling the milk from that morning's milking. A small child lounged on a motorbike outside the family home, a fragile-looking structure of cardboard carton walls and tarpaulin roof.

Coconuts were on sale at another stall. A fat, hairy, black sow grubbed past followed by her family of piglets. Young men sat in the shade of the trees playing cards. Or they lounged idly on the sea wall watching a fisherman casting his nets close inshore, between the rusting remnants of a sunken ship and the four-deck floating Central Hotel. Previously an inter-island ferry, it was moored just off-shore and linked to the shore by a 100-yard floating walkway. Others watched as a happy crowd of youngsters dived and swam off another sunken ship. The beach itself was, of coarse sand studded with lumps of coral.

On the landward side, past a row of magnificent banyan trees and over the main road, stood evidence of the colonial past. These were smartly restored government offices shining in fresh white paint; an adjoining barracks equally smart behind ochre-colored walls; a refurbished Portuguese embassy and a well-maintained garden. In the center stood a memorial marking 500 years of Portuguese rule.

Back at the hotel, I joined the weekly meeting of the Rotary Club of Dili. Nearly all 20 members were aid workers representing various NGOs. One of the two local members was about to leave for Australia to attend a university course. The speaker was an American Rotarian who wanted to bring in donated hospital equipment but was frustrated by difficulties in getting it past Customs. Other NGO personnel agreed there was a huge hold-up at point of entry. It seemed that, in the past, many dutiable commodities had been smuggled through in containers; now Customs officers were inspecting everything. Other problems were poor maintenance and lack of trained local staff. I learned the population of East Timor was about 800,000, of whom 91 per cent were Catholic. They spoke Tetum and other local dialects, as well as Portuguese, English and Bahasa Indonesian.

I was up early on Friday, and eating breakfast, a simple continental buffet, at 7.00 a.m. in the garden patio, sitting with an Australian, Rod, a legal expert. He was working to make a coherent whole of the Land Rights legislation; at that time, it consisted of an incompatible mix of native tribal law, Portuguese law, Indonesian law and United Nations law. Many freedom fighters had been displaced from their land by the Indonesians;

then, when the country regained its independence in 2002, many others who had sided with the Indonesians had been displaced.

At 7.30 a.m., Chico, the Megatours guide, arrived promptly, driving a four-wheel drive, six-seater Land Cruiser. A native East Timorese, he spoke good English, having spent some years in Australia during the Indonesian occupation. We drove inland through the center of the city. Chico pointed out the dramatic contrast between buildings restored to their original Portuguese splendour and others still derelict after destruction by an Indonesian-backed militia that had damaged 90 per cent of the city's buildings.

We quickly came to the hills behind the city and started the long climb up a narrow two-way road. A car passed us coming down the hill. It was carrying President Xanana Gusmao on his way to Dili from his temporary residence, a pleasant group of bungalows set in colourful gardens that we saw farther up the hill. What used to be the Governor's palace situated nearer the foot of the hill had been reduced to a shell by the militia. The day before, I had been turned away from the gate by a security guard when I tried to take a photograph. But I took one anyway from a higher vantage point farther up the road, from where I had a panoramic view of the destruction.

We saw, walking along the side of the road, groups of children neatly dressed in uniforms, on their way to school, some barefoot. I learned a tremendous effort was being made to give both boys and girls a basic education. We passed the sort of homes they came from—shacks with plaited bamboo walls and grass thatch or corrugated iron roofs, and a patch of cultivated ground growing corn, bananas, sugar cane and mangoes; they were accompanied by hens, goats and pigs. Bougainvillea and hibiscus bushes added color. Further up, we came to plantations of coffee trees, planted under the shade of tall Samtuku trees.

The road became progressively worse, steep, winding and studded with potholes — and this was very near the end of the dry season, which would have been the best time to make repairs. It brought home the country's extreme lack of funds. Aileu was the first significant town we reached; it was a district administrative centre, set in a wide valley of rice fields, some flooded, the green stalks of young rice a welcome contrast to the dusty dryness everywhere so far. The town itself was an unattractive string of houses on either side of the road, many destroyed; the only smartly restored one was the government administration building. A large memorial commemorated the deaths of the many freedom fighters.

Farther into the mountains, we reached Maubisse, dominated by the former residence of the district governor, placed on a semi-fortified hilltop. It was a colonial-style bungalow, square, with wide verandas, and set in a square garden with servants' quarters to one side. I had hoped to eat lunch here, but Chico insisted that my 'all expenses paid' tour did not cover expensive meals at pousadas (inns) such as this building had now become. Instead, we drove back down the hill to the village and ate at a restaurant facing the main road and village square. Here we had an excellent bowl of soup stacked with meat and vegetables, washed down with mineral water. The meal was enlivened by the arrival of a young Austrian woman, an anthropologist who had been traveling around Indonesia for four months. She had spent all of $2 to travel from Dili on the back of an open truck — an unpleasant experience in the dust and heat — and planned to return the same way later that day. Truck transport was the basic means of travel; one grade up were the buses. In the wet weather, the roads were often closed, so the country people had to walk or ride horses.

A War Memorial, dated 1943, to the Portuguese dead in the

war with Japan marked the turn off from the main road to the pousada. A packed cemetery also had gravestones marking the deaths of fighters in the war of independence against the Portuguese in 1974, the Indonesian invasion in 1976, and the struggle leading to independence from Indonesia in 2002. One gravestone carried a photograph of a young guerrilla in battle fatigues carrying a gun, with relief carvings on either side of daggers, dripping blood. How sad it was that, in such a beautiful area, this graveyard should be a witness to such prolonged fighting and death.

The road wound up and out of the wide valley. At the top of the ridge, a side road led towards our destination, Mount Ramelau. Looking back at the valley, I thought that this was a prime place for a golf course—it would be a first in East Timor. If the road had been bad already, it now became much worse—a single track with passing places, pot-holed, areas washed away by last year's rains and not repaired. Chico was an excellent driver, but even he was beginning to feel the strain. We climbed higher, now through conifers and native eucalypts until we came to a crest; from there, looking west across the next valley, I could see for the first time Mount Ramelau, rearing up high on the horizon, a reassuringly gently rounded summit with wooded slopes and free of cloud cover at 2.00 p.m. I looked forward to the climb.

An hour later, we had negotiated a way through the potholed road, round the top of the valley to the lower slopes of the mountain, and reached Hatu Biluico, a hamlet of half a dozen buildings by the roadside. An ex-district official residence perched on top of a shoulder of the mountain overlooked the valley. Like the one in Maubisse, it had been converted into a government-run guest house. My lodgings were just below the road, about 30 yards from the house of the landlord, the farmer who owned the land in the valley. There was also a church and small graveyard, a school house and a football pitch at the floor of the valley.

The Pousada Alecrim Namrau, Rua Gruta Ramelay Hun No.1, was the impressive address of my lodging for the night. It was a wooden structure on a stone base, one floor for living and a storeroom below. The front entrance led straight into a lounge furnished with comfortable sofas and many cushions; through this lay the main living and dining room with a long table in the centre of the room, the walls painted sky blue and decorated uniquely with children's soft toys. Off this room were bedrooms, one single, one double and one with four beds. The bathroom was of bare cement, containing a cistern of water, a plastic bucket and two squat-down toilets.

Chico and I were greeted by Julio, aged 13, second son of the owner, who brought a welcome pot of coffee and bread. I learned that he had five uncles and two aunts and was one of eleven children, nine surviving; the oldest was sixteen. I also learned that East Timor had one of the highest birth rates in the world. After our snack, I strolled down the road taking pictures. The nearest house was a dilapidated wattle and daub construction with a corrugated-iron roof, and with a hollow tree trunk outside for storing water. The young owner was happy to pose for me in front of his home.

Outside the farmhouse of the innkeeper, some of his many children were pounding coffee beans in another hollowed-out tree-trunk, while others were chipping bits of firewood off a large fallen tree. At 5.30 p.m., the farmer and owner put a bulb in the light socket hanging in the centre of the room. The electricity generator was switched on from 7.00 to 10.00 p.m.

Supper was brought from the farmer's house by a column of children, each bearing an item; coffee, rice, spinach, sliced fried potatoes and portions of chicken—wings and thighs off a small bird, a retired fighting-cock perhaps. We started the meal by candlelight, under the watchful gaze of the children, and were happy to have the electricity when it came on later. The children themselves looked well fed.

At 9.00 p.m., we turned in for a brief sleep; we planned to rise at 4.30 a.m. to prepare for the summit attempt the next day. I wore all my climbing clothes in bed because, even near the Equator, the altitude of 6,300 feet meant the temperature was low. We were the only two guests. The guest book recorded 83 visitors in 2004, of whom 42 had climbed Mount Ramelau.

Saturday, November 6
I was up before 4.30 a.m., drank tepid coffee and ate biscuits by candlelight. Outside, I found a clear, still night, a half-moon shining and a brilliant array of stars, with Venus the brightest light in the east. Chico had suggested starting even earlier, so that we could watch the dawn at the summit, but I had stated firmly that reaching the summit was the objective, not the dawn view. Julio joined us as mountain guide. Chico had been up once before and believed he could find the way himself, but had felt it politic to accept Julio's services.

We drove in the Land Rover to the end of the trail at 7,400 feet. We climbed on a well-marked path rising steeply at first along the southern flank of the mountain, using head torches, until the arrival of dawn lightened the sky. With dawn, the wind started blowing strongly from the east. Once we had turned onto the western face, we were sheltered from the wind and could enjoy a gentler climb through a parkland of mature trees.

The remains of a bamboo stage marked the spot where, on October 7 every year, hundreds of people come to celebrate the feast day of the Virgin Mary. I noted a species of Erica, heather, by the trail, and eucalyptus, many of them dead. Deer and monkeys are reported to live on the mountain, but I did not see any although deer tracks were visible on the soft earth, along with the tracks of cattle.

At 7.20 a.m., we reached the summit, (2,986 meters, 9,797 feet); it was dominated by a life-sized statue of the Virgin Mary in white stone, on a five-foot-high stone platform supported by four stone pediments that enclosed a shrine. It had been erected in 1997 during the Indonesian occupation. Plaques raised by various Indonesian and Portuguese military groups were placed nearby to commemorate their ascents. On every side rolled rank after rank of mountains—no wonder the guerrillas were so difficult for the Indonesians to control. Disappointingly, the distant mountains were obscured by a haze of smoke from hill-fires set by farmers clearing the land and burning off the dry grass before rains came to stimulate fresh growth.

During our descent, I lectured Julio via Chico on ecological awareness and suggested that, during his next climb, he bring a rubbish bag to clear the admittedly sparse number of tin cans and plastic bags. In Hong Kong, I told him, the fine for littering was $600, probably more money than he had seen in his lifetime. I gave a second homily on the benefit of exclusion fences to keep deer and cattle from eating seedlings, so that forests would have a chance to regenerate.

Back at the pousada, breakfast awaited us, consisting of locally grown coffee, large bread rolls and butter and fried sweet potato chips. On the road again in the Land Rover, we headed back along the route by which we had come. We stopped to take photographs—a villager and her two young children coming back from foraging in the forest. They carried heavy bundles of branches balanced on their heads. A group of cheerful primary school boys dressed in colourful shirts and shorts, one wearing trainers, two with plastic flip-flops and two barefoot. Fighting cocks were tethered in a group, to be used for that day's sport in Maubisse.

We stopped for lunch at the same roadside café in Maubisse, watched hopefully by an extraordinary-looking dog. It was Dachshund shape with brown and black stripes vertically down its body, a thin ridge of hair along its back like a Ridgeback, and lesser ridges down the side of its neck. At Aileu, we stopped to look round the covered market. It was a small affair, with stalls selling cheap clothing — but not the Che Guevara t-shirt that I was looking for. Vegetables on sale included carrots, onions, potatoes, chilis, and light brown sun-dried coffee beans. Elderly women were sitting on the ground behind their little piles of produce, chatting to neighbours and enjoying their weekly market day.

After Aileu, Chico took a left turn off the main highway onto an even worse secondary road that ran along the crest of a mountain ridge, through a very poor farming area. The villagers' main source of income was firewood, gathered from the rapidly depleting forests, stacked in great piles by the roadside waiting for purchase. The walls of the houses were made from plaited palm fronds, and the roofs were thatched.

We passed a wide valley where there was the remnant of a large lake, with horses grazing on the grassy fields where rice had previously been cultivated. Unexpectedly, in this deprived area, we came across a road improvement scheme, with a park full of expensive heavy earth-moving machines, all painted white in the United Nations Aid colour. Descending from the mountains, we came to Gleno, devastated by the militias; many of the houses were still empty shells. Then we went through Ailaco and thence down to join the coast road back to Dili. Altogether it was a round trip of about 160 kilometers.

Chico and I reached the Hotel Turismo and parted the best

of friends after our brief expedition. I asked Chico to pass on to his boss that I did not have the energy for another long day in a car the next day being bumped around the awful roads. After a long bath, I went down to enjoy the Saturday barbeque as advertised — only to find the garden restaurant deserted, despite all the UN-type cars in the parking lot. The only person there was the 'fat Momma' type bar-tender cum waitress. I ate an excellent fish and chips washed down by bottled water, the meal accompanied by the meowing of a cat, the whining of mosquitoes and the chirruping of a tree lizard.

The next morning I found that the hotel telephone line was not functioning so there was no telephone, fax or e-mail. It was one time when I would have been happy to have a mobile phone. In the fifty rooms in the hotel, there were only fifteen guests. After breakfast, I walked along the beach and watched fishermen casting their surface nets from dug-out canoes with out-riggers, made from bamboo or PVC piping; the boys diving off the wrecked ships. I renewed my acquaintance with the hairy black pigs, and also spied a large white sow. I walked onto the Central Hotel, the ship moored in the bay, and took photographs of the shoreline and boats.

I lunched at the One More Bar, a pleasant first-floor restaurant near the government offices, cool on the veranda frequented by non-Timorese. I enjoyed a large dish of baked potato with vegetables, a Coca-Cola and an iced-coffee, all for $10.50 Down below on the waterfront main road, there was a constant stream of traffic — Toyota taxis cruising for customers, packed minibuses, each with a young man hanging out of the door calling for customers, small buses brightly painted, motorbikes and heavy SUVs. There were many white UN vehicles — cars, minivans and minibuses.

From Chico and others, I now knew that East Timor had

been inhabited by tribes isolated from each other by the rugged topography, speaking thirty-two different languages. Since independence in 2002, with outside help, East Timor had made enormous strides to recover from years of warfare and economic neglect. It appeared to me to be in the Backpack phase of tourist development—only small hotels, minimal tourist development, terrible roads but with great diving and fishing possibilities. Oil revenues should in a few years make a vast difference. East Timor claimed Australia was robbing it of oil revenue, Australia claiming it had rights up to the edge of the continental shelf, rather than up to the mid-way point between the two countries.

November 8

At 8.15 a.m., I was picked up by Rui of Megatours who drove me to the Merpati office to change my flight to that day, then to his own office where I paid his bill of $360 in cash, including the hotel at $40 per day. I assume he was paid something by the hotel, because he gracefully declined my offer to pay for his time driving me around Dili. He took me to the Oxfam office at Matadouro, opposite the Obrigado barracks, in a partially restored building. There I talked with Frank Elvey, director of the Hong Kong projects. Oxfam has groups from Australia and UK all in the same building, cooperating on aid efforts. On the drive to the airport, Rui pointed out the large US and UK embassies and the smarter clubs, hotels and residences in the western part of Dili, rebuilt and looking smart in new paint. He told me that the hotel boom-time was when 20,000 aid workers were in the country: the number had since dwindled to 8,000. Departure tax was $10.

Altogether it was a fascinating trip, well worth the detour. The country had a terrible time of it but was now rapidly repairing the war damage, and improving public health and education. It enjoyed an elected government and the prospect of much better things to come with the arrival of oil revenue. Tourism would be the country's other source of revenue; large cruise boats were expected to start calling soon. What the country needed was golf courses.

INDONESIA, BALI
Gunung Agung
Height: 1,558 metres (5,112 feet)
Date: 2004

Next came Gunung Agung, the highest peak in Bali, Indonesia. The flight back to Bali was uneventful. My arrival visa, this time for 30 days, cost US$25. All flights to Lombok were full, so my plan to climb Mount Rinjani (3,726 m) had to be put on hold. The taxi ride to the Sanur Beach Hotel cost Rupiahs 60,000, or US$6.70, nearer the market rate than my first trip. The hotel tour desk had not managed to make arrangements for my climb up Gurung Agung; so I spent time on the phone making arrangements with the Perama Tourist Service to be guided up the mountain; the cost was Rupiah 1.8 million, about US$20. I had a long swim in the larger pool, then ate a fine meal in the hotel's Basilico Italian restaurant. A long phone call home to Judith was a pleasure, setting her mind at rest about my safe arrival in Bali from the wilds of East Timor. That evening there was a monstrous thunder-lightning and rainstorm—the monsoon rains were due soon. I decided that, if the weather was too bad for the climb, I would leave for Perth earlier than planned.

Tuesday, November 9

I was up and out by 6 a.m. I walked along the jogging track next to the beach going north round a headland so that I could see Mt Agung. It had cloud cover but looked clear enough for my climb planned for that night. I enjoyed an excellent full English breakfast in the restaurant situated between two swimming pools, in a typically open-style Balinese building; hardwood pillars supported an intricately ribbed roof of bamboo, covered with grass thatch. Checking with the travel agent, I found that flights to Perth were full; I would have to keep to my reserved flight on 13 November. I swam in the sea, off Sanur Beach, gently shelving, protected by a reef from the heavy rollers hitting the shore on the southern shore of the island. I saw a large pink starfish ornamented with purple protuberances, and a few long worm-like animals amongst the sea grass.

I had a solitary lunch, with poor service, the under-occupied waiters gossiping noisily. They were a charming crew, but not efficient. For supper, I stoked up on carbohydrate with a large plate of pasta at the Basilica restaurant. Then I rested in my room, watching television, until my guides arrived at 9 p.m. Their old Rover car had a driver and two guides, Didi and Nyuman, both students at university in Denpasar. Didi was in his final year studying Law, with a brother in first year Accountancy and a married sister: his father was a farmer. He spoke excellent English, but Nyuman was quieter having less of the language. We drove round the coastal plane to the north; then, after Klungkung, we gradually climbed up through Selat and Sebudi until two hours later we reached Pura Pasar Agung, a Buddhist temple, where we parked the car. It was too early to start walking; our plan was to reach the summit just before sunrise and avoid having to wait there where it was much colder. The others stretched out in the car; I lay down in a dormitory. The two wide beds had wooden slats covered with a dirty blanket. A prime habitat for lice and flees I suspected, but I came away unscathed.

Wednesday, November 10
I dozed until 1 a.m., when other climbers arrived with their guide — two young Germans. I was well equipped for the climb, carrying in my backpack: food, water, compass, whistle, head torch, GPS device, camera, spare film and batteries. First, we ascended a broad flight of stone steps; I wondered whether the entire route would be paved. Very shortly, I realised that the steps led to a forecourt from which a further stairway led to a Buddhist temple. At the small shrine at the foot of this stair, my guides knelt to make offerings for the safety and success of the climb. They presented small bamboo and flower offerings, lit incense sticks, prayed and invited me to do likewise; they splashed a little holy water onto my head and poured water into my cupped hands "to drink".

Our first obstacle on the climb came immediately — skirting the temple, we had to struggle through a huge heap of bamboo and flower and fruit offerings dumped there after a religious ceremony the previous day. Once clear of the temple, we climbed more or less straight uphill following a path through rainforest; we clambered over roots and grasped at branches to help us up the 45-degree slope. I asked Didi if it got better further up — only to be told that it would get worse! After two hours, we halted at the "half-way point" beside a large tree marking the edge of the treeline. By that time, I was hot, wearing just a T-shirt, short-sleeved shirt and jeans; and thirsty.

Above the treeline, the climb was over very rough terrain, rock and hardened volcanic ash from the last serious eruption in 1963. We stopped at hourly intervals for short rests. After four hours, we were ahead of schedule, with only 90 minutes climbing left and sunrise not until 6.10 a.m.; we lay down and sheltered as best we could from the wind. By now I was wearing all my cold weather gear. The clear sky was brilliant with stars; below us the lights of the towns outlined the curve of the shoreline. Lightning flashed and glowed in the clouds further west, a strange feeling to be above the storm.

After a further hour of climbing, Didi decided he had come far enough; the cold was getting to him, so he went back down to a warmer elevation to wait for Nyuman and me. For the last half hour of the climb, the light in the sky was sufficient for us to do without torches. That was just as well, because the going was very steep. I was glad to get to the safety of the mass of larval boulders at the southern rim of the crater. The sunrise was spectacular, lighting up the clouds far below us in roseate colours. Peaks of lesser volcanoes spiked through the cloud further to the west.

Looking back down the mountain, I could just make out the temple from which we had climbed, in the trees clothing the lower slopes. The crater wall plunged vertically down to a flat base, holding a small lake, strewn with rock-falls. The wall opposite to us was striated with layers of lava coloured in red and ochre and yellow, brilliant in the rays of the dawn sunlight. At 6.30 a.m., we started our descent, going slowly because the gravel between rocks was slippery; even so I fell once, happily without doing more damage than a laceration on one hand. On the way down, we stopped for a snack, joined by Didi, now warmer and more cheerful in the sunlight.

By 9 a.m., we were back at the temple car park where we were greeted by the driver who had spent the night sleeping in the car. Altogether, the climb had taken five hours, including half an hour waiting to do the final leg; it took half that time to descend. It had been harder than I liked, climbing over rough ground by torchlight; a backpack added to instability, which was not pleasant. Next time I will make that sort of climb in daylight. The most dangerous part of the expedition was yet to come. In his haste to get home, the driver nearly killed the lot of us. He careered downhill on the wrong side of the road into the path of a large lorry. Only last-second evasive action by both drivers avoided an horrendous collision. Despite this near escape, he continued to cut corners in a frightening manner. It was with relief that I arrived back at the Sanur Beach Hotel and stepped out of the car, grateful to be in one piece. In a fit of bravado, despite aching legs, I climbed the four floors to my room rather than take the lift. After a welcome bath and change of clothes, I had my hand dressed, very competently by the hotel nurse. Once she learned that I was a doctor, she declined to charge a fee.

Thursday, November 11
Before my flight to Perth, I had two days to enjoy Bali. On the first day, I had a large and leisurely breakfast and relaxed until 11 a.m. then walked slowly through Sanur village on the landward side of the resort hotels. Predictably, prices were cheaper on the street — for example, laundry was one fifth the price of that in the hotel. I stopped at the Hyatt Hotel for lunch with the oldest Rotary Club in Bali, founded in 1983. The simple meal of chicken, rice and fruit cost the equivalent of HK$60, a far cry from the Rotary lunch at the Peninsula in Hong Kong at HK$275. They were a friendly bunch of Indonesians, animatedly discussing aid

projects. My neighbour at the table translated the salient points.

On the way back to my hotel, I picked up the four rolls of film I had left with a camera shop for developing. The rest of the day I spent labelling the photos. The climb had left me with stiff thigh muscles and abrasions on my hand, but no blisters on my feet. I was in bed by 11 p.m., just as a severe squall swept in from the sea; it brought a heavy downpour and a wind that had the palm trees bent over, the flags flying horizontally and the fairy-lights on the trees dancing: a good night not to be on the mountain.

Friday, November 12

My pre-breakfast walk was along the beach. The hotel staff were digging holes in the sand into which they piled the sea grass and other flotsam dumped on the beach by the storm. Boatmen were preparing their brightly-painted outrigger canoes for the day's outing. At the back of the beach were a number of high bamboo poles each with a rattan decoration at the top like a fish and a two bladed wooden propeller, traditional wind-vanes, functional yet decorative. Other tall bamboos had no decoration, but vertical slits cut at regular intervals in a spiral up the shaft. When the wind was strong enough, there came a melodic hum from the bamboo, a strange musical instrument. Between the hotels were a few of the original private residences, wooden-walled thatched-roofed, in mature gardens, one with two small deer, like the barking deer in Hong Kong.

In the afternoon, I took a taxi to Legian, to 'Ground Zero', the spot where the bombs set off by islamist groups Jemaah Islamiyah and; al-Qaeda, on 12 October 2002 killed 202 people, mostly holiday-makers. It was situated at the intersection of two main roads, five stone steps led up to a platform with a fountain at its centre; behind, against the background of a curtain of stone, was a Balinese sculpture in white stone of an impressionistic tree of life rising to the height of a three-storey building. At the base of the sculpture was a plaque of black marble with the names and countries of origin of all the victims of the bombing. It was well done, a sombre reminder of a terrible act. I was saddened to see holiday-makers treating it as just another tourist photo-opportunity.

Legian merges into Kuta, the original backpacker's paradise and now again thronged with tourists. I walked through the narrow streets, keeping clear of motor bikes and squeezing past taxis in the narrow streets; they were lined with small shops selling Balinese crafts, paintings, jewellery, silverware, carved wooden objects, music shops, surf boards and beach clothing. "Osama Don't Surf" was a popular message on the T-shirts. The area was interspersed with bars and restaurants—all a lively contrast to Sanur.

I passed the ornate stone and coral decorated entrance to "Poppies", the original beach lodging house. Further on, I stopped for a much-needed haircut. On entering the "Lotus Hair Beauty Salon, Ladies and Gents", I was disconcerted when the hairdresser rose from a couch on which she had been breast-feeding her baby and put the babe down. I asked for a light trim and became even more nervous when she set to with an electric razor. However, she soon switched to a comb and scissors and completed a very satisfactory trimming. The whole scene took no more than 10 minutes and cost the equivalent of HK$15.

Through the maze of streets, I made my way to the long curve of beach that has made Bali famous. The tide was right out and wind offshore so there was little surf. I sat at the Kuta Inn beach café and drank slowly an iced tea, watching the human drama taking place around me. An English family was having the full Bali experience. Father was lying on a rattan mat on the beach having a massage and eyebrow-pluck. His 20-year-old son joined him for another 45-minute massage. His wife was sitting on the steps to the beach, holding her baby and having a back and neck massage. At the same time, she was trying to bargain with three different hawkers who thrust garment after gaudy garment at her for approval. Having bought several items, she sat down on a rattan mat and started to have a leg massage; she handed over the baby to her teenage daughter and younger son. Before long, the baby's persistent crying became too much for the daughter, who decided he was hungry; she handed the baby back to her mother. Mother started breast feeding — while still being massaged and mobbed by hawkers. I was reminded of the first visit Judith and I made to Bali, when we stayed at the Kuta Palace Hotel — alas now no more. Judith's enjoyment of a massage on the beach was totally spoilt by over-persistent hawkers. This scene had been re-enacted countless times over the years and always will be in the future. I walked away west along the beach to watch the sunset away from the crowds.

In the distance, I could see flags and a crowd of people dressed in white. Walking closer, I found a religious ceremony taking place. I learnt that this was the second day of a Hindu ceremony to invoke the blessing of the rain god and bring a good rice harvest. At the centre of the ceremony were two tables covered with white clothes and bearing ornate rattan and grass offerings, jugs of holy water and bowls of fruit. Sitting on the sand in front were a row of seven priests dressed in white with white head-dresses; in front of them were 40 or so more rattan and grass offerings. To the left was an "animal", a grass-covered beast decorated lavishly with golden pieces of cloth sparkling with mirrors, a golden tail and an ornate face with moving jaw. Red pom-poms on all protuberances added further colour.

Seated to the left were dozens of women in white blouses and colourful sarongs, with circlets of golden flowers in their hair. Behind the centrepiece were about 200 men dressed in white. Leading down to the water's edge from either side of the ceremony were two rows of bamboo poles carrying long flags. Running around and having fun were groups of young boys smartly dressed in white shirts and coloured sarongs. The ceremony went on for some time, with chanting led by the head priest, dances by the priests carrying the ornate offerings, dancing in unison by about 50 women, and a dance by the "lion-like animal" supported inside by two men. The priests rang bells, then went round the crowd blessing each person by sprinkling water on their heads and pouring a little water three times into cupped hands—just as I had experienced two days before during my climb. The ceremony ended at sunset with the tide beginning to come in, floating off the myriad little floats of rattan bearing flowers that had been placed at the water's edge. It would have to be an uncaring god that did not respond to such a ceremony.

Back at the Sanur Beach Hotel, I dined in splendid isolation on the balcony of my room; it directly overlooked the open-air stage where there was taking place a Legong Dance. It was performed by a troupe of nine dancers dressed in rich colours, predominantly gold jackets and red or green sarongs, with exotic headdresses. They were backed by a 20-piece gamelan orchestra. The setting was perfect, with the dancing area flanked by tall palm trees and the backdrop of an ornately carved stone temple entrance.

Altogether, the day was a perfect finale to my stay in Bali.

NEWS FLASH: That day, an earthquake hit East Timor, 7.2 to 7.4 on the Richter scale and everyone was advised to stay away from the beaches.

CAMBODIA

Phnom Aural
Height: 1,813 meters (5,948 feet)
Date: January 2006 (I was aged 70)

This was my second visit to Cambodia. I made the first in 1996, when I accompanied Judith to the National Workshop on Tobacco Control Strategy and meetings in Phnom Penh with government officials on smoking control policy, sponsored by the World Health Organization. At that time, travel outside the capital was hazardous because of widespread banditry, remnants of Khmer Rouge forces and land mines. Despite that, we were determined to visit the Angkor Wat temples, Cambodia's most famous tourist attraction. We were advised to travel by air to Siem Reap because travel by road or boat was too dangerous. Siem Reap is the country's second-largest city and close to the temples. I am glad we went when we did; it was an unforgettable visit.

Ten years later, there was still a perception of land mines everywhere and that it was a dangerous country to visit. But contacts with Zeman McCreadie of Cambodia Expeditions convinced me that it would be perfectly safe to attempt an ascent of Cambodia's highest mountain, Phnom Aural; it was in an area that had not been fought over and therefore was not covered with land mines.

We chose January for the climb because it was well into the dry season and still cool. The same anticyclone that had brought cold weather to Hong Kong was reaching down to Cambodia, giving maximum temperatures of only 28 degrees Celsius. My Dragonaire flight left at 4.00 p.m. and flew across the South China Sea until it reached the coast of Vietnam. Showing through the clouds were the mountains dividing that country from Laos. The flight turned south as far as the Mekong River and then followed it up to Phnom Penh.

Zeman was at the airport to give me a friendly welcome; he was easily identified by his Cambodia Expeditions t-shirt. In his late thirties, he was stockily built, with short, light brown hair and a well-trimmed moustache and beard. He was an interesting character. Welsh, he ran jet-boat bird-watching trips in the 1,000 islands area off the Pembrokeshire coast of west Wales during the summer, and dirt bike tours in Cambodia in the winter. To get through the congested traffic, he had come to the airport on his dirt bike. He put me in a taxi and arranged to meet me at my hotel, The Sunway. We set off on the main road, but, to my alarm, the taxi turned off onto an ill-lit gravel road. In Manila, this would have meant certain robbery, and possibly kidnap. I questioned the driver, who spoke good English; he told me that we were on a ring route that was still under construction and would avoid the heavy traffic on the main road. And so it proved.

Zeman was already at the Sunway Hotel. We discussed the trip. I was impressed with the thoroughness of his planning, including two reconnoitres to the base of the mountain to confirm feasibility and hire guides and porters. I handed over the balance of the money in payment for the trip; in return, I received an expedition T-shirt and a Kamar, a scarf-like garment which is used for everything, including a headdress, scarf, waistband, and loin cloth when bathing. We arranged to have breakfast together at the hotel at 6.30 a.m. the next morning. I phoned home to confirm that all was well. And so to bed.

Thursday, January 12
In response to my wake-up alarm, I was up at 6 a.m. and a phone call from Zeman. We met at 6.30 a.m. for a large buffet breakfast; on offer was food to suit English, American and Japanese tastes. At 7.15 a.m., the transport arrived—a Toyota Pajero, roof-rack piled high with luggage. The driver was Mr Se, a Cambodian who had spent seven years in Russia learning agricultural engineering; he had also worked as a palace guard. A quiet, amiable man, he spoke French, English, Russian and Khmer. The passengers were the two assistants to Zeman. One was Sima, aged about thirty, who had spent ten years in the police, doing spells as palace guard alternating with fighting Khmer Rouge; the other was Chea, 23, who was studying computer science. Both spoke good English.

Driving north, we followed the western side of the Tonle Sap River, through a Cham area. The Cham are Muslims from a kingdom that used to occupy southern Vietnam and once were constantly fighting the Khmer who had controlled their land in Angkorean times. The women wore head shawls, and there were several mosques. Carpets of fish were lying out to dry and a second crop of rice with fresh green shoots were sprouting in the paddy fields; all showed that this was a relatively prosperous part of the country.

At forty kilometres from Phnom Penh, on Route 5 to Battambang, we stopped at Udong, a small village of roadside shops/houses, previously a capital of Cambodia. We bought offerings for a Buddhist blessing ceremony. While Sima and Chea went to make the purchases, I watched the main-road traffic. There were smart luxury tourist buses, petrol lorries, battered public buses, private cars, motorbikes, bicycles; and private enterprise transport—motorcycles pulling long, flat, trailers equipped with wooden boards for passenger seating.

Purchases made, we drove off the main road to the south on a dirt track to a low ridge, the remnants of a volcano. At the 200-foot summit was a huge, ornate Buddhist stupa from which I had wide views over the flat surrounding floodplain. This building and the others in the temple complex were all recent restorations of previous ones destroyed by the Khmer Rouge. At the foot of the ridge, we entered a temple for the blessing ceremony. We presented our gifts of fresh fruit and lotus flowers; we put them on silver chalices in front of two monks who were sitting cross-legged on the floor. We sat in front of them as they chanted for about ten minutes and scattered the lotus petals over us. Finally, we placed incense sticks in pots standing in front of a bier. Resting in a glass coffin on the bier was the perfectly preserved body of the previous head priest. In the centre of a large rectangular formal lake was the golden figure of a woman standing on a crocodile. The legend was that she was a princess who saved the flooded world by riding in on the crocodile and soaking up the water in her long hair.

We were back on the main road for only a short distance before turning west onto a potholed dirt road, Route 136, leading to Phnom Aural. Distance in Cambodia is best measured in time, not kilometres, because of the state of the roads. The land rose gently, leaving the flood-plain behind; dry rice stubble in the fields marked the end of the harvest. Coconut and oil palms dotted the landscape. Later there were more trees and saplings; intensive logging was denuding the forests. In one area, every hamlet had villagers loading charcoal logs onto carts to take to market; further on were piles of cut logs for sale, for fence stakes, house building, and fuel.

At mid-morning, we stopped for lunch; Zeman explained that, if a Cambodian did not eat rice every four hours, he would become cranky. He and I ate sandwiches brought from Phnom Penh while the others ate rice and dried fish lightly grilled, a staple food. The 'restaurant' was a single room of a wooden house with eating area at the front on wooden tables, and a kitchen stove at the rear. The walls were colourfully decorated with posters of television and film stars and fashion models. A raised wooden platform served as a bed for two small children. In a corner was a stack of electronic equipment, a television, VCR and karaoke machine. This was clearly the social center of the village. In the cluttered backyard roamed unhindered pigs, chickens, dogs and cats; surprisingly, behind this was a hygienic squat-down dunny.

As we came nearer the mountains, the road became narrower, rutted and with even deeper potholes. At this point, the only other traffic was the occasional motorbike or bullock cart. We forded one river. At intervals, the original road was blocked by a fallen tree which we had to drive around.

In the early afternoon we reached our destination, Phum Aural (Phum meaning village), at an altitude of 183 meters, 110 kilometers from the capital. It was a hamlet of ten houses strung along the road, all made with wooden board walls and thatched roofs and set up on stilts, and with one barn-like schoolhouse.

Tents were set up for Zeman and me on a sandy patch of ground between the houses and the road; the others strung hammocks under the houses. Everyone in the village was watching. Then we walked the 200 yards to the Aural River for a welcome bath in its clear, cool water. A host of butterflies were enjoying the damp sand at the river's edge. Just before sundown, Zeman and I ate an excellent meal pre-prepared by Deborah, his partner—kebabs, rolled leg of lamb and tea; we were sitting at a camp table and observed by the villagers. We chatted for an hour and admired the full moon as it came up. I had a folding camp bed with a sheet and two blankets in a mosquito-proof tent and so looked forward to a good night's sleep.

Friday, January 13
But it was not a good night's sleep. At 3.30 a.m., I was awakened by a cock crowing noisily—perhaps thinking the full moon was daybreak. Also, as the night went on, it became steadily colder. Two blankets were not enough. I was up at 5.00 a.m., before dawn, and made use of the squat-down dunny; I picked my way carefully through the cow pen by torchlight to get there. We breakfasted on muesli and coffee. At first light, we all piled into the Pajero for a drive closer to the mountain. Zeman, Sima, Chea and I were now joined by two porters and a guide recruited at the village. After fording the river and a short drive, the cart track had deteriorated to such an extent that the car could go no further. We started a long walk. On the first shoulder of a hill, we stopped for another Buddhist ceremony; the prayer had been given to Sima by the monk at Udong. We left bananas and lighted incense sticks—I hoped we would not be the man-made cause of a hill fire, as so commonly happens in Hong Kong following grave-sweeping rituals.

The climb now began in earnest, up steep slopes, first over

granite boulders and grassy open spaces between sparse park land tree cover and later through groves of bamboo. At 10.30 a.m., we stopped for lunch beside a stream. We filled water bottles through a filter pump and added chlorine sterilizing tablets. The pattern of progress was already established. The lead guide climbed at a fast rate followed by Sima, Zeman and then me and a porter; at a slower pace came Chea and the last porter. After every twenty minutes, the leaders stopped and sat down to wait for the last two. Despite good-natured abuse from Zeman in terms of "lazy city fat boy", Chea could not go any faster.

An hour later. we reached a shoulder from where we could at last see the summit ridge through the trees. And what trees— the bamboo had given place to a mixed forest of deciduous and fir trees, the mature firs rising eighty feet before branching. For the next four hours, we worked our way upwards along barely discernible trails left by animals; we climbed over two high points on the ridge before reaching at 4.15 p.m. a suitable campsite. We had heard gibbons calling, seen evidence of wild pig diggings and seen droppings of a large herbivore and broken trees suggesting elephants. But we saw no signs of the tigers reputed to be in the forest. The guides had no anxiety about landmines underfoot, because the forested area was not a scene of conflict. Neither did we see any snakes, possibly because of the citronella fruit which we had each been advised to carry.

That night I slept in a hammock for the first time. Happily, I managed very well. Before sleep, I gazed up at the stars shining between the silhouetted trees and the full moon shafting light onto the bushes underneath. Unforgettable.

Saturday January 14
At 3.00 a.m., I woke up feeling cold and was pleased to get up at 5.30 a.m. once Zeman had a lighted a fire and heated water

for morning tea. He enjoyed fires, and had stayed up for two hours the night before, after I had turned in, to build up and enjoy his fire. Others in the group had their own fires to keep animals away. At 7.00 a.m., we were on the trail, lightly laden, intending to return to the same camp that day. Even so, with only a water bottle to carry, Chea lagged behind. Climbing along the ridge line was marginally easier than the climb the day before. There was even more evidence of wild pigs, the ground being heavily dug over, and muddy wallows created in the hollows left by fallen trees. Fresh hoof prints of pigs in the mud and of a large cloven-hoofed animal, perhaps a kouprey or wild ox, were easy to see.

At 10.30 a.m., I followed the first three into a clearing to find the guide sitting down. He reported this as the summit; but, looking through the trees. I could clearly see another peak at a higher elevation. On further questioning, he said that, from his village, the peaks looked the same altitude, but that yes, the other one was a few meters higher. So on we went.

An hour later we were at the true summit. Zeman checked the location on his GPS device, at 1,806 meters. A small, ruined stone structure marked the summit. The guide did not know its origin but thought it might have been built by the French. We had no view, since the summit was clothed in a thick growth of young trees. To mark our presence Sima chopped out 'TOP' on a tree-trunk; Zeman, Chea and I took team photographs.

Returning to camp, we took our time, walking very quietly in the hope of seeing game. We heard more gibbons, but that was all. We returned to camp by 1.00 p.m. The porter we had left to guard it had filled the water bottles with boiled stream water. The rest of the afternoon Zeman and I spent separately exploring the area, hoping to see wildlife. In the evening, I washed in the stream and changed clothes; in doing so, I picked up a host of bites round my ankles, I thought by midges. It had been a perfect day for climbing—dry, sunny and cool under the shade of the trees. That night I used the waterproof sleeve over the sleeping bag and all my clothes on as usual.

Sunday, January 15

I slept well, warm all night, but disturbed by itching of insect bites and noises of pigs foraging. I was up at 5.30 a.m. for the usual breakfast of muesli and tea. The camp was packed, all refuse burnt and fires extinguished before we left at 7.30 a.m. Going down was certainly easier than climbing up, and faster too because we went down a more direct, more precipitous route. Even so there were viciously spiked vines to avoid and creepers ever present to trip you up, and the marginal trail disappeared entirely when interrupted by a fallen tree. Chea again lagged; finally I had him walking in front of me, urging him forward and determined that all seven of us would reach base unscathed. The porter who stayed with Chea did not mind the slow pace; he took advantage of the time to collect bark and roots and cuttings to make medicines and food.

Reaching the valley floor, we knew the Pajero would not be there; instead, Zeman had asked the driver to send four motorbike riders to meet us and ferry us for the last six kilometres to Aural village. Our delight at meeting them as planned was short-lived. They demanded $10 each to take us. Considering that he was paying the porters only $5 for a strenuous day's climb, Zeman rightly declined to be pay these cowboys twice that wage for a one-hour ride. It was now midday, hot, and our water supply was running low, but we set off to make the best of it. Happily, after half a mile, two other villagers rounded a corner on their bikes, and agreed to take Zeman and myself for $0.50 each. Delighted, we climbed onto the pillions, I wore my pack and held a porter's heavy backpack in front of me; my driver balanced another pack in front of him. This, my first ever motorbike ride, was memorable. We whirled along the dirt track, swerving from one side to another to avoid holes, ducking under low bamboo — no helmets of course — just me holding on for dear life. We made excellent progress trying to keep up with Zeman's driver; he was holding on casually with one hand, as he tried to photograph me behind him.

Progress halted when we came to a stop halfway across a river. I got off while the bike was pushed to the bank, passed over to Zeman one of the heavy packs and we set off again; we arrived at the village without further mishap at 1.00 p.m. An ice-cold a can of Coca-Cola was very welcome as we waited for the others to appear on the return trip of the motorbikes. After lunch, it was a very real pleasure to go back to the river for a refreshing dip and change of clothes. Zeman found he had a tick on his leg, a black crab-like creature about three millimetres across; he had difficulty getting it off despite use of iodine liquid and the flame of a lighter. Eventually, using the blade of my penknife, it came away complete with its head.

While the crew put up the tents, we walked around the village, passing a herd of cattle, white with a hump above the shoulders, possibly a Brahmin cross with a French Charolaise, and a water-buffalo drawn cart. Dinner that night was a special celebration — chili beans and rice, washed down by an excellent red wine. The 'city boys', Sima and Chea, celebrated with the villagers by drinking copious quantities of palm wine and singing to the karaoke machine. Zeman finally closed them down at 900 p.m. so that we and the rest of the village could go to sleep.

Monday, January 16

Up at 6.30 a.m., we had a slow start, all except Sima who slept in his hammock until it was time to pack up to leave. The nearby school was summoned by the teacher striking a metal lorry wheel with a steel bar. He was a young man who had arrived on a motorbike, wearing a football shirt with a '10' on the back. On the road at 8.00 a.m., we crawled along the appalling cart track retracing our route as far as Trapeang Track, then heading south to Kampong Spueu. Part of this road had been upgraded and smoothed since the rains and showed how fast the roads could be, if properly maintained.

The countryside was much the same except for one large lake covered with lotus flowers, with dug-out canoes moored at the bank. At Kampong Spueu, an unprepossessing town of new buildings, we joined a tarmacadam highway again; this was Route 4 from Phnom Penh to Sihanoukville. We stopped here at a roadside café to have a bowl of one of Cambodia's national dishes, tasty, marinated beef, green beans and rice. On the next forty kilometers into the capital, we passed an emerging light industry park, and even a golf course.

Back at the Sunway Hotel, I said farewell to Zeman's crew, giving each of them a tip equal to one day's wage. I arranged to meet Zeman and Debora for dinner the following night. Once in my room, I stripped off all my filthy dust-covered clothes and sent them for express laundry, just meeting the 3.00 p.m. deadline. They were back at 7.00 p.m., immaculate. I telephoned home and spoke to our maid, Lucy, to pass on the news of safe completion of the climb. After enjoying the luxury of a wonderful hot shower, I settled down to have a careful look at my insect-bitten legs. To my horror, I discovered one crab-like tick and several smaller mites. I must have picked them up at the mountain camp and had hosted them as they worked their way up my legs for the following two days. This resulted in at least 100 bites on each leg; the ones on my left foot had already produced large blisters.

The tick was the most difficult to remove, since its head was buried in my skin. Eventually, after dousing it in insect repellent, I prized it loose with my penknife—an unpleasant postscript to an otherwise great trip.

Tuesday, January 17
I spent most of the day with my feet up, literally. Apart from a large breakfast in the hotel restaurant and dinner in the evening, I lay down with my feet raised in an attempt to shrink the blisters. It made no difference. In order to walk out to dinner, I pierced the blisters and covered them with plasters. The time passed very well; I read a book by Joseph O'Connor, called *Star of the Sea*, based on the Irish famine in 1847. The farm clearances and forced migration of the starving peasants brought echoes of the holocaust in Cambodia under Pol Pot.

Zeman and Debra joined me for a drink at the hotel. Then we went out to dinner at Milas, a very new, very upmarket restaurant in the city centre. We sat in the walled patio beside an ornamental pond with fountain playing, in front of the white three-story building. The service was excellent and the food Cambodian, beautifully presented. I arranged to meet Zeman the following day for lunch at the FCCC, a clone of the Foreign Correspondent's Club in Hong Kong.

Wednesday, January 18
Leg inspection showed no new bites, the refilling of the blisters, but no sign of secondary infection. By mid-morning, I had breakfasted lavishly, packed up and checked out of the hotel, leaving my luggage to be collected later on my way to the airport. A taxi down to the National Museum cost $5. Ten years earlier, my impression of the museum was of an elegant building in classical Cambodian style housing a dusty and scanty display of artifacts,

and droppings from a million bats. This time the bats were not in evidence and the display was well set out and labelled. After an hour there, I walked down the street to the waterfront road, the Preah Sisovath, to the Foreign Correspondent's Club. The club was a bright airy place on the second floor with heavy lounge chairs on an open veranda looking over the river; it had a bar and dining area, pizza oven and a TV alcove showing Cambodia's most popular programme, All-In-Wrestling.

On the walls were historic photographs, one was of a barefoot Khmer Rouge soldier patrolling a street in Phnom Penh. The photographer had been trapped by the Khmer Rouge advance into the city, had survived to tell the tale and was today sitting along the veranda, a small wiry man with a shock of grey hair and a beard. Zeman joined me and shortly afterwards, a friend of his, who was on the FCCC committee. He was helping Zeman put up a new website for Cambodia Expeditions.

I talked about the Phnom Aural climb, while Zeman took notes for publication in the FCCC newsletter and took my photograph. In the conversation that followed, there were interesting snippets.

At Cambodian New Year, a bull from the King's herd is brought to the lawn behind the club where it chooses between several food crops, his food choice sure to be blessed with good growth during the coming year.

The skeletal palace across the Tonle Sap River was the convention center planned for the Association of Southeast Asian heads of meeting some years ago. Once the bribes had all been paid, there was no money to finish the building.

The medical system received millions of dollars of aid money, of which only eight per cent actually benefited the poor. The education system was better — only 50 per cent disappeared.

After this pleasant and instructive interlude — I paid for the lunch — Zeman took me back to the Sunway Hotel on the back of his dirt bike. I filled in the time before going to the airport by strolling round the corner to Wat Phnom where I photographed a statue of the fierce Kouprey that we nearly saw on the mountain, a large beast like a Spanish fighting bull with enormous horns; a pavement seller of lotus flowers and incense sticks, and a memorial to the 1907 Treaty between France and Cambodia. I did not have the heart to photograph the sad elephant on hire to take people for rides, nor the cage packed with little birds whose release would cost a few dollars and bring merit to the Buddhist faithful, nor the amputees begging on the steps — a continuing reminder of the horrors of the country's many wars.

(The taxi to the airport cost $7 and took half an hour. The Departure Tax was $25). My Dragonaire flight left on time and provided the familiar pleasure of the South China Morning Post with which to catch up on the news. Our Filipino helper Oscar met me at the airport at 11.00 p.m. and I was home by midnight. The trip had been a success. I had climbed the highest mountain of one more country, this one well off the tourist path. In so doing, I had enjoyed myself, learned a lot about Cambodia — from the basic life of the village to the growing sophistication of the capital.

BURMA (Myanmar)
Mount Victoria
Height: 3,109 meters, (10,200 feet)
Date: January 2008

My target was Mount Victoria, the highest peak in Burma accessible to trekkers. The country's highest peak is Hkakabo Razi, 5,881 meters or 19,296 feet. It is in the far north, part of the Himalayas; it is difficult to access and difficult to climb — not a trekker's peak. It had taken the first international climber, a Japanese named Takashi Ozaki, three attempts before he succeeded — and he had already climbed Everest, twice.

January 16 Hong Kong to Rangoon (Yangon)
Judith and I left for the airport together, Judith flew Air India to

Mumbai for a three-day conference and I took Thai Airways to Bangkok. From there I would fly to Rangoon for a two-week visit during which I hoped to climb Mount Victoria. After a three-hour flight, I arrived in Bangkok at 5.00 p.m. local time, just in time to board another Thai flight for the eighty-minute flight to Rangoon. There was a ninety-minute time difference from Hong Kong. I was worried about my backpack making the connection; fortunately, it arrived — and was easily spotted as it was bright green.

Lwin, the Burmese guide for the trip, met me at the airport. He immediately made me feel welcome, chatting while the driver took us the half-hour trip through the city. The roads were good, and the traffic was light; we had a glimpse of the Shwedagon Pagoda, brilliantly floodlit and shining above the trees to our left. Our destination was the Traders Hotel, just three years old, a five-star hotel managed by the Shangri-La Group. There I met Leo Murray, a Hong Kong friend and organizer of the trip. An inveterate traveller and rock climber, Leo, then 65, was an American who had lived in Hong Kong for many years. Previously, he had flown aircraft for the Auxiliary Air Force of the Hong Kong government. The group had seven other members, of whom I knew two, in addition to Leo. They were Ron Clibborn-Dyer, 68, and his wife Veronica, 65. He was British and formerly a Chief Superintendent of Police in Hong Kong. Veronica was South African and a primary school teacher. They had lived in Hong Kong for many years and were, like me, keen gardeners. I was the oldest member of the group at age 75. The other five were Stephen March, 61, formerly a dentist and Olympic Luge competitor at the Sapporo Olympics in 1972; his wife Marion, 63, a former dentist who lived with her husband in Guernsey: Marit Kleppa, 67, a librarian at the Norwegian Parliament; Kerry Ferris, 59, a tour guide at Kakadu National Park in Australia;

and Julian Armstrong, in his 60s, formerly a British banker with HSBC and resident of Kuala Lumpur.

I took my gear up to my room and returned at 9.00 p.m. to meet the others and the director of the Travel Agency, Shota Kanazawa; a Japanese. He had lived in Burma for many years and in good English, he briefed us about the trip. A tall Norwegian, Marit, told us the sad story of her friend Kirsten who should have been with us. A day earlier, as she tried out her new boots, she had tripped and fallen flat on her face receiving severe lacerations; she was in hospital for repairs.

Rangoon to Mindat

I was awakened by my alarm at 4.15 a.m. after a good sleep and was in the lobby by 5.00 a.m. to meet the others and pick up a lunch box, before climbing into the bus to the airport. Built in 1975, the domestic airport was crowded with early morning travellers. At 7.00 a.m., we took off for the central city of Bagan in a new Air Bagan ATR propjet. During the seventy-minute flight, we had a smartly served snack.

After our arrival, a bus took us along well-tended avenues to the local government offices. There we waited for half an hour, while Lwin went through paperwork with the officials. We had to show special permits to enter Chin Territory where Mount Victoria is located. In the meantime, we observed the traffic — trucks hugely overloaded with goods and people, horse-drawn two-wheel tongas, bicycles with sidecars for passengers, motorbikes and bicycles. Once we had completed our business, we drove past some of the famous temples and stupas of Bagan to reach the Irrawaddy River. The water was low, so there was a wide strip of bank leading down to the boat. On the bank were pottery makers, a man pounding rice into flour and people carrying loads of stones in baskets balanced on their heads from a riverboat to a waiting lorry. Our ferry was a long thin boat with a dramatic outboard propeller/rudder like the ones at Bangkok. It took forty minutes to cross the river, passing a large ferry boat going upstream and a huge barge loaded with teak logs going downstream. Fisherman in small boats were casting their nets; other nets were hung up to dry on the sandy banks.

On the far shore, four Jeeps were waiting for us; old and covered with dust, they did not look prepossessing. After much discussion, all our luggage was stowed and we packed in, two scrunched into the narrow back seat and one in front. Having the longest legs, Julian claimed the front seat, while Kerry and I were in the back. The roads were awful, packed earth, and the jeeps raised clouds of dust. As the last vehicle, we had to hang back from the dust clouds to avoid being smothered. Sometimes the roads were sealed but full of potholes, and so narrow we had to go onto the shoulder to let oncoming traffic ease past. Slower buses in front of us were reluctant to let us pass, so our driver had to make a charge to overtake when he could. The trip took about six hours, first across very dry plains, and across rivers running low between wide sand banks where vegetables were being grown, to be harvested before the rains started in April. Then we went over rolling hills and finally up steep wooded slopes.

We stopped once in a market to buy fruit and towels, visit the dunny and give the driver a break. He appeared to keep going with the help of a betel nut wad in his mouth. His discoloured teeth bore evidence of a long-term habit. We stopped again for lunch—multiple dishes of chicken and beef and vegetables all served at once; they were preceded by vegetable soup, backed by liberal helpings of rice, and concluded with fresh fruit. We would have the same meal with slight variations for lunch and dinner for the rest of the trip. Our third stop was because the leading Jeep had broken a shock absorber. A roadside repair shop mechanic took off the broken parts, welded them together again and replaced them on the Jeep, all for $4. It was just amazing. Our route had taken us from the ferry through Wetkyun, Wunbyi, Tamandua and Pruk.

Our destination was Mindat, a long thin town of single-story, mostly wooden huts strung out along a high ridge at 4,800 feet. There we established ourselves in a couple of rest houses. We had individual rooms with ensuite bathrooms; they consisted of a toilet, wash basin with outlet spilling onto the tile floor, a large tub of water and a scoop with which to douse oneself, while standing on a platform of wooden boards. I was provided with a basin of hot water, so I was able to enjoy a good wash down. Electricity for us and the rest of town was on from sundown until 9.30 p.m. At 7.00 p.m., we ate our evening meal at The Rising Star restaurant a mile along the ridge, still boasting a 'Merry Christmas' gold and silver banner. It was a simple wooden structure perched on the side of the hill and facing the road. The kitchen stove was an earthen affair with room for three pots, heated by firewood. The meal was excellent — toasted peanuts as a starter, soup, beef, chicken, potatoes, snow peas, various spices, tea and sweets. Back at our rest house, Ron and Veronica Clibborn-Dyer, Julian and I joined Marit for a nip of Southern Comfort (whisky) provided by her friend Kirsten. With the sundown, it was now so cold that we were quickly into bed inside sleeping bags and with thick Burmese blankets covering us. We also had mosquito nets, although the insects were not around.

Chin village celebration

The next morning, I was up at 7.00 a.m., washed and into a Jeep by 7.25 a.m. to go to breakfast; it was a filling meal of potato samosas, soup noodles, bread and tea. On the way back to the rest house, we passed a long line of saffron-robed monks with their bowls held out, to be filled with rice by benefactors keen to earn merit for their next incarnation. At 8.30 a.m., we set off in a Jeep convoy, down a winding, dusty, dirt road past a hillside burned off the preceding dry season, from which wood was being gathered. Down 1,000 feet, we crossed the river on a good fifty-meter long bridge and climbed up an equal distance on the other side of the valley until we reached a huddle of houses. The road had been repaired and graded since the last rainy season, but there were still two patches where landslides and overflowing streams made driving difficult.

The houses were perched on the side of the hill, supported on tree trunks; they were made of a bamboo frame with rattan walls and grass-thatched roofs. The Chin women all had tattoos on their faces. The practice reportedly started so raiding parties from other tribes would find the women unattractive and not take them away. The practice was now officially banned. Many of the women smoked tobacco through long-stemmed pipes. The many children were not tattooed, and looked healthy enough, playing among the dogs, chickens and pigs of the hamlet. From our vantage point, we could see a village on the other side of the valley, where we were about to witness an extraordinary celebration.

To get there, we walked down a steep trail through fields of corn, castor oil plants, banana groves, tea bushes, coffee trees and patches of vegetables, beans, cassava and sweet potato. After crossing the river at the bottom of the valley on a bamboo bridge, we ascended the other side until we came to Kyardor village. Our first view was of the graveyard, a mass of stone 'toadstools', four supporting stones holding up a massive flat stone, the ashes of the deceased being placed under the stone.

At the center of the village was a large hut with a bamboo

deck; outside it, village elders were sitting clad in G-strings with colourful blankets over their shoulders, and bright red head scarves adorned with white cock feathers. Women were fully dressed and turbaned. Both sexes smoked tobacco in long pipes. One man was carving decorations on a ten-foot tree trunk at the point where it divided and formed a Y-shape. This was to join nine others already standing in a row in commemoration of previous sacrificial ceremonies. There was a surrounding mass of women and children from other villages in the valley.

The ceremony about to begin was a harvest thanksgiving event not held every year and only held by villages that could afford to show off to their neighbours. Rice wine was passed around in buffalo-horn goblets. We all had to take a sip. The first sacrificial victim was a small black dog that had its head and then paws chopped off on the sacrificial log. The next to go were two fine white cocks, their necks deftly twisted and then held up till they stopped twitching, so the shaman could predict the future. Their tail feathers were cut off to make new headdresses. An egg perched in the cleft of a branch stuck in the ground was the next divination object; the pattern of cracks when it was broken was the key. The chief subject for sacrifice was a fine-looking young bullock. It was secured to the line of commemorative stakes by a halter round its neck. The elders took turns to try and kill it by firing arrows tipped with steel heads, using a bamboo bow. After half a dozen arrows had been fired in, and pulled out again without any effect, an elder stepped up with a gun and shot the poor beast. It was immediately butchered, and pieces of meat handed out to visiting villagers. The final victim was a pig that succumbed to the third arrow, which passed right through it. This gruesome slaughter of animals horrified most of our party, myself included.

Next came the music provided by drums and cymbals, and

dancing by the elders. They leapt around waving their knives in the air in a ferocious exhibition of fighting off Nats (spirit people). All males over the age of four carried a knife and small basket slung from a waist belt. Amid much shouting and beating of gongs, men now came up the hill carrying the large stones to make two new toadstool burial chambers. Successful completion of this task was followed by more wine-fuelled celebration.

The villagers were animists and believed in shamanistic divination, despite the presence on the hillside above the sacrificial scene of a Baptist church. At this point we left, walking for an hour down the valley to the bridge; there the Jeeps were waiting to take us back up the mountain to Mindat. The evening meal was again at the Rising Star, then back to the rest house, where I was able to get clean with a basin of hot water. A final tot, with the others, of Kirsten's Southern Comfort completed the day.

January 19 Mindat to Aye

I was up at 6.30 a.m. and ready to board the Jeeps with the rest of the party to go to the Rising Star for breakfast. It was the same meal as on the previous day—soup noodles, tea or coffee with condensed milk, and a rather greasy 'baguette'. Before returning to the rest house, we visited two unusual villagers. One was an elderly woman with ears pierced and the lobes expanded by bamboo cylinders about four centimetres across. Festooned with multiple bead necklaces, she was a colourful sight. The second was an even older woman unable to walk upright; she sat on a stool and played a long wooden flute blowing through her nose, her fingers only just reaching the keys.

At the rest house, we completed packing and set off for the first leg of our two-day climb to the summit of Mt Victoria. The two Jeeps were loaded with luggage; four people who were not strong trekkers—Ron and Veronica, Julian and Marit—had opted not to climb what was reportedly the most difficult section. The road would take them over the same ground that we had covered the day before, and further up to Aye, near the crest of the mountain ridge across the valley from Mindat. I chose to walk with the remainder of the party and the porters. The descent to the valley floor was steep walking but interesting, passing villagers on their way to Mindat with loads of wood, others harvesting beans, and patches of brilliant red wildflowers. We paused at the bottom of the valley to allow the porters to catch up, before crossing the bridge and starting the ascent on the other side.

Instead of following the road, Lwin took us up very steep villager tracks. In the heat, I found it difficult to keep up with the others; after an hour, I took the opportunity of taking a lift in one of the Jeeps at a point where the path cut the road. The others took another three hours to reach Aye, exhausted. At Aye, 5,700 feet, we found several bamboo village shacks, and a schoolhouse with wooden walls and a corrugated iron roof built by CARE, a humanitarian NGO. It faced onto a flattened play area and, behind it an immense view over the valley back to Mindat. While we waited for the others to appear, Marit and I walked on to the crest of the hill, finding the first rhododendrons in flower that we had seen. We admired a view over another steep valley, the forest scarred with patches of slash-and-burn agriculture.

The four others and I established ourselves in the schoolhouse, while three of the others opted for tents. Camp established, there was time before the sun went down for our party to join the village children in games of football and in flying a frisbee. We ate our evening meal at dusk, sitting out in the open beside a roaring bonfire. Afterwards we were joined by the porters and villagers round the fire for a singsong. We sang snatches of what we could remember of school songs, such as *There's a hole in my bucket*, ably led by Ron, Veronica and Sam. The village schoolteacher responded by leading her dozen children in several songs, about the beauties of nature, pride in their country and, poignantly, one about care for people with AIDS. When the cold started to bite, we turned in, the wind rattling the schoolhouse.

Aye to Mount Victoria

I slept poorly because of the cold and the howling wind. We were up at daybreak. Lwin already had three slices of toast, a fried egg and cups of tea waiting for us. We had a climb of 4,500 feet ahead of us. It was to be an all-day trek. At first, we had a packed earth road to walk on along the crest of the ridge and into Natmataung National Park. There were magnificent old trees, firs, rhododendrons, teak and Ashoks, rather like oaks. After three hours and at 8,300 feet, we stopped for lunch of vegetable soup, oranges and sweets. Leaving the road, we branched off onto difficult-to-follow, partly overgrown mountain paths, occasionally blocked by fallen trees. We climbed up and down but steadily higher.

A guide led, followed usually by Sam and Marion and Kerry, the fittest and youngest of us. Julian oscillated back and forth depending how many times he stopped to take pictures; Leo oscillated also, up with the leaders sometimes, falling back to encourage stragglers. Ron was usually last, as he stopped at every new plant and carefully took a picture and tried to identify it. I spent much of the climb with Marit and Veronica who found it hard going.

I reached the summit by late afternoon. It was marked by a single steel pole standing on a cement base. To the west was a vista of ranges of mountains of Burma and then Bangladesh and to the north the mountains of Chin State in Burma. To the east, the mountains dwindled down to the foothills and the Irrawaddy plains, with a faint outline of the Shan Hills farther east. A few feet lower on another peak to the north stood a golden stupa.

I was delighted at having finally made it to the summit. Several years before, I had planned to go but had been obliged to cancel.

We pitched our camp in a clearing just short of the summit, all of us in tents. I had spent the day climbing in a t-shirt and trousers, but I knew that, as soon as the sun went down, it would be very cold and so I put on all my warm clothing before the light failed. I joined the others at 6.30 p.m. for a hurried evening meal by a bonfire and retired to my tent by 7.30 p.m. I was already chilled, and the wind was howling. The five female porters, the youngest aged fifteen, shared one tent; many of the male porters spent the night chatting round the fire.

Mt. Victoria to Bagan

I was up before sunrise after a poor night's sleep; I listened to the wind coming in waves—like lying on a beach and hearing the breakers roaring towards the shore then sighing away, their power spent. Breakfast was the usual hurried slices of toast, fried egg and tea. The walk down was a pleasure, blue skies, a gentle breeze once the sun was up, and time to 'smell the roses'. I recognized sweet-smelling buddleia, brilliant gentians, daphnia and the bright red rhododendrons. After a walk of ninety minutes, we arrived at the road head where the Jeeps were waiting for us. We bade farewell to the porters, all nineteen of them; they were a cheerful and hard-working group who had carried as much as twenty kilos of supplies along sometimes precipitous paths, wearing flip-flops. They had earned their pay. Packed into the Jeeps, we now had a seven-hour drive back to the Irrawaddy River. The route took us through teak forests until we reached the plains passing through the villages of Saw, where we had lunch in a restaurant, and Aing-gyi. The roads were poor, some were very poor, and the rest were appalling. The bridges were so fragile that the heavy teak log transporters had to use slip roads that forded the rivers. No wonder that transport largely ceases during the wet season.

We bid goodbye to our drivers at the ferry landing. They had driven well over difficult roads and turned up on time at all the planned meeting places. On the eastern bank of the river, at Bagan, we came back to the tourist world of hawkers; in the mountains, there had been none. We checked into the Bagan Thande Hotel opened in 1922, it was a lovely riverside collection of single-story residential blocks set in gardens with huge mature trees. Phoning home turned out to be a problem. International calls could only be made from the reception area under the supervision of a member of staff who had a stopwatch to time the call, $3 per minute. There were only two outside lines, so it required multiple attempts before I got through — and Judith was out, so I had to leave the message with our domestic helper Lucy that all was well. For dinner, we were taken by bus to a restaurant in Bagan where we sat out in the garden. We had the standard Burmese meal and were entertained by a clever string puppet group backed up by a band consisting of gamelan, flute, drums and gongs and cymbals. Back at the hotel at 9.00 p.m., I was at last able to have a hot shower, get really clean for the first time in four days and to wash some clothes.

Bagan

I slept so well that I did not wake up until 8.21 a.m. I had to rush to join the others at 8.30 a.m. in time for the day's sightseeing. I grabbed an orange from the room for breakfast, missing out on the lavish buffet laid out at the riverside restaurant under the trees enjoyed by everyone else. Our first stop was the Nyaung-U Market. On getting out of the bus, we were immediately surrounded by peddlers of trinkets, cheap jewellery, 'golden' butterflies, scarves, longyi, lacquer boxes and a book by George Orwell called *Burmese Days* that I wanted to read anyway. The asking price was $5, but I got it for $3 after protracted bargaining; the vendor followed me around the market for twenty minutes. One purchase I had to make was glue to mend my climbing boots where the rubber sole was separating from the leather uppers. The market was a lively place. There were tourists shopping for mementos — lacquer goods, Buddha images in wood and clay and metal, puppets and dolls, opium-smoking sets, clothing, knives and swords. There were also local people buying fruit and vegetables, ten varieties of rice, and all sorts of household commodities.

I was happy to get away from the scrum of vendors into the bus and on to our next stop, the Shwezigon Pagoda. From the 11th Century, this enormous temple was one of the oldest in Bagan. The gold on the lower parts was painted, but on the upper parts was gold leaf. The central pagoda was surrounded by a courtyard paved in marble and ringed by numerous other stupa, each one exotically different. On one side was a red brick stupa naked of all the coverings of white stucco and gold it would originally have had. Sam and Marion had visited seven years before and found several of the stupas then in red brick; they had since been restored.

Our next stop was a village factory for making lacquerware. It took eight months to complete one piece. There were many steps in the process, from making the base — either of wood, woven bamboo or woven horsehair, the finest and most malleable — to applying the various layers of lacquer and etching the different colours; each was followed by a week in the kiln. We watched the craftspeople doing exquisitely fine work in poorly lighted surroundings. The final products in the showroom were varied, colourful and some exceedingly beautiful. The lacquer was not applied deeply as in Chinese ware; the emphasis was on intricate design.

Our last stop in the morning tour was the Ananda Pahto Temple. Built between 1090 and 1105, it was one of the largest and best-preserved temples in Bagan. Only the central fifty-two-meter-high spire and minor spires were gilded; the rest was dirt-stained whitewash. I spent time outside in the large, paved courtyard watching monks coming and going, villagers sitting in the shade chatting, children playing, and tethered cattle grazing on grass. Inside was a covered walkway leading to four standing Buddha images, gilded, 9.5 metres high. Inside the south entrance was a double bed richly draped and protected by mosquito nets. A monk was sitting inside, he was broadcasting Buddhist texts on a loudspeaker.

For lunch, we were taken to The Beach View Restaurant, an up-market establishment recently opened by a German. It was on the banks of the Irrawaddy and overlooked a great expanse of beach, during this dry season, anyway. During the meal, we were entertained by a young man brilliantly clothed in sequin-covered silver and pale green; he performed a classical dance with hand movements reminding me of Thai dancing. True to form, Julian spent much of the meal using his newly acquired digital camera to photograph the attractive young waitresses. We were back at the hotel at 3.00 p.m., with the afternoon free from organized activity. I repaired my boots and watched CNN coverage of the US Presidential primaries and of the stock market's 'free-fall'.

By 4.30 p.m., it was cooler. So, armed with my camera, I wandered out of the hotel and headed for the nearest temple, the tallest one in Bagan, called Pahtothamya, as I was informed by a small girl who attached herself to me as a guide. She said she was eleven but looked about nine; she feared she would have to leave school after one more year because the family was so poor and she would have to go into domestic service. Her ambition was to be a tour guide. In good English, she told me her father and elder brother fished, earning 10,000 kyats, equivalent to $10, on a good day. We walked through her shanty-town village, met her parents coming back from market and went off to look at more temples. Not far away, we came to the only Hindu temple in Bagan, Nathlaung Kyaung from the 11th Century, it had Vishnu reliefs inside and remains of murals blackened by smoke. Statues that had been there had been stolen by a German in the 1890s. A great many artifacts had been stolen over the years; the British army used the temples as living quarters during one of its wars with Burma. We climbed halfway up a nearby temple to watch the sunset, before heading to our homes, the girl was happy, I hope, with a payment of 1,000 kyats.

For dinner, we were taken by bus to the Green Elephant Restaurant, in a delightful outdoor garden south of Old Bagan, by the river. The meal was the same as ever, nicely served and tasty.

Bagan to past Kalaw

Breakfast was a special experience. At 6.00 a.m., a full moon sinking in the west reflected sparkles of light off the rippling Irrawaddy River. The full buffet meal I had missed the morning before was worth getting up for. It was a great start to a long day.

As we travelled on the bus to the airport, we saw three hot-air balloons gently rising in the still morning air of a clear day — chariots from which their passengers (paying $275 each) could view the morning sun on the spires of the many Bagan temples. We took off shortly afterward in an Air Bagan plane heading for He Ho, crossing ranks of mountains until we reached a highly cultivated plateau in the eastern highlands of Shan State. A bus took us from the village of He Ho on a seriously bad single-track road over a range of mountains to the town of Kalaw in the next valley. It was perplexing why this particular road was so bad, because it was a trunk route from Burma into Thailand, used by heavily laden trucks. Coming into the town, we passed a new 600-bed hospital built for the army. The tribes along the border with Thailand had been in a state of rebellion ever since independence in 1948. Before that, they fought the Japanese. Before that, having conquered the plains, the British left them to fight among themselves.

At 4,330 feet on the western edge of the Shan Plateau, Kalaw had been a British hill resort. It had become an army base, a trekking center and a market town of about 20,000 people. Exploring the market area, I found a number of internet cafes, and IDD phone shops; I used one of them to phone home and speak to Judith, getting through more easily than from the hotel. The shops were bright, with highly coloured thick blankets that I had come to appreciate for their warmth. Trekking companies advertised their presence. We had come to Kalaw specifically to pick up porters for the next part of our journey—a trek to Inle Lake. We ate lunch at the Everest Restaurant serving Nepali food. The owner was a Nepali descendant of the Gurkha soldiers stationed there in colonial days. He had seven daughters who staffed the restaurant. The meal was excellent, washed down with Nepali tea, thick and sweet and flavoured with cinnamon.

After the meal, we were driven to the edge of town where we were met by nine porters, fewer than before because the terrain was easier than in the west. There were fewer tents to carry because the plan was to stay in monasteries overnight. We set off walking on gentle, undulating cart tracks; we were passed at intervals by oxcarts carrying loads of lime, mined from the limestone rocks by the roadside. We had not gone far when we came to an agricultural village, a prosperous one judging by the new building going on; rattan and thatch houses being replaced by sturdy wooden-frame houses on concrete bases, the lower floor walled with breeze-blocks made locally and the upper level wooden floored and walled, with roofs of corrugated iron.

Here we were entertained to tea with the villagers, and Veronica headed for the village school. By the time we were ready to move on, it was getting late; we stopped at the next monastery at Shar Bin, a Dan-U tribal hamlet. The porters were a long time in catching up with us. It was clear we did not have enough and that they were not of the calibre of the Chin mountain people. By next morning, we hired three more, which made all the difference. The monastery where we had planned to stay was in a dilapidated condition, judged comfortable enough for the porters, but not for us. Next door was a new and very fine building half- completed, but not habitable. In the end, six of us ended up sleeping in the living room of one of the wealthier villagers; the other three slept in tents in the courtyard. The owner and his wife had five sons and two daughters; large families were the norm. The ground floor of the house was a storage area—not a livestock pen, thank goodness. Upstairs in the living room was a Buddhist shrine, at which both parents prayed morning and night. They had a television and a radio. A partition separated two more rooms that they used. Goodness knows where all the children went to that night. With great kindness, the family provided rattan mats for us to lie on, pillows and blankets.

Once we had settled in, the games began. Leo and others blew up balloons and launched them from the balcony to a throng of children in the courtyard below. He then went down to play with them and take pictures. No wonder he has such a store of smiling faces from his travels. We had our evening meal in the old monastery, watched by the monks sitting on the dais at the end of the room, on which stood the Buddha images and ceremonial artifacts. The village dunny was halfway down the hill. Regrettably, several of us had to get up in the night and edge our way down by torch to make use of it. The other impediment to a good sleep was the snoring of four of the others. I solved that problem on subsequent nights by using ear plugs.

Monastery to monastery

We were up at dawn as usual and breakfasted on bread, fried eggs and tea at the monastery. As we ate, villagers carrying great bundles of dried flowers set off for market. With the additional porters, we made better time that day; even so, it was an eight-hour trek over undulating hills, clad in fir or great stands of bamboo. The uplands were dry with hedges of cacti and fields of wheat harvested or ready to be so—all by hand; herds of cattle roamed the higher pastures. The mountains were all of limestone, thrust up from the sea with the movement north of the Indian tectonic plate. The valleys were filled with brown or reddish earth washed down from the mountains, turning to a fine dust on the paths. In places, loss of forest cover to create farmland had led to dramatic erosion.

Hamlets were widely placed. In one, the chilli harvest was being dried in carpets of brilliant red. In another, the skin colour of the villagers was really dark—they were Pa-o tribespeople. We stopped at a rare roadside shop selling cold drinks, snacks and cigarettes. There were cigarette advertisements on the walls—the only ones I saw in Burma, where they must have been officially banned. As the day wore on, Marit became more and more exhausted, despite plenty of fluids fortified by sachets of rehydration powder. I stayed with her at the tail end of the party, with Ron happily taking pictures and Lwin the guide. With much encouragement and great determination, she completed the trek to our overnight destination, a monastery at Hti Thein. It had two main halls built on plateaus cut into the side of a wooded mountain. We stayed in the upper building, about ninety feet wide and seventy-five feet long. The ground floor was a storage area and the first floor a huge hall with the Buddhist shrine along the back wall on a raised dais. We slept in an area to the left, shielded from the rest of the room by seven-foot-high rattan screens. We slept on mats and blankets provided by the monastery. The roof of corrugated iron rose up in tiers to about forty feet under the central spire

Across the beaten-earth courtyard was a well from which water was pumped to two troughs in separate roofless cement-floored rooms, shielded by five-foot-high walls. This was the washing facility. Throwing scoopfuls of icy cold water over myself was a monastic discipline to be endured rather than enjoyed. I felt tingling fresh afterwards, though. The dunny was even further away on the hillside. We ate our evening meal in a wooden outbuilding, warm and smoky with a blazing wood fire. We went quickly to bed as darkness deepened and the brilliant stars came out. A dozen novice monks chanting evening prayers and kneeling in a line in front of the shrine lulled us to sleep.

Monastery to Inle Lake
With ear plugs in place, I slept well and was awakened at 6.00 a.m. by the chanting of the monks. By 8.00 a.m., we were on the road again, climbing over more undulating highland country. We passed through Ngoat, a Pa-O tribal village, where all the women wore red headscarves, and then Than Taung that was Inn-Thar tribal territory. We paused for the stragglers to catch up at a village at the rim of the plateau, where a ravine cut through a range of mountains and led down to Inle Lake.

The path down was steep and rocky through the heavily

wooded ravine, with the roar of a river below. By the time we reached the bottom, we could see stretching out south before us a wide expanse of coastal plain, heavily cultivated with fields of sugar cane, and bamboo, garlic and onions. We paused again at the banks of a large river, which we had crossed on a very rickety bamboo bridge and watched as buffaloes wallowed happily in the water and small boys bathed. One of the guides cut a length of sugarcane, stripped off the skin and gave it to me to eat. It was very tough, fibrous, with an unrewarding amount of sweetness.

Later, we went to a sugar factory, where the cane was pressed in a mangle; the resulting juice was boiled in metal pots and the impurities skimmed off with the foam. The syrup that came out was then boiled again in a wok to concentrate it, before it was poured onto a rattan mat dusted with sugar powder where it solidified. I tasted the resultant slab of brown sugar — sickly sweet. After hours walking across the plain, we suddenly came to the end of the trek. Four boats were waiting for us in a narrow waterway by the road. We paid the thirteen porters with 7,500 kyats, about $7, clambered into the boats with our luggage and were off. The porters would get home by bus from a nearby town.

The boats were about twenty feet long and three feet wide, able to seat five people one behind the other. Sitting at the rear behind a very noisy two-stroke diesel engine, the boatman controlled the combined propeller and rudder. We threaded our way down the canal, past fields, village houses, a monastery and then around islands of floating grass and water hyacinth and past a hotel on stilts over the water. Finally, we sped over open water to our destination, The Golden Island Hotel, at the southern edge of the lake. We were greeted at the landing stage of the main hotel building by a line of staff beating gongs and drums. Spreading out from the reception, lounge and dining hub were four arms — irregular lines of wooden cabins with thatched roofs on stilts, linked by wooden walkways. The rooms were well appointed with a double and a single bed, both with mosquito nets, a fridge, hair dryer, tea-making equipment and mosquito coil burner. Each had a private porch for sitting out, and an ensuite bathroom tiled in white with instant hot water for the wash basin, bath or shower, sockets for electric shavers and a proper pedestal toilet.

After a late lunch and rest, five of us — Leo, Sam, Marion, Kerry and I — decided to watch the sunset from a nearby hill topped by a small temple of five white spires tipped with gold. With a guide, we took a boat round the coast to the nearest onshore village. From there, we climbed up the hill, passing trees from which the villagers collected sap to lacquer the hulls of their boats. From the temple, we had a wide view of the lake, a central area of open water fringed with a wide border of grasses; the whole was reported to be twenty kilometers long and ten kilometers wide. As soon as the sun was down, we scrambled down the steep hill and back to our boat. On the lake, we passed a fisherman laying his nets, standing on one leg and paddling with the other — a remarkable balancing feat. Our evening meal was the same as usual but highlighted by the failure of the lighting system — on the one evening, I hadn't brought my torch. Happily, the lights came on before I had to make my way back to my cabin, at the very end of the long walkway.

Inle Lake

I was awakened by the Buddhist chanting on the loudspeaker from the monastery a mile across the lake, and by the sound of motorboats. I did not feel well, aching and mildly nauseous. A rather soft bowel action prompted me to take an Imodium capsule, which I hoped would control any developing digestive upset while we were sightseeing. I ate little but soup and soft fruit for the rest of the day. After breakfast, we piled into the long boats and were taken across the bay to the western shore and up a river to a market at Indein. Local produce on sale was fruit and vegetables, and fish straight out of the lake, all of the same breed and the largest about nine inches. Over the teak bridge and upstream was Nyaung Ohak, a crowded collection of ancient shrines and stupas; it was overgrown, damaged by earthquakes and weathered over the centuries. Despite this, there were still remarkably preserved bas-relief figures of gods.

Nearby, a long corridor lined by stalls of tourist merchandise stretched uphill to another temple, Shwe Inn Thein. A field of hundreds of stupas commemorated the efforts of previous inhabitants to gain merit for the hereafter. The effort by present-day seekers of merit was shown by the number of stupas that had been restored to their former white and gold splendour; plaques showing the names of the benefactors were placed before each restored stupa. Crossing back over the bridge again, we stopped to watch a farmer in the river scrubbing down his buffalo, and women bathing; the younger ones demurely covered themselves with their black longyis, but a pair of old ladies went topless. By the time we got back to the market, all the fish had been sold. The riverbank where we had landed was a mass of longboats, as tourists from farther away arrived. Back near the lakeside, among the houses on stilts, we visited craft workshops, harassed all the way by floating hawkers. We saw paper being made, a coarse kind from pounded sugarcane stems; parasols made from the paper; jewellery of silver and gold inlaid with precious stones from Burma — ruby, sapphire and jade, crafted most skilfully. At a handicrafts shop, I finally bought something — a silk scarf for Judith. At this shop there were women of the Kayah tribe with their necks stretched by multiple layers of copper wire. I lifted a sample neckpiece and found it very heavy. The Kayan had been fighting the government for years, so tribal members had taken refuge in Thailand and Inle Lake, exhibiting their unique neck ornamentation as a way of earning money.

We had lunch on the second floor of a restaurant overlooking one of the main canals. An enormous meal was served; I ate very little. Near the restaurant, we visited the Phaung Daw Oo Pagoda, the holiest religious site in the southern part of the lake. It was the site where five gold Buddha images were kept; once a year, four of them were carried round the lake in an elaborate golden barge that had belonged to the former king and was housed in the boathouse next door. Next, we visited a factory that wove imported silk, locally grown cotton and a coarse thread made from the stems of the lotus plant. Their showroom had a wonderful array of fabrics for sale. By then I was tired, and happy to sit in an easy chair while the ladies did their shopping. The last stop was a shipyard where hand-built teak longboats were moored

Back at the hotel I slept from 5.00 p.m. to 7.00 p.m., getting up for a light dinner. I then enjoyed a remarkable display of native dances performed by the staff of the hotel. There were two very contrasting styles of dance, a melodic graceful style performed by Pa-O women, and another with drums and cymbals backing suggestive of Chinese music, which accompanied a two-man Lion Dance, but with a golden-fleeced deer instead of a lion. The most accomplished act was a performance of a Puppet Dance by a young man, possibly the one we had seen at the restaurant in Bagan—really excellent.

I slept solidly and went for a big breakfast. We motored down the river below Inle Lake to a second lake to visit the 'non-tourist' market at San Kar. Until the 1960s, there had been two separate lakes. But, as an act of post-war reparation, Japan had built a hydroelectric dam for the Burmese. This raised the river's water level by forty feet, creating the lower lake, and raising Inle Lake by about ten feet. This has caused the loss of much agricultural land and the relocation of many villages, allegedly without compensation from the government.

The market town was on the very edge of the lake, with ancient stupas partially submerged. The market was indeed a local affair with farm produce and local handicrafts for sale. I bought Judith a brilliant red cotton headscarf such as those worn by Intha and Pa-O women. One stall was attended by a young woman in a US Army blue jeans jacket, selling betel nut wads. A pepper tree leaf was smeared with lime and then sprinkled with powdered betel nut and various other sweetening flavours and folded into a parcel. No tobacco was used by the women. Our guide was from the hotel. He told us that his father was a Karen and his mother a Pa-O. His father had fought first with the British against the Japanese, then with the Karen against the government and, when they made a truce, for the Pa-O against the government. The guide had his primary education in a monastery and his secondary education while staying with a rich relative and working as a houseboy. He had partly financed his BSc at Mandalay University by herding cattle twice a year from Burma into Thailand. Twelve young men took fifty head of cattle across mountains and the swift-flowing Salween River. When the conditions were good, it took a week, but in difficult conditions, it could take nearly a month.

On the way back up to Inle, we stopped at Kyauk Taung noted for its pottery making. We watched the potter winding snakes of clay onto the rim of a pot designed for food storage, without using any turntable. She could make twenty a day. The pots were placed in an underground room and fired continuously for twenty-four hours; they were lightly glazed with lead taken from batteries. Further along, we came to a village that distilled rice wine. Rice was first boiled, then allowed to ferment with yeast on rattan mats; then it was placed for a week in large open pots. Then it was heated in closed pots, the vapor being siphoned off through bamboo tubes into a cooling pot. The pot had a double thickness with cooling water in the center that condensed the alcohol vapor circulating around it in the outer sleeve; the liquid was finally collected in bottles. One distillation produced 40 percent alcohol, two distillations 60 percent. We were all obliged to take a sip, my first alcohol since the Southern Comfort at Mindat. I preferred the latter.

We took a short walk past another part of the village where they were making breeze blocks from lime and gravel. We reached another monastery, Thaung Tho Kyaung, with many stupas, some of them restored. From the monastery pier, it was a short boat ride to the Golden Island Restaurant on stilts in the bay. The manager, a local man, had spent three years studying taxidermy in England. He lamented that there were few wild animals at Inle to work on—everything that moved was eaten by villagers. Next stop was a metal workshop that produced knives and swords. One man held a piece of metal on the anvil, while three others pounded it into shape; a fifth man worked hand bellows to heat the charcoal. Lastly, we called in at a cheroot-making workshop. Tobacco shreds were hand-rolled in a tobacco leaf, with a filter inserted, to make the cheroots many men smoked. The fastest worker could roll 800 per day, earning $0.1 cent each. The youngest worker was thirteen. Nowhere did we see any very young children working. Dinner that night was delayed because of a power failure. They had candles at the ready. Lwin was given a fond farewell, and a handshake worth $180, because he had done a terrific job for us. The director of the tour company chastised Leo the next day for being so generous. I had finished all twelve reels of film. The weather that had given us unbroken sunshine all the time we were trekking started to deteriorate. On the trip down the river, there had been wisps of rain from a cloudy sky; at night, a fierce wind blew, rattling the walls of my cabin as rain pattering on the roof.

January 28
Inle to Rangoon

My alarm went off at 5.45 a.m.., The wind had dropped but it was still raining. Thank goodness it had not been like this on the treks; trudging, soaking wet, along muddy, slippery paths would not have been fun. Breakfast was at 6.15 a.m., and half an hour later we were packed into the boats with our luggage. I opted to be the windbreaker for our boat, sitting in the front seat, because I had more waterproofing than the others. We skimmed over the mirror-calm lake, escorted by swifts, and watched flights of ducks coming down to feed. Fishermen were pulling in their nets ready for the morning market. We travelled the full length of the lake before entering a canal leading to the town of Nyaungshwe. There we transferred to a bus heading to the He Ho airport. Ron identified trees decked in brilliant orange blossoms as Tiger's Claws.

The Air Bagan plane was on time at 9.30 a.m. to take us to Rangoon. When the land below was visible through cloud, I could see the streams and ditches full of water. The storm had been unusual because the rainy season was not due for another two months. We arrived at Rangoon an hour later and boarded our waiting bus. Instead of heading for the hotel as I had imagined, we set off on more sightseeing. First stop was a most enormous Buddha image, seated, carved out of a single block of marble quarried in Karen State and ferried down river on a barge to Rangoon; then it had been transported to the hilltop site over a specially built railway line. The figure was enclosed in a glass case with air conditioning to control the temperature and humidity. To get to it, we climbed a long flight of marble steps to a marble courtyard. A tall, elaborately decorated stupa housed the Buddha. This impressive structure was financed by the country's leader, General Than Shwe. The guide was dismissive; he suggested the general thought of himself as a king and was buying merit in the royal manner. On our way down the marble steps, Leo was persuaded to buy the release of three caged sparrows and gain merit for himself. After some hesitation, they did fly off into the trees, but we all knew they would be back in the cage within hours.

Not far away was an enclosed garden, wild with long grass and trees, surrounding a pavilion; inside were three albino elephants captured in the border area between Burma and India. Albino elephants are believed to bring good fortune and are used in ceremonies. They were each shackled round an ankle by a chain leading to rings in the ground, so the elephants were just out of reach from one another. They were rocking backwards and forwards in a repetitive movement, usually indicating distress. We were all put off by this treatment and hoped that they were only on show like this temporarily and could enjoy the surrounding parkland the rest of the time. This was the only place in Burma that I saw an armed soldier, a guard for the elephants.

We lunched very well at the upmarket Sabai Thai Restaurant in an old house on an avenue of large colonial era houses set in large gardens. The change in food was welcome. At 2.00 p.m., we were back at the hotel and found we had been upgraded to top floor rooms — perhaps because the manager was an ex-Hong Kong policeman known to Ron. While the others went off on a conducted tour of market areas, I opted to go to the Shwedagon Pagoda, which the others had visited on the day before the trek started. I bought more camera film and took a decrepit old taxi to the temple for 2,000 kyats. I was glad I had left this temple to the last. It is quite the most spectacular temple in the country. In legend, it was reputed to have been the site of a temple built 2,000 years ago to house hairs of the Buddha. In fact, it may date from the 10th Century AD, and had been rebuilt many times after damage from warfare and earthquakes. Stairways on the North, South, East and West led to a platform on top of the hill in the center of which is the main Stupa, or Zedi; the lower parts were painted gold, the higher parts covered with gold leaf and the highest parts plated with solid gold and studded with thousands of precious stones. At the apex was a 76-carat diamond.

Surrounding it was a profusion of shrines, temples, stupas, each different and more exotic than the other. I spent two hours walking round, clockwise, watching the crowds and taking pictures. It was very much a civic center; tourists were far outnumbered by residents. I took a dilapidated taxi back to the hotel in time to join the others for the bus trip to the Green Elephant Restaurant for our last meal in Burma. It was a very jolly affair, with much picture-taking and an excellent poem composed and recited by Kerry about the trip.

January 29, Rangoon to Hong Kong

At breakfast, I said goodbye to Sam and Marion who were off to see a different part of Burma: Kerry, off to Thailand and thence Australia; Marit, off to Norway; Leo, spending another day in Rangoon to tidy up the administration, and Julian, on his way back to Kuala Lumpur. I boarded a taxi to the airport with Ron and Veronica. The smart new airport was a surprise, with one serious design fault. Once through immigration, there were no shops, money-changing booths or charity collection boxes; so I could neither spend nor change my last 4,000 kyats worth

\$4. At Bangkok, Ron and Veronica left to have check-ups at Bumrungrad Hospital before returning to Hong Kong, while I transited straight back. It was a pleasure to be home again.

The trip had been memorable and enjoyable. Traveling with a group had been a new and stimulating experience; on previous expeditions I had always been just by myself, or with guides and porters. I was happy to find that, despite being between five and fourteen years older than others in the group, I was by no means the slowest.

Postscript: My heart bleeds when I read of the disasters that have affected Burma since my visit. Just four months after I left came Cyclone Nargis that created a tidal wave that inundated the delta, swept forty kilometers up the Irrawaddy River and killed 138,000 people. The Rohingya genocide followed. Then the 2021 military coup has caused fighting and bitter social conflict.

SINGAPORE
BUKIT TIMAH
Height: 163.63 meters (536 feet)
Date: March 14–18, 2010

This short trip was an outing with friends to play three golf matches on three different courses in Singapore. I joined the group to see Singapore, which Judith and I last visited thirty-four years earlier. I wanted to play golf at three courses new to me; to climb Singapore's highest mountain and to see how I handled a 'boys only' tour.

Sunday, March 14
The flight down was on a Singapore Airlines Airbus 380-300, the newest and largest passenger plane flying, carrying 470 passengers. The food in economy-class was just adequate; the

leg room was good as was entertainment on a personal screen. I watched *The Blind Side*, an American feel-good film about a white middle-class woman who takes in a black teenager; he becomes a college football hero. Sandra Bullock won an Oscar for this true story. The non-stop flight time was three hours and fifty minutes; we arrived at 8.00 p.m. It was the same time zone as Hong Kong and China and one hour before Malaysia. Changi Airport Terminal Three was new and vast, spoiled by a horrid, but no doubt practical black and white carpet. Driver Norman and his minibus were waiting for us and took us direct to the hotel, the Landmark Village Hotel, 390 Victoria Street, entrance on Arab Street. The hotel clientele, like the area, was Malay. By the time we had checked in, I was ready to go to bed, the others chose to go out for drinks and a meal.

The next morning, Norman took us to the Singapore Island Club, in the Bukit Timah area near the center of the island, for our first match. We were to play against The Tanglin Club, one of the oldest and most prestigious clubs in Singapore, founded in 1866 and having 6,000 members.

The original Singapore Golf Club had been founded in 1891 and—like the original Hong Kong Golf Club—consisted of nine holes built inside a horse racing track. Again, like the HK Golf Club, the course was once 'Royal'. It later moved to the Bukit Timah location, expanded to two courses, took over a third course, the Island course, and was named the Singapore Island Golf Course. The clubhouse facilities were huge. We played on the Sime course, set in rolling parkland with water and trees everywhere, 5,578 meters off the white tees. My partner and I won our match, as did the other pairs; the score was 4-0. Our own opponents were a large American and a much smaller Japanese, Yuji Ono. Both could out-drive us but suffered from bad slices. We had a meal and prize-giving at the club. Norman returned us to the hotel at 8.30 p.m. I went to bed, the others spruced up and ventured to check out the nightlife.

On the second morning, I was up early, breakfasted and explored the neighbourhood. The Arab Street area of two-story shop-houses, red-tiled, with covered walkways and a couple of mosques, was the only remnant of the old city. The rest was gleaming skyscrapers as high as 40 floors, with wide avenues, canals, and flyovers. Down by the river, there was parkland and views across to stylish apartment buildings, the revolving 'Eye' and the grandstand for the Singapore Grand Prix Formula 1 Racing circuit. It was hot and humid, so I rehydrated, had a shower and lay down to rest, before joining the rest of the team at 11.00 a.m.

Norman and his bus took us out west past the new spectacular Sands Casino complex, past the Jurong high-tech manufacturing area, to the Tuas district at the southwest tip of the island, and the Raffles Country Club. The beautiful, spacious clubhouse overlooked a large lake. The courses were designed by American Robert Trent Jones Jr. and opened in the 1980s. We were to play on the Palm course, used by PGA Asian Tournaments, off white tees 5,558 meters; it was an interesting layout with many water hazards.

Membership lists were closed but membership could be acquired in the open market or via the club waiting list. A Term Membership was available to expatriates only, good for one year for roughly HK$100,000, with no monthly fees. Our opponents were the American Club, which had also co-opted a number of out-of-work Australians to complete the team. With my same partner, we were facing two young, long hitters, but were one up at the 9th. Unfortunately, on the third hole, I realized my heart was fibrillating again. I kept on playing, but not well and almost fainted once. On the 9th, I was particularly proud to have made a par five despite heavy rain. We stopped play at that stage to wait for the storm to pass. I was grateful we were driving round the course in electric carts. I rested lying down in the changing room for half an hour, but the fibrillation continued; I took a taxi back to the hotel. With rest, an aspirin and beta blocker, I reverted to normal heart rhythm. The rest of the day, I rested. The team had halved one game, won one and lost one.

On Wednesday, I felt fine the next morning, had breakfast by 7.30 a.m. and set off by taxi in search of Singapore's highest mountain, Bukit Timah. Half an hour later, the taxi had reached the car park at the foot of the ascent. The climb up the steep road took around fifteen minutes walking briskly. Views were obscured by heavy first-growth rain forest. At the top was a large rock on which was painted 'Bukit Timah Summit 163.63m' and the map reference. There was a steady stream of climbers, several of them going downhill backwards. I felt pleased that I had another country to add to my list of ascents. At fifteen minutes, this was my shortest ascent.

By 9.30 a.m., I was back at the hotel, showered, lay down to rest, and read 'The Teachings of Buddha', provided by the hotel along with a Gideon's Bible. For the next round of golf, I made sure I took salt tablets with plenty of water to avoid an episode such as the one on the previous day. At 11.30 a.m., Norman took us to the Jurong Country Club. The first nine holes opened in 1975. It was the first course to be flood-lit for night playing. Term Membership for one year was about HK$50,000. Surprisingly cheap by Asian private golf club standards.

Our opponents on that day were from The British Club founded in 1987. I was playing with a new partner, against Stephen, a giant of a man from Birmingham, and Gary from Belfast with a unique grip — the left hand being below the right. They both hit their drives about fifty yards past ours. We lost, but the team won 3-1. The first nine holes, lined by mature trees, were more attractive than the younger second nine, flanked by younger trees and more water. Interestingly, the golfers walked while the caddy had a motorised bag-carrier to ride on, a speedy way to progress. Dinner and prize-giving afterwards at the club finished by 8.00 p.m. Norman drove us back to the hotel. I went back to my Buddhist readings. The others went, variously, to dine with Singapore friends and explore Harry's bar (too noisy), Muddy Murphy's (heaving with St Patrick's Day crowd), Boat Quay (packed, noisy, everyone age 30 or younger) and Brix (quieter).

On our last morning, I went for an early swim in the pool. For once, we were all present at breakfast. Our driver was on hand for the last time; he drove us the thirty minutes to Changi airport at the eastern tip of the island. The road was lined with trees, jacarandas mostly, excellent shade trees; the center divider of the motorway was brilliant with bougainvillea and azaleas. The flight back in a Boeing 777 was uneventful, arriving back to hazy Hong Kong on schedule at 5.15 p.m. The total cost for me, including hotel, air ticket and golfing fees, was about HK$10,000, about US$1,300.

Altogether, it was a good outing, marred for me only by my ill-health in the second golf match. My companions were congenial and good fun, however, I never felt part of the 'boys-on-the-loose' gang.

NEPAL
EVEREST
Height: 8,848.86 meters (29,031feet)
Date: 1992

In 1951, the Kadoorie Agricultural Aid Association (KAAA) was set up to help the hundreds of thousands of Chinese refugees who had flooded into Hong Kong, fleeing the communist regime established in 1949, following the defeat of the Kuomintang under Chiang Kai-shek. The aid was provided as financial loans or livestock; training courses in animal husbandry and agriculture; breeding programmes to upgrade the local animals such as swayback pigs and the building of wells, drainage ditches and roadways.

In 1968, the Association also provided training courses in farming to Gurkha soldiers of the three battalions stationed in Hong Kong who were completing their service with the British Army and returning to their native Nepal. At the same time, the

KAAA started small training farms at resettlement centres in Dharan and Pakilhawa in Nepal. From this small beginning, the Association expanded its aid to Nepal, through the British Gurkha Welfare organization; it used the same self-help philosophy that had proved so successful with the New Territories farmers in Hong Kong.

Each spring, directors of KAAA from Hong Kong went to Nepal to inspect progress of their many projects. In 1992, I was invited to accompany them to provide medical back-up. We flew to Kathmandu in a Royal Nepal Airlines plane and were lodged in the British Embassy. Next day we boarded a Super Puma helicopter and flew west to Pokhara. From the army camp where we stayed, we had a magnificent view to the north – there was Macchupuchre, 6,995 metres, in the foreground and the Annapurna range with its snow-capped peaks behind rising more than 8,000 metres. For two days, we visited villages to inspect KAA projects, flying to their remote locations in minutes rather than the days it would have taken on foot.

We flew back to Kathmandu for one day to prepare for the long final day of the tour, to the east. In the helicopter bound for Lukla, our 45-minute flight took us east from Kathmandu, quickly past the rice terraces, steadily climbing over lightly forested mountains, with no game to see; on our left, we saw the snow and ice peaks of the Himalayas. Eventually we skimmed over a high pass and dropped into the valley of the Dhud Kosi, the gateway to Mount Everest. We flew up the valley for a short distance before landing at Lukla, 9,000 feet. There we had to unload excess fuel and three passengers, so we could climb to the Everest View Hotel at Namche Bazaar at 12,000 feet.

Lukla must have one of the most spectacular airstrips in the world. It is about 250 yards long, inclined at an acute angle from the edge of the cliff up the crest of a ridge and ending against the mountain wall. There is a level parking area to the right at the top. Landing a helicopter was no problem but fixed wing planes also fly in. Evidence that they do not always fly out again was the broken shell of a plane to the left of the runway. Level with the top of the runway was a huddle of stone dwellings, lodges for climbers and Sherpas, and houses for the villagers. The flight up the valley to Namche took 10 minutes. An American couple we met there had taken three days to walk up. Huge rock walls plunged down to the river boiling white—the Dhud Kosi (Milk River)—in the ravine below and soared up above us towards the snow.

It was a relief to find that the landing at the Everest View Hotel was on a grassy clearing amongst trees, part of a plateau at the point where the river swings south. The hotel is perched on the edge of the plateau with a panoramic view up the valley to Mount Everest itself; a plume of cloud whips off the summit in the jet-stream and the lower slopes are hidden by the Nuptse—Lhotse ridge. We breakfasted in style looking out toward Everest—it was the nearest I ever came to the 'roof of the world.'

Back in Lukla, we picked up the three people and freight that had been off-loaded so that the helicopter could fly higher in the thin air. We visited two villages on our way back to Kathmandu. After this most spectacular day I was happy and relieved to be back at the Embassy.

In 1993 Gurkha Col Mike Kefford and ex-Gurkha Major Kit Spencer showed us pictures of the Joint Services Expedition that Mike had led the previous year to climb Mt. Everest by the difficult West Ridge. They had failed, just short of the summit, because of bad weather. We were all impressed by the hazards of high altitude climbing. Three years later nine experienced climbers were killed in a storm while climbing the regular East Ridge approach.

('Into Thin Air' by Jon Krakauer.)

NORTH KOREA (DEMOCRATIC PEOPLE'S REPUBLIC OF KOREA–DPRK)

Mt PAEKDU
Height: 2,774 meters (9,101 feet)
Date: 2012

In 2012, Judith and I made our first visit to one of the world's most secretive countries—North Korea. What attracted me was curiosity about a largely unknown country, and a desire to climb Mt Paekdu, its highest mountain at 2,774 meters.

In 2006, we had made contact with Koryo Tours specializing in tours to North Korea. Judith had heard that the living members of the North Korean football team in England for the World Cup in 1966, required some funding. She made the tour viable with a donation of about £4,000. In the summer of 2006, while they were staying in Middlesbrough in northeast England, we hosted a luncheon party at the Spa in Saltburn for the Korean team, young Korean team players, male and female, their escorts and Nick Bonner from Koryo who had organized the trip with the BBC.

In 2012, we went to two talks on North Korea by the Royal Geographical Society (RGS) of Hong Kong. One was by a schoolteacher in Hong Kong who had taken parties of school children into the country, and the other by Simon Catterall of Koryo. Both speakers emphasized the beauty and safety of the country, and the emerging middle class. Research on North Korea was confined to a well-researched book by an American reporter about survivors of the 'Arduous March', a famine in the 1990s, *Nothing to Envy* by journalist Barbara Demick; and an anthology in the Asia Literary Revue of Spring 2012. Amazingly we did not have the *Lonely Planet* book, much of it written by Koryo members. Visas were easily obtained from the DPRK consulate in Hong Kong

September 5, Hong Kong to Beijing

On September 5, Judith and I flew from Hong Kong to Beijing. We landed at the huge Beijing airport at noon and were nearly conned into paying CN¥600 for a minibus ride into the city, instead of the 100 yuan regular taxi fare. As usual, the taxi driver had no idea of the location of Hotel G, our destination. We arrived eventually after studying a map, asking passersby and phoning the hotel. It was owned by Hong Kong people and run by French management — 110 rooms, very comfortable. We walked a couple of blocks to the Koryo office to attend a briefing session at 4.00 p.m. The room was crowded with about sixty people, a mixed bunch, none of our age and many young backpackers. Hannah Barraclough gave the presentation and introduced us to Christopher Graper who would be our other guide. Hannah was English, in her 30s and vivacious with a voice used to being heard; Christopher was Canadian, older and genial.

We walked back to the Hotel G in a pleasant 20 degrees Celsius evening, dined at the Scarlett Restaurant, chatting with the handsome young Lebanese manager. We were introduced to Vincent God, the hotel owner. That night we watched CNN — it was the British TV personality Piers Morgan interviewing people at the US Democratic Convention. He was as dominant and opinionated as ever.

China to DPRK September 6

We slept well in a comfortable bed and breakfasted royally in expectation of more frugal fare to come. At 8.30 a.m., we took a taxi to Yashaw Market just beside the Koryo office, where we boarded a coach for the airport. We were in Group B, under Christopher. The airport check-in was very slow. We eventually got through and boarded the Air Koryo plane to take us to Pyongyang. It was a Russia Ilyushin 62, the first version launched in the 1960s. The seats were very close together. Take-off scheduled for 1.00 p.m. was delayed by an hour, because many planes were queuing to depart. The flight path was northeast close to the coast of China, north of the Bohai Sea and turning south at the China-DPRK border. This avoided South Korean airspace, but at double the distance and a four-hour flight. The land in the China part of the route was dry, mountainous and wooded, with agriculture in the valleys and narrow strips along the coast. Over the DPRK, it was at first heavily wooded, mountainous and uninhabited, but later along a coast that was heavily agricultural.

A bus took us from Sunan Airport through a modern city, along wide streets with scant traffic and lined with imposing buildings. Our hotel, Yanggakdo, was a gleaming new forty-seven story building surrounded by gardens on an island in the

River Taedong. The rooms were four-star quality. We had just time to check in and unpack before we were back in the bus again on our way to the Arirang Mass Games at the May Day Stadium. It was dark by the time we got there, a 150,000-seat venue; it was a stunning building of sweeping white arches. Outside were thousands of people, many in military uniform—performers or audience was not clear—and fleets of buses. A huge fountain of coloured dancing waters enhanced the festival feeling. Inside the stadium, we had excellent seats at 150 euros each, not cheap. The far side of the stadium was already filled by thousands of school children holding placards, white on one side. At intervals, the coloured sides of the placards were presented, accompanied by pounding of feet and loud cheers—a warm-up routine. During the actual performance, the white placards combined to make a giant screen for camera projections. The next ninety minutes were pure magic—a swift series of tabloids, colourful masses of maybe 10,000 people moving in unison, dancing, doing acrobatics and swirling in complex patterns. The overall theme was the 100-year history of Korea from the birth of Kim Il Sung in 1910. We emerged, dazzled by the performance, to a chaos of people and buses. Eventually, we made our way to the correct bus and sped back to the hotel through deserted streets. We had a light buffet supper, then back to our room to download the pictures, before a welcome bed.

Pyongyang Day 1

We slept well and were up at 7.00 a.m. to be ready for our 8.30 a.m. departure. From our 30th- floor vantage point, I took pictures up and down the river; it was devoid of traffic, apart from barges dredging sand from the riverbed. In the morning haze, details of the city were indistinct. Breakfast in the ground floor dining room was a buffet. There were many hot dishes of vegetables, tofu, rice, rice-soup and breads designed for Asian tastes, and a European selection of yogurt, tea and coffee, omelettes, tomatoes, toast, butter and jam, sliced apples, but no cereals, which I missed. In every hotel where we stayed, this was the choice.

Our party, Group B, had twenty-one people of various nationalities—Dutch, French, Polish, Czech, South African, Australian, a Canadian and two Americans. The Americans were treated like everyone else, despite their government being Public Enemy Number One. However, they were not allowed to take the train out of the country, having to fly out the same way as we flew in. They also were not permitted to overnight in a Korean home, the two times we did not have guides with us. Our guides were Christopher Graper from Koryo Tours, a Canadian who read Philosophy at university; he had worked as a bus driver, bus company manager, tour guide and was on his first year with Koryo. Local guides provided by KITS, Korea International Tourist Service, were Mrs Kim, an experienced guide with good English, petite, always beautifully dressed and wearing high heels; Mr Kim, in his 40s, efficient, the organizer with adequate English, thin and intense; Mr Han, the apprentice, around 30, good English, smartly dressed with a languid manner, and the driver, another Mr Kim, in his 40s, quiet, no English and a good and careful driver. All the men smoked at every opportunity. All three guides had parents who had been in the North Korean diplomatic corps, and we suspected they too were destined for a diplomatic future. Their stint as tour guides was to familiarize themselves with westerners and their questions and to practise the language.

Our sight-seeing tour led off appropriately with a walk through Fountain Park, enroute to Maesong Park, a place of pilgrimage for Koreans; it was the site of enormous bronze statues of Kim Il Sung and his son Kim Jong Il. The statues dominated a wide-open area leading down towards the Taedong River. They were flanked by monuments depicting life-sized figures of military and civilian heroes of the revolution against the Japanese and South Korea. Christopher bought flowers to lay at the base of the plinth, while we lined up, then all bowed as a mark of respect; before and after us, other groups of people did likewise. As we walked away, we passed a bridal couple smartly dressed in formal wear on their way to pay their respects to the two leaders. Kim Jong Un, who inherited the leadership from his father in 2011, had decreed that his statue and portraits would not be placed alongside those of his illustrious ancestors. Our second destination was the Museum of Gifts to the Leaders. It was situated in the outskirts of the city, up a long straight avenue leading to a grandiose building set back behind a tall steel gateway guarded by soldiers. We were warned that photography of soldiers was not permitted. The museum's many palatial rooms displayed of some of the huge number of gifts to the two leaders; many were exquisite, others mundane.

Back into the city, we were taken to the Arts Center at Mansudae where chosen painters and sculptors work. It was the sight of the only equestrian statues of the two leaders. As ever, we were greeted by a guide dressed in the traditional high-waisted, wide-skirted gown, a Hanbok; it was made of a nylon-like fabric, Vinalon, a fibre created out of limestone and anthracite by a North Korean scientist in the 1930s. She told us how the institution was inspired by the benevolence and foresight of Kim Il Sung and his son Kim Jong Il. Inside the building, we were shown two studios where artists worked, and then a gallery where works of art were on sale. There were well executed works in oils and water colours of landscapes, portraits of the leaders and heroic scenes of workers and the military. There was no abstract or modern western-style art.

We had a picnic lunch at a site on Mt Ryonggak, Dragon Mountain, guarded by two immense cement dragons. The waitresses provided a song and dance routine, accompanied by an accordionist. Many of the party walked up the road to the crest of the mountain. Judith and I went part way to a pagoda where we talked with Mr Han about the Korean social structure. He was happy to chat and asked us what we thought of his country. We replied that, after just one day, it was too early to say — Mr Han was not the only diplomat — and suggested he ask us on our last day. But we did point out that we had come to the DPRK to learn for ourselves. Back in the city, we visited the museum of the Metro Construction. We were given a briefing in the usual laudatory terms about General Kim Il Sung's brilliant initiative to have the metro built deep enough to withstand American bombs, in the 1970s. A huge cavern in the museum depicted the construction, with hundreds of figures painted on the walls. Our last visit of the day was to the riverside Juche Tower in the form of a torch, built in 1982 to commemorate Kim Il Sung's 70th birthday and his philosophy of self-reliance, Juche, for the individual and the nation. The white granite tower soared 170 meters, with a flame forever burning at the summit. Beside the tower was a thirty-meter high bronze monument of three giant figures — a worker holding a hammer, a peasant holding a sickle and an intellectual holding a pen. Judith and I sat on the steps, enjoying the calm of twilight, the view across the river and watching bicyclists silently making their way home from work. A security guard hovered in the background, agitated that we had not taken the lift to the top of the tower with the rest of the party. During dinner back at the hotel, we had an interesting briefing about the DPRK.

Day two of our exploration of Pyongyang started with a visit to Cine City near the edge of the city. At the statues of Kim Il Sung and Kim Jong Il, we were given the welcome address extolling the leaders who had developed a thriving film industry for entertainment and propaganda. Kim Jong Il was given personal responsibility for the industry by his father. We watched a 1920s black and white drama about building a dam, and were taken around the streets of the film village with examples of Korean, Japanese, Chinese and European architecture. Next stop was The Grand People's Study House, a palatial building in traditional Korean style with a blue tile roof, which opened in the early1980s. It contained a library of thirty kilometers of books, lecture halls and computer rooms filled with students at work. Entry was free.

We lunched back at the hotel. Then we were driven to a Science Park, with six buildings of strikingly different designs, housing different disciplines from chemistry to astro-physics, set in immaculate gardens. We were taken around the Heavy Industry Hall where we saw mock-ups of mining areas and real examples of heavy machinery and vehicles, motor bikes, cars and railway engines—impressive. At 4.00 p.m., we arrived at a magnificent new building housing the circus. The acts included skating, juggling, an animal act involving clever dogs and a sad bear pulling chimps on a sled. At one point, the bear became fed up and was taken off stage, to return later, performing as trained. The finale was performed by a dramatic trapeze troupe. At 5.30 p.m., we were at our next venue, an embroidery workshop housed in a classical Korean building; we watched women working on exquisite tapestries, very fine work, and embroidered copies of paintings we had seen earlier. The iconic, pyramidal, unfinished Ryugyong Hotel was in the background. It was designed in the 1980s as the largest luxury hotel in the world, with 105 floors, 330 meters high. But building stopped in the 1990s at the time of the 'Arduous March', or economic collapse.

We dined at the No 1 Restaurant—vegetables, chicken, noodles, soup and rice coming at the end of the meal; there was no dessert or fruit. By 8.00 p.m., we were back in our hotel. Judith and I and five others of the older group elected to stay at the hotel; the others went to a fun-fair at Moranbong Park. We spent time exploring the basement area of the hotel, the swimming pool, sauna, karaoke lounge, and bowled badly at a twenty ten-pin bowling alley. In the adjoining lane was a very good bowler, a middle-aged local man; his exploits were applauded by two acolytes. We were told the bowler was an Army officer. It had been a long day, with events crammed in to make way for the optional circus performance.

National Day

We had a more relaxing start to the day, a drive to near Kim Il Sung Square and a walk on the bank of the Taedong River. Men were fishing from the steps below the esplanade; a couple of fishing devices stood unattended, each trailed six lines in the water. We did not see anyone catch anything; the water looked dirty. We were told that it was the women who always prepared a feast for National Day. Some hired boats that were being rowed inexpertly on the river; they were the first craft I saw on the river apart from dredgers. We stopped at the Taedong Gate, a 1635 reproduction of the original 6th Century walled city's eastern gate; it was a solid stone structure about fifteen yards wide, with a pagoda on top.

Further along the riverbank was another traditional structure, built in 1111 and rebuilt in 1670, the Ryuongwang Pavilion, a teahouse. Steps led up to a wooden platform with surrounding balcony seats; from there, one could gaze at the ornately carved and painted wooden ceiling, or out over the river. Nearby was the only other remnant of historic value to have survived the country's wars — a huge bronze bell built in 1726, to be rung as a warning in the event of attack or fire.

We spent time here, waiting to see if there would be a National Day Parade in Kim Il Sung Square. It was not to be, so we climbed back into the buses for a drive out of town to the Martyr's Monument, built in 1975 on the Jujak Peak of Mt Taesong. A magnificent gate opened onto a wide flight of steps up past rows of bronze busts of martyrs of the wars against Japan, leading up to a monumental red stone in the shape of a fluttering flag. On either side were life-size sculptural groups, one depicting battle and the other mourning. At the foot of the stairs, our guide placed a bouquet of flowers, and we all lined up and were expected to bow. From the top of the hill, we could see across the city. On our return journey, the bus stopped so we could take pictures of the Kumsusan Memorial Palace where Kim Il Sung used to work, now his mausoleum, and later also that of his son.

We passed an old amusement park with rusting equipment: we were told Marshall Kim Jong Un visited it recently and criticized its rusting condition so it was closed for upgrading. Apple orchards lined the road; no other fruit appeared to be grown in the DPRK; the winters were too harsh for citrus or soft fruits. Vegetables were grown outdoors in the summer, in greenhouses with a solid wall on the north side and curved retractable screens on the south side. Back at Kim Il Sung Square, we visited a bookshop with books in English of Korean history and of the writings of the leaders, scrolls and picture postcards. I bought *Korea in the 20th Century*, a fascinating account of history from the North Korean viewpoint. Lunch at a nearby restaurant was a fine banquet of eight side dishes and a main course of either the local equivalent of nasi gorin goreng or fried rice, or the spicy local delicacy, cold noodles.

Our guides obtained tickets for us to go to a special National Day concert by the Korean National Symphony Orchestra in a new concert hall, a handsome glass and concrete building. The orchestra of 100 musicians, in formal western evening dress, gave us a succession of immaculate short pieces under three conductors, ending with the stirring Kim Il Sung March. A gentle walk in hilly Moran Park followed. The road led up through trees, past a playing field and small groups of students dancing and singing to boom boxes: then up to a pagoda at the top of the hill, in times past, a defensive look-out where a bonfire would be lighted at the approach of the enemy; it signalled to towers on other hills to raise the alarm. Walking down the hill on the other side, we passed the Kim Il Sung Stadium, the first one built after the 1950-1953 war. Other walkers with children were happy to have their photographs taken with us. In a wide parade ground near the stadium, an open-air concert was in progress. A choir, smartly dressed in military uniforms were singing patriotic songs before an audience of thousands of people, some shading themselves from the hot sun with colourfully decorated parasols. After the concert, the music started again and everyone jumped to their feet to take part in a mass dance, simple dances in line or in circles, with some of the ladies in the colourful, voluminous national dress, the Hanbok.

Dinner on a boat in the river was a disappointment because the boat was firmly moored to the bank, and the food not great. For drinks, there was always a choice of bottled mineral water or the local bottled lager. For the last event of the day, we had a choice of going back to the Arirang Mass Games, or to a new fun fair nearby. We chose the fun fair, and watched people on the eight Italian-designed rides, quantifying a 'scream index'. Some youngsters in our group tried them all; we only rode the dodgem cars. The people were in holiday mood, with some happy to try out their English with us.

Pyongyang to Nampo, September 10

Our first outing was a pilgrimage to the birthplace of Kim Il Sung, Mangyongdae Native House. We were told his grandfather was at that time the warden of an area where the rich and famous were buried. Our bus took us out of town, into attractive parkland and to a thatched cottage facing south, with barns on either side of a courtyard exhibiting farming implements. The whole place was immaculate. We were briskly conducted around by a beautifully dressed guide, and ushered out to make way for the next group. I looked around for evidence of gravestones, but saw none.

Back in the city, we entered the subway system, down a very long escalator, spotless and with no advertisements and no graffiti. The platform was spacious, with murals on the walls and chandeliers. We boarded a train more akin to the London underground than Hong Kong's. It was crowded. After four stops, we disembarked into another lavishly decorated station, and took the escalator to the surface. The Metro was built in the 1970s on the orders of Kim Il Sung, deep enough to provide a bomb shelter. It was tunnelled using manual labour through soft sand and limestone rock, on the west side of the river only. In total, there were fourteen stations, of which foreigners could only use two. On our way back to the hotel for lunch, we visited a large department store with goods of every kind; but we were unsuccessful in finding a colourful parasol. No photographs were allowed. After lunch, Judith successfully concluded her missing sock saga. Her pair of Nike socks had not been returned from the laundry the previous night; in their stead came a very inferior pair. In the morning, the two maids on our floor could not understand what was wrong, it was not until the afternoon when the tour guide talked with the front desk that the message got through and the missing socks reappeared. We were careful not to get anyone into trouble for issues such as this.

We were scheduled to spend the night at Nampo, a spa outside the city. So we packed the minimum necessary and paid the hotel €5 to keep our room till our return. The bus drove down an eight-lane highway with a tarmac surface that was breaking up, so progress was not that fast; we headed for Chonsam-ri Agricultural Commune. It was set on a plain surrounded by ripening crops of rice and corn. Our introduction to the farm took place before a large statue of the Dear Leader Kim Jong Il. Guides said his father dwelt on the fact that Kim Il Sung had visited the commune seventy-five times and had inspired the workers with his good advice. We were shown round a worker's comfortable house; we observed grain drying on the road, vegetables, and a bullock cart pulled by an orange/red coloured cow. We saw no other farm animals.

The village primary school children, about fifty of them, were assembled in the playground in front of the schoolhouse and entertained us with a well-rehearsed routine of callisthenics. They all seemed healthy and happy. A second visit was to the Kangso natural spring bottled water factory, the largest in the DPRK. The workers were still on holiday so we did not see the bottling process. It looked a clean and efficient place.

Back on the road again, we continued to head west, through the delta area of the Taedong River. We stopped at Ryongang Spa at Nampo; individual chalets were hidden from each other in thick trees and from a central dining building. Hundreds of egrets were coming in to roost, covering the trees with their white plumage. We had time to enjoy a luxurious, cleansing, hot spring water bath, before joining the rest of the group for an outdoor Petrol Clams BBQ. Two fire-resistant mats were on the ground, covered with clams. They were sprayed with liquid from hand-held bottles and burst into flames—very dramatic. When they were judged to be cooked, we were invited to sit around the mats and eat those clams that had opened during cooking and wash them down with locally distilled 'vodka'—soju. I was put off by the whole procedure and ate nothing; Judith ate some. Dinner inside the club house was excellent and predictably convivial. Trying to find our way back to our chalets was not easy. Poor lighting and thick forest had us walking in circles.

Nambo to Pyongyang

We were up early on the 11th to have another soak in the hot tub before breakfast, and were ready to depart at 9.00 a.m., as scheduled. Some confusion about chalet keys meant that we had to wait for others and did not leave on time for our visit to the Western Barrage. This was an eight-kilometre-long dike carrying rail and road traffic that encloses the delta of the Taedong River; it was commissioned in 1986, with lock gates for sea-going vessels weighing as much as 50,000 tonnes. The bus driver had to accelerate to get us over the locks before they closed for the shipping; it was close. An hour later, we reached Sinchon and the Atrocities Museum. A guide dressed in sombre black and white led us through several rooms of pictures of horrific carnage and dead bodies, allegedly on instruction of a General Harrison, US Army, during the Korean War; 35,000 civilians were killed in 1950, she said. It left us all upset and reluctant to talk. How much was collateral damage and how much deliberate it was difficult to say. At the end of the tour, the guide asked what we thought of it. Everyone was reluctant to speak. Eventually, Judith said very diplomatically that the exhibition showed that disputes should be resolved by negotiation, not war. It was a good answer but a disappointment for the guide, who no doubt expected a diatribe against the Americans.

Another two hours in the bus took us through rich farmland. On the plains were rice fields, with tied-up stems having been flattened by a recent typhoon; on uneven ground corn and soy were growing. Further up the hills were orchards of fruit trees. Village houses looked well built, detached, in orderly rows. We lunched at the Sariwan 38 Hotel, commemorating Women's Day, August 3. Later, we visited a city public park laid out round a volcanic core jutting out of the plain. A long mural depicted the history of Korea; a small lake held a turtle-shaped boat with oars and up the hill was a pleasant pagoda where we sat and relaxed, looking out to the horizon over rice fields. The drive back to Pyongyang took about five hours through sparse traffic. In the city, we stopped at the side of the Taedong River and went on board the USS Pueblo, a survey and spy ship captured in 1968 by the DPRK navy that claimed it was within their coastal waters. We were shown the shell holes in the ship and went into the wardroom to watch a film of the capture, arrest of the crew, their confessions and their release many months later. We arrived too late at our next target location, a micro-brewery and the Paradise Department store. Instead, we stopped at a 'German' Beer Cellar, where Judith and I had ice cream. Dinner was at a Korean hot pot restaurant. We were told this style of cooking evolved during warfare when the troops used their tin helmets to boil vegetables and rice in a hurry during combat. Back at the hotel, we did housekeeping, loading the camera photos onto the computer, washing clothes and packing for our trip the next day.

DMZ September 12
We were on the road at 7.30 a.m., intent on getting to Maesang and the DMZ, Demilitarized Zone, before other visitors. Traffic was light on the double-lane highway. We stopped for a few minutes at a gaunt concrete rest house spanning the road. There was no

running water in the toilets; a small stall outside sold apples and bottled drinks. By the time we reached the check point at the edge of the DMZ, half a dozen buses were there already. We were obliged to get down from the bus and walk through the barrier before re-joining the bus. The road was narrow, just one lane; the first few 100 yards were guarded by concrete pillars and massive concrete blocks. They were poised to fall on the road when their support was removed by a hawser attached to a concrete ball, whose fall would pull them all down.

There was a two-kilometre separation between the check point and the actual border, and the same on the South Korean side. Local people farmed with special permits. We passed what we were told was the highest flagpole in the world, with the DPRK flag on top. A large plaque showed the signature of Kim Il Sung on the day he died, July 7, 1994. The plaque were 9.4 meters wide and 7.7 meters high. At the border, we were allowed to take photographs of the building straddling the border and the soldiers on guard at each side.

An expert gave a Taekwondo martial arts demonstration.

A junior officer showed our party into the building and allowed us to sit at the North-South negotiating table. He posed for photographs with us afterwards, a genial fellow who appeared to enjoy his job. We gave way to the next group of tourists and moved on to the building in which the Armistice Treaty was signed. Our guide was pleased to point out that the UN flag was faded, whereas the DPRK flag still looked good as new. Pictures and documents round the walls told the story of the Armistice proceedings and participants.

We travelled back to Maesang for lunch at the Ginseng Restaurant, where a King's Feast awaited us, the table laden with each place having eleven copper bowls with lids on, containing food fit for a king. In Maesang, we visited the 5,000-year-old

Confucius University. It was rebuilt 400 years ago, but some trees in the gardens were older than 1,000 years. The layout was that of a typical temple: the entrance building opened into a courtyard leading to another building and another courtyard behind. The present university was housed in a large, modern building nearby. The area was not bombed during the Korean War because, at the start of hostilities, it was on the South Korean side of the 38th Parallel.

Our next stop was the gravesite of King Kongmin in a beautiful twin-domed tomb of the 31st King of the Koryo dynasty and his Mongolian wife. It was situated in what was then a perfect geomantically oriented position, facing south down an enclosed valley with a lake at the bottom and an opening to the far left for his spirit to travel to the hereafter. The king's wife died first, in childbirth but he loved her very much and so he did not remarry. Their grave mounds were side by side surrounded by heraldic animals. Mrs Kim, one of our guides, gave us a dissertation on birth and marriage customs. After birth of a child, mother and child are confined to the house for three months. At one year, there is a party at which the baby is named.

Marriages used to be arranged by parents, now people married for love, she told us. Marriage ceremonies and feasts take place at both parent's homes. Registration was required within three months and separation before that date was not regarded as divorce. Mrs Kim and her husband did not register their marriage for a year because of busy careers. Interestingly, the local guides at Maesang and the grave site did not mention Kim Il Sung or his family.

The trip back to Pyongyang was 160 kilometers. We reached the Friendship Statue at sunset: there were white marble statues of two women reaching out from either side of the road to release a dove from a cage—a striking image.

Dinner was at a BBQ restaurant housed in the prefab equivalent of a worker's mess hall. I was having mild gastro-enteritis so I ate little. After the meal, there was singing and dancing to karaoke music. On the bus back to the hotel, the guides sang again. Mrs Kim sang a Korean song beautifully; Mr Kim sang, surprisingly, *Edelweiss* from *The Sound of Music* and Mr Han the theme song from the film *Titanic*.

Pyongyang September 13

Judith and I both had diarrhoea, so it was congee for me that day. Judith also had possibly broken a toe in the bathroom. We set off on the morning tour to a maternity hospital, the tertiary referral center for the DPRK; it had 1,500 beds, a palatial building inspired by Kim Il Sung. We were conducted round several departments — clean, organized, with good equipment — impressive. For the first five days, fathers were only allowed remote contact with their wives and children via a video screen and telephone, to minimize infection.

It was a rainy day, so we went into a 'Viennese' coffee shop, a bare room with coffee at €3.50 a cup, very expensive by DPRK standards and strictly for tourists. Judith and I were tired after the morning tour, so we skipped lunch; we had biscuits and water in our room and slept. In the afternoon, we visited the national art gallery. Pictures were hung chronologically, starting with copies of wall paintings from the tombs of kings thousands of years old and moving on through the centuries, in an artistic style akin to that of the Chinese, until 1910, when Japan took over. Since 1945, the paintings had been of a heroic, socialist realism style, lauding Kim Il Sung, workers and soldiers — art in the service of the state.

Our second event was a visit to the Children's Recreation Palace. It was a palatial building where we saw children enjoying free instruction in dance, netball, chess, and musical instruments.

We sat in a 1,000-seat concert hall and watched a one- hour performance; a remarkable show of music, dance and acrobatics performed by the youngsters. It appeared that the Recreation Palace was a training ground for young people. At the end, Judith presented a bouquet of flowers to members of the choir — their teacher was overcome by the gift. We finally made it to the Paradise Department store, just before closing time, and found a suitable umbrella, a present for our helper in Hong Kong. It was here that Judith watched as a well-dressed Korean woman tried to pay for a suite of furniture; she offered U.S.$1,000. The counter clerk did not have enough US dollars for change. The purchaser paid with a credit card. Later, Judith commented on this to our guides who said they all had credit cards and asked Judith whether she had one. They said the woman purchaser must have been the wife of a trader or businessman; no government employee would have that much money to spend, he said.

We then spent ninety minutes at a nearby microbrewery watching others drinking beer, before moving on to a restaurant run by the Korean International Tourist Organization. Of the lavish meal, I only ate rice; much food was left over. I am sure it did not go to waste. Finally, after a long day, we were about to climb into bed at 11.00 p.m., when Judith received a call from the WHO representative in the DPRK — he had been trying to contact her since early evening. She went upstairs to the 47th floor restaurant and had a very good meeting. She came back excited by the fact that she had obtained permission to meet government officials regarding their tobacco control policy. We all got on well with our guides, but Judith had admonished them pleasantly regarding their smoking habit — to no avail. At last, to push the message home that more than 50 percent of smokers die from a smoking-related disease, she said to Kim and Tan, "One of you will go to the other's funeral!" Only momentarily taken aback, they challenged each other to a Stone-Paper-Scissors competition to see which one would attend the funeral.

East Coast

We had a bus ride of two and a half hours from Pyongyang to the east coast to Hamhung, a major industrial city. It had been closed to foreign tourists from 1945 until 2010, when Koryo Tours became the first company to take people there. The highway had four lanes of bumpy concrete slabs. We drove through a range of limestone mountains, heavily wooded with secondary growth. We stopped for a picnic lunch at the foot of the spectacular Echo Waterfall. The water was crystal clear. Brendon, the Canadian, went for a swim to the foot of the waterfall. Coming down from the mountains, we reached the coastal plain; the crops were the same as on the east coast. We saw bullock carts carrying the harvested corn. We stopped at the King Li guest house; he was the first king of the Li dynasty and lived there as a retirement home. The garden was dominated by an ancient fir tree. Mrs Kim coyly announced she was unable to translate the commentary of the guide, the task falling to Mr Kim. A tea house in the garden had eight steps to reach the elevated platform. If the king developed an erection before a lady of the court could make it to the top step, she would entertain him for the night!

The beach hotel we had been booked into was holding an international conference. So we were given a choice of staying at the newest hotel in the DPRK. It was called the Majon but looked in every way a Sheraton—its name was on the toiletries—or we could choose a lesser establishment in Hamhung. Some of our party, including us, chose the Sheraton for an extra €100 for the night, and luxuriated in what was a new four-star hotel. This was new territory for our guides; it was the first time Koryo had run a tour there. A pop music group famous in the DPRK was having a great time; they were noisily playing a game I had not seen before—throwing four dice onto an oblong table covered in green baize with diagonal lines across it and shifting a pile of counters depending on the dice.

I woke up at dawn after a very comfortable night in the luxury of the 'Sheraton'. I went out to the beach, a wide expanse of meticulously clean sand. A cement walkway clear of sand led to a volcanic outcropping jutting into the sea and affording a landing place for craft, and a fishing spot for a cormorant. I noted a beach house changing room and a beach soccer pitch. These splendid facilities triggered the thought of a full western breakfast—but it was not to be, only the usual DPRK oriental-style buffet. Our bus took us to the other hotel where the rest of the party stayed, uncomfortably; no rooms were ready, no running water and there was a power outage for one hour. Together we visited the Hamhung Grand Theatre; it was the iconic building of the city, dominating the central area and bordered by a pleasant park. The next destination was the large Hungnam fertilizer factory. There were the obligatory statues of the leaders, who were proudly announced as having visited several times. The buildings were old but well maintained and the machinery was functioning. Posters exhorting the workers were on the walls. The smell was not good, so we were pleased to make our next stop back at the beach we had first visited; some swam, others sat on the piles of shells on the beach. The hotel where we were to have stayed was indeed holding a meeting of a UN agricultural agency—to judge by the fleet of white Toyota cars and vans parked outside. Inside, the hotel lobby and dining room were decorated with colourful murals of beach scenes, mountains, flowers and of the biggest concert hall in the DPRK in Chungjin.

After lunch, we visited the Tung Bing Cooperative Farm. The usual long introduction was followed by an inspection of a worker's cottage, with five small rooms, meticulously clean, with an indoor toilet and surrounded by a small garden bursting with healthy-looking vegetables. At last, I had a good photograph of a bullock cart. The next three hours we spent in the bus traveling over steep mountains, mostly tree-covered, with what looked like Scots pine, some old trees but mostly young plantations. The river delta flood plains were fully cultivated, guarded by high flood barriers from the rivers where scant streams were flowing over silted-up channels. We stopped at an agricultural college established in 1960 and housing 5,000 students, set in a forest of 800 varieties of trees. Greenhouses — a joint venture with Belgium we were told — with plots of trial crop varieties showed that serious work was being done.

Our last visit of the day at Wonsan was the Songdowon Children's Recreation Palace, a grand building facing onto a huge parade ground surrounded by lakes and parkland. It could accommodate 1,250 children. We were shown bedrooms of four, six and eight beds, each with a TV and ensuite bathroom. The children from different provinces stayed there for free to take part in all sorts of sports. They were dressed in standard blue shorts and white shirts with red scarves. We were taken to a 1,500-seat theatre where the children put on an impressive performance of music, dance and acrobatics. My impression was that this was another example of the State control, but using encouragement in the training of children to create excellence.

Our hotel in Wonsan was the Songdo (Pine Tree), set on the seafront, an attractive old-style building painted green. Inside was a disappointment. It was run down, the rooms were smelly, the lights were not working, the water cistern dripped and there was no hot water. We had dinner at a restaurant across the main road. It was crowded with tour groups, so we had to wait; it was noisy but served a good meal. There were eight courses, plates of vegetables, fish, two kinds of meatballs, potatoes, soup and rice and watermelon for dessert. I was still anorexic and ate little. Back at the hotel, the lights were working and hot water was available.

Kumgang

I slept badly on a hard bed and did not enjoy the breakfast of a cold omelette and toast. We travelled 120 kilometers down the east coast over a range of mountains to the Kumgang area. This scenic area was developed as a resort for Southern Koreans for family reunions during the Sunshine Policy of former South Korean President Roh Moo-hyun from 2003 to 2008. After Roh left office, the policy collapsed and the border was sealed off again. There is a story that a southern visitor wandered out of the hotel in the early hours of the morning, did not stop when challenged by guards, and was shot dead. We did not wander. We stopped at Sunil Lagoon, named after the visit of a former King of Korea who came to visit for a day, and stayed for three. It was a delightful spot with pine and bamboo-clad hills surrounded a lagoon with many bays.

We lunched at the Mongnan restaurant perched over a river tumbling down a rocky ravine from Mount Kumgang, 1,690 meters in height. The range extends sixty kilometers from north to south and forty kilometers from east to west. After lunch, we set off up a path along the river that led to the famous Kuryong and Pibong waterfalls. Judith and I lagged behind the others. She turned back with a retired Belgian couple Andre and Karin. I carried on until it started to rain and returned to the restaurant to join the rest of the party. Our resort hotel, the Sijung, was a great step up from the previous night. Judith spent time at the local spa, enjoying all except a brutal massage that involved agonizing pinching of the skin and resulting in bruises all over. We learned that our bus had damaged a fuel pipe; repair overnight was unlikely, so we might have to spend another day at this location. This would be a disaster for our future programme that involved a charter flight on the following day from Pyongyang to my goal, Mt Paekdu.

Kumgang to Pyongyang

We awoke to the good news that we had transport back to Pyongyang. Another KITS driver drove across country, leaving at midnight and reaching us at 6.00 a.m. He had had one hour's sleep and was preparing to drive back to the capital, leaving at 10.00 a.m. A three-hour drive over the mountains took us back to Sangam where we had a good lunch at the same restaurant where we dined before. My appetite was returning, so I enjoyed the meal. We left Sangam at 2.30 p.m. and reached the outskirts of Pyongyang, just as the sun was setting under the fringe of the typhoon cloud that had dumped rain all the previous night and for much of the day.

The driver handled the bus skilfully, stopping once because of fatigue, and delivered us to Pyongyang's one pizza restaurant at around 7.00 p.m. We waited an hour for our pizza. Two female chefs worked hard to fill twenty-plus orders at once. We were entertained by a female singer, backed by a karaoke machine. She had a good voice; her finales were *Edelweiss* and *O Sole Mio*. It was not till 9.00 p.m. that our driver delivered us to our hotel. Conscious of the extraordinary job he had done – unhampered by trade union regulations – we all contributed to a tip of €100 and various food items. Judith and I had just settled into our previous room, 3022, when the phone rang. This was the WHO representative and the Director General of Health of the DPRK waiting to talk with her in the hotel. The original meeting time had been scheduled for 6.00 p.m. and they had been trying to make contact since then. Judith had thought that the meeting had been postponed. The meeting went well and she was invited to return to the DPRK and advise the government again after the snows had melted.

Mount Paekdu September 18

We were up at 5.40 a.m., ready to board our bus at 7.00 a.m. for the trip to the airport. Check-in was slow, with all baggage inspected but not weighed. At 9.20 a.m., we boarded an Ilyushin18 chartered by Koryo Tours; the plane with four turbo-prop engines was produced in the Soviet Union from 1959 to 1976, so this one had to be at least forty years old. The seats were close together and free seating meant a scramble for window seats. All the baggage was packed into the cabin, with other cargo in the hold. The weather was clear, so from 13,000 feet I had an excellent view of the country. We flew northeast from Pyongyang over the central mountains till we reached the coast, and then up the interesting coastline, over white sand beaches, rocky headlands and islands. Around Chongjin, we turned inland northwest to Samjiyon airport in the forest near Mount Paekdu. The flight took a little over one hour, during which we were offered a glass of tea, fruit juice or water. The airport had a single runway, a terminal building, a row of fighter jets parked to one side and camouflaged hangers. I assumed that the parked jets were decoys, and the real jets were in the hangars. The sixty passengers were made up of three Koryo Tour groups, A and B doing the Ultimate tour, C in Korea for one week. We piled into six minibuses and headed for the mountain, a one-and-a-half-hour ride. First, we went through thick forest, pines, larches and birch trees beginning to show autumnal colours. The trees thinned out as we climbed, giving way to alpines blooming red and yellow, and possibly heather. Finally, the alpines gave way to a bleak, sea of volcanic ash.

The buses parked at the base of the volcanic cone, with the top shrouded in cloud. We all waited for permission from the border guards to proceed further up a road marked with a 'No Vehicles' sign. When word came that the senior officer was away having lunch and that no permission could be granted till he came back, and even then, only if the cloud had lifted – I became seriously concerned that, having come all this way, I would at the last minute be unable to make the summit of Mount Paekdu, a major reason for the trip. A funicular railway lay disused and rusting to our right. I set off alone, after the few that had already started walking the rest of the way to the top. The road was winding, paved with lava stone blocks, easy walking. The road paving ended just short of the crater rim, so I proceeded on the dirt track round the rim of the crater; a low fence separated me from a drop into the unknown through the cloud. I walked slowly because of the altitude, 2,744 meters or 9,100 feet. I finally reached the top, marked by a structure of four metal bars embedded in a concrete slab, holding an object about twenty feet higher.

We had been shrouded in fog and unable to see the volcanic lake. But just as we were leaving the area, the cloud began to lift, giving views of the crater lake and the shore at the other side, which was Chinese territory. Judith was already in the bus, ready to descend but the guides came and encouraged everyone back up to the crater rim. Judith hurried up but suddenly started to get very breathless with altitude sickness. It was the same acute reaction she had in Colorado in 2000. Quickly the buses drove back down, and, as they did so, Judith started to recover. We paused at the lower car park, while the early climbers had their picnic lunch, then descended further into the forest to visit Kim Il Sung's Secret Camp at Paekdusan. Only then did Judith feel more comfortable.

The Secret Camp was a group of three log cabins deep in the forest where Kim Il Sung lived, planned his campaign against the Japanese and trained his guerrillas. They were solidly made and immaculate with a maple tree in autumnal red behind each cabin. Next stop was the Rimjongsu waterfall, tumbling down from a rift in the rock over a width of thirty yards, into a small lake created by a dam. It was an attractive spot, but on looking up the valley, I saw another dam and wondered whether or not the waterfall was a product of a pipe running from the upper dam. We passed a large village of comfortable looking detached villas and a school, with women washing clothes in the river — possibly a base for forestry workers.

More forest roads of packed earth took us to the Pegaebang Hotel for the night. It was a large, handsome building with large rooms with TV and fridge. It was substandard, however, with hot water only from 9.00 to 10.00 p.m. and 8.00 to 9.00 a.m. Judith found to her cost that, at 10.00 p.m., the hot water was very promptly switched off, and finished with a cold shower. However, our evening briefing warned us that there would be no running water at all at our next two hotels.

Homestay night, September 19

I had a good night's sleep despite the thin duvet, because the room was comfortably warmed by the floor heating. We were up at 7.00 a.m. and on our bus at 8.30 a.m., with a long day ahead. The first stop was only twenty minutes away through the forest — the Samjiyon Grand Monument, a shrine to the heroes of the Anti-Japanese War. It was a huge open, parade-ground area paved in concrete, dominated by the second largest statue of Kim Il Sung, on a high plinth, flanked by phalanxes of life-sized soldiers and civilians. A Juche tower stood behind Kim Il Sung. A fringe of trees separated the site from a large lake, forest and mountains behind. Driving on through the forest we passed two Swiss-style ski villages. A downhill piste was visible on an adjacent mountain, and there was, no doubt, great opportunities for cross-country skiing. Our bus took us back to the hotel to pick up our belongings, and on to the Paekdu airport; the chartered Ilyushin was waiting to take us the one-hour flight to Orang, the airport of Chongjin on the east coast. It was the second largest city in the DPRK, a manufacturing center and port.

Buses took us a three-hour trip south to Mount Chilbo area, first up the wide valley of a large river, flanked by hills of sandstone and limestone and in places capped by layers of lava rock and columnar granite. We climbed out of the valley into fir-clad mountains. Near the summit of the range, we stopped at the Kaesim Buddhist temple dating from the 9th Century, where a monk showed us around and invited some to sit at the shrine where he chanted a blessing for the travels. I was told he was an employee of the government. Behind the temple, we walked up to the top of the ridge and admired a vista of limestone mountains, weathered into pinnacles and castles, and saw two lovers embracing. The drive down the other side of the range to the sea took us through a spectacular gorge. At intervals, gangs of laborers were repairing the road damaged by the flooding from the recent typhoon. We drove along the coast, past fine beaches with occasional lava headlands. We had elected to have a homestay night, living with a Korean family; others had opted to stay at a hotel halfway down the gorge through which we had descended.

We were pleased with our choice. The Korean family had two teenage children, two dogs and a goat. They lived in one of a row of detached bungalows, with a sitting room, two bedrooms with bathrooms and a kitchen, surrounded by a healthy vegetable garden. Throughout the DPRK, house gardens invariably grew vegetables rather than flowers. Only about 20 percent of the DPRK is arable, so there is a never-ending need to grow food. Our room had plenty of space for two rolls of bedding laid on the floor. The bathroom had a large drum of cold water and a scoop, a washbasin and a western pedestal toilet. Floor heating kept us warm. We dined well at a communal building. Judith showed the wife her photographs of Pyongyang on her computer; she was fascinated, but said she had seen these sights herself.

Chongjin

We slept poorly, for the bizarre reason the floor was so hot that we had to move our bedding to the edge of the room away from the heating. It was only in the morning that the lady of the house showed us the point at which we could have unplugged the heater. I was up early and went down to the beach to watch the sunrise, a beautiful moment. Back at the house, we were given a thermos of hot water, with which I shaved and Judith had a sponge down. Back on the beach, we felt free for the first time, able to wander around without any guide hovering around. I gathered attractive shells, fan-shaped, coloured white and pink. After breakfast, we went back to house number 17 to say our farewells and leave little gifts—raisins, a tin of corned beef, sweets, thick warm gloves and two bottles of mineral water.

We drove back up the spectacular gorge, picked up the others from their hotel, and drove north. The packed earth roads and crops showed signs of typhoon damage. At the side of the roads were small piles of earth or gravel to fill the potholes. Roadside trees had white-painted trunks to guide motorists and deter insect pests. I saw for the one and only time a family of pigs, a horse and a tractor. We got onto tarmac again at the outskirts of Chongjin, which we reach at 2.30 p.m. The city was poorer than the showpiece capital, Pyongyang. Along the six-lane main road,

I only saw one building that was ostentatious, not just functional. There were few cars on the roads; instead, there were bullock carts and many bicyclists. Our hotel backed onto a railroad, but there were few trains to disturb our sleep. The rooms were all right, but there was no running water, the bath was full and the vital plastic scoop was at hand. Judith had an upset stomach and decided to miss the afternoon tour; our guide Mrs Kim was also indisposed and grateful that it was her duty to stay at the hotel to be with Judith.

A building on the square housed the Chongjin Revolutionary Museum, a shrine to seventeen guerrilla soldiers who lost their lives in a forest fire, supposedly protecting trees with Kim Il Sung slogans written on them. The tree trunks were on display in glass cases, with patches of bark peeled off to provide space for the slogans. Also displayed were the photographs and names of the dead fighters, male and female. On the opposite side of the square was the city library, free to all, with books on the second floor and 300 computers on the first floor, and many students reading. Through an internet link, the students could access all the books at the National Library in Pyongyang. At a kindergarten, we were treated to an hour-long exhibition of precocious musical and dancing talent by children aged five to seven.

Our last stop was the Naval Club by the harbour where we had Japanese-style showers. A large room had a dozen or so showers and hoses at intervals along the walls at which we could wash down and clean with soap. A large tub in the centre of the room was filled with cold water rather than hot, so I settled on just a tepid shower. We returned to the hotel in time for supper, which Judith skipped. We were in bed by 9.00 p.m.

Chongjin to Pyongyang, September 21

I slept well, undisturbed by trains. From the window, I watched a gang of women working on the railway line; they were putting back by hand stones that had been displaced from the track. Other people were hurrying off to work on foot or bicycle on the road by the railway, emerging from the alleyway running between the single story low-cost houses; and a man was tending to the rice that grew between the two rail tracks. Judith was still unwell and skipped breakfast; she was on a fluid diet and taking medicine to cope with the travel she still had to do.

First stop south of the city was an 'historic site', a small fishing village that was once visited by the wife of Kim Il Sung. A twenty-ton white marble plaque commemorated the visit. We were shown a well where his wife had tasted the water and pronounced it good — the well-head was a forty-ton block of carved granite; a simple wooden windlass for drawing boats ashore built at her suggestion; and the rocky headland from which she fired a rifle to hit a target fifty meters away, demonstrating what an excellent shot she was. Along the beach were wooden fishing boats lying above the high tide mark, and nets being repaired by fishermen, something that must have been done here for generations.

The Dutch couple, former-Navy, tried to say that windlasses were also common around the world, and not 'invented' by the DPRK leaders, but facts got short shift.

Back in the bus, we drove on earth roads over a low range of hills, the driver going fast, blaring his horn and clashing his gears in a disturbing way; but he got us on time to Gyong Song Hotel near Orang airport. There we lunched very well, the best meal of the trip, on vegetables grown in the garden and the biggest fish we have seen so far, just out of the sea. At Orang airport, our chartered plane was waiting, an Ilyushin 62. Our luggage was loaded into the hold by hand. The flight to Pyongyang covered 450 kilometers and took an hour. We returned to the hotel we had stayed in before, to the same rooms. It appeared the hotel had blocked off two floors for our use throughout our trip whether or not we paid the €5 retainer fee.

For our final meal, we were taken to a very smart Korean duck BBQ restaurant. There was much drinking of rice wine and toasts to all the guides who had looked after us so well. The older group returned to the hotel, while the youngsters went on to The Diplomatic Club for a karaoke party. The next morning they reported the party was not great because most of the songs were Korean. At 9.45 p.m., Judith received a call from the lobby that the package she had been promised by the WHO office has arrived. What was that? We did our packing for the train trip the next day.

Train ride, September 22
My last breakfast in Korea was congee, bread and butter. A last bus ride took us to the station. The forecourt of the station was thronged with people, cars and buses; a very large video screen displayed colourful, touristy scenes of the country. As foreign guests, we received priority entrance past the guards into the station. Inside the station was a mass of people, through whom we made our way to the front of the train where a sleeper carriage had been reserved by Koryo. There were four berths to a compartment; we shared one with our new Dutch friends Andre and Karin. There were flushing toilets at both ends of the carriage and running water for the hand basin—a luxury. We were advised that photographs could be taken at Pyongyang station and of the countryside but not at stations up the line. We said farewell to our guides. Americans in our group were barred from traveling on the train, and had to return to Beijing by air. At 10.00 a.m., the train pulled out slowly, all twenty carriages. Our route took us along the coastal plain, through rich agricultural land with neat villages, like those we had seen in the south

and east. The train stopped several times at stations, unloading dozens of passengers, all with heavy bundles of luggage. Each river we passed over had a ruined bridge in view, all casualties of the 'American War'. We were advised the Korean border customs officials would check all our cameras for photographs derogatory of North Korea, so Judith had downloaded the film each day onto her computer, leaving only a few on the camera.

Four hours later we reached the Korean side of the border on the south bank of the Yalu River. We stopped for two hours at Sinuiju, while the inspection was completed. The official was polite and friendly. He was more interested in looking at pictures of our children and grandchildren than the pictures of our trip. The train crossed the Yalu River as the sun was setting, sparkling on the water as it flowed under a ruined bridge to our left. In Dandong, on the Chinese side, we stopped for another two hours, while the wheels were changed to fit the wider-gauge Chinese tracks. We were allowed out of the train for the first time and walked along the clean, spacious platform to the best public toilets we had seen for three weeks.

The train pulled out of the station at 6.30 p.m. We and Andre and Karin headed for the dining car, nine carriages further back, squeezing our way past all the people standing in the corridors. The Chinese meal was very good, a welcome change from Korean cuisine. We had skipped lunch during the first part of the train trip, feeding on the remains of the biscuits we had been carrying around the DPRK as emergency supplies. By the time we finished the meal, it was dark and our return trip up the train was unimpeded, the passengers having by now returned to their compartments to rest. We all turned in shortly after 8.00 p.m., Judith and I on the bottom bunks, warm under a clean duvet and with a soft pillow.

Beijing to Hong Kong September 23

After a good sleep, I awoke up at 6.00 a.m. It was misty outside as we rushed past the factories and skyscrapers of Tianjin. There was a short interlude of countryside and then we entered the edge of the Beijing metropolis. The station was crowded, noisy, with advertising hoardings everywhere, reminding us that we had left the simplicity of North Korea. All the members of the Koryo group joined together in a ring for a group hug and cheer and farewells. There was a long queue for the taxis, so four of us hired a minibus from a tout at CN¥300 to take us to the airport; the usual taxi fare was 100 yuan.

Our flight to Hong Kong on Dragonair was not scheduled to leave until 1.00 p.m.; with gentle persistence, Judith managed to get us on an earlier China Airlines flight. We had time to enjoy a rest and snack at the Business Class lounge shared by Dragonair, Air China and Cathay Pacific. Judith tried to access the internet but failed — then she realized that Google was banned in China and she could get through with a different search engine. We had a good meal on the flight south, and a spectacular descent into Hong Kong in the evening light, clear skies giving us great views over the islands around Hong Kong Island and of Clearwater Bay Golf Course. A rapid taxi ride and we were home at 6.30 p.m., glad to be back and delighted at having had such a great adventure.

IMPRESSIONS

Pyongyang is a designer city, built entirely new from the rubble of the Korean War. It was designed to impress with wide streets, palatial buildings and modern architecture. Every major public building had a statue or portrait of Kim Il Sung, and sometimes also his son Kim Jong Il. The population had for many years been so indoctrinated to respect the leaders that their images were places of pilgrimage. Television, radio and internet connection with the outside world were blocked.

The 20 percent of the country that is arable and the floodplains of valleys and delta areas were intensively cultivated and appeared to be heading for a bumper crop that year of rice, corn and soybeans. The rest of the country was mountainous and well covered with trees. Many hours traveling in buses across the country revealed that rural villages were all well planned, and neat with individual dwellings. We saw no squatter huts, no starving children and no people in rags. There was no mechanisation of farm production and buffalos pulled the ploughs and the farm carts; everything else was done by hand by the plentiful workforce.

Petrol was in short supply. I did not see a single western-style filling station. There were plenty of cars in Pyongyang, many run by officials, diplomats and NGOs as well as some taxis and private cars. Trams and trolleybuses were powered by electricity, as were the major rail tracks.

No individual paid income tax. The government raised money from corporate taxes and exports. There was free schooling for eleven years, free medical care, and free housing for people working for companies. But people were assigned jobs and needed permission to travel from one city to another, disposable wages were minimal and people were required to accept all the rules and not criticize the government. For those who could accept these limitations, it was a socialist utopia.

I enjoyed the tour Judith and I made. Our Korean guides were efficient and, over the three-week trip, friendly and helpful. We were mindful of the limitations, took no photographs of military subjects, we did not wander off unaccompanied and showed respect for the many statues and portraits of the political leaders. As a public relations exercise, the tour was a great success, showing us a country doing its best, clean, no beggars on the streets, people enjoying themselves and capable of a uniquely spectacular event like the Arirang Mass Games.

Mount Paekdu was a bonus.

PHILIPPINES
Mount Apo
Height: 2,954 metres, (9,691 feet)
Date: 2012

The purpose of this trip was to climb Mount Apo, 2,954m, the
tallest mountain in the Philippines. It is in Mindanao, in the
south of the country. This was the last mountain in south-east
Asia that I had planned to climb to complete my chosen itinerary;
the highest mountain in Laos was the only other trekkable one
left but was closed to climbers because of rebel activity and a
profusion of land-mines. Previously, I had not climbed Mt. Apo
because of a Muslim secessionist rebellion in Mindanao. It was
just a year since I had undergone a heart atrial ablation operation
to control increasingly frequent bouts of atrial fibrillation. Since
then, I had been well and, two months earlier, had climbed
Mount Paekdu in North Korea with no ill effects. I felt I was
ready to make this climb.

Day One Wednesday 21 November

I flew from Hong Kong to Manila, where I changed planes for the flight to Davao, capital of Mindanao; this took me over myriad islands to Mindanao, almost as large as Luzon. We passed over the mountainous, wooded centre of the land and reached Davao on the coastal plane at the south of the island, arriving at 4 p.m. I declined the offer of an airport limousine to take me to my hotel for Pesos 500—a regular taxi cost P200. The ride was depressing—bad roads, wooden shacks along the road and many petrol stations; unlike in North Korea, fuel was abundant. The traffic on the town roads was heavy, flanked by dilapidated buildings. To the right, I could see an outline of the range of mountains that included Mount Apo.

My hotel, booked through Ogden, an agency in Singapore, was conveniently in the centre of town on Jose Camus Street, opposite the People's Park. It was an oldish, five-storey building that fronted right onto a busy street. The guard at the entrance checked me for firearms. The small lobby had a reception desk, a sofa and chairs; to the right was a small dining room dominated by a large-screen TV. My room 204 was clean, appointed with modern requirements—fridge, safe, multi-channel TV, en suite bathroom and air conditioning; but the furniture was cheap and the ambience shabby. I ate a good meal in the hotel, watching a spirited game of Filipino netball. In my room, the only channel available appeared to be a Filipino one.

Day 2 Thursday 22 November

I had a leisurely buffet breakfast in front of CNN news on television, then went out to explore. I walked round to the far side of the People's Park on intermittent and uneven pavements, past a profusion of little shops selling food, medicines and DVDs. I also walked past offices of doctors and dentists to the Marco

Polo Hotel on the corner of Recto Claveria and Roxas Avenue; its gleaming white tower block was strikingly visible from a distance. I went in for a refreshing soft drink and to get out of the heat, over 30 C; I found it very smart inside, with spacious public rooms, swimming pool and health club. Next door was the new Red Cross centre, and, opposite, an office block housing the Post Office and the Philippine Airlines office. I went back to my hotel and collected my camera and flight reservation for my return flight; the run-down nature of the city apart from a few buildings around the Marco Polo convinced me that, as soon as I had finished the climb, I should return to Hong Kong.

What was a surprise were the anti-smoking posters and No Smoking notices for all indoor areas and in the People's Park itself. The jeepney minibuses were uniquely colourful and noisy, while motor bike three- wheelers were also common. I lunched at the Royal Mandaya Hotel, an excellent buffet. Before leaving Hong Kong, I had checked up on Davao Rotary clubs. So, at 6.00 p.m., I returned to the Marco Polo Hotel by taxi, concerned that, walking along the irregular pavement, I might injure myself before even getting to the mountain, and also because of warnings of the high crime rate. At the entrance, armed guards inspected the taxi, inside the boot and underneath using a mirror device, and frisked me down. There were only five other people at the Rotary meeting, including PDG (Past District Governor) Salvador Angala, a retired wood exporter, mostly to Japan, and his son President Anthony, an orthopaedic surgeon. They were very friendly and gave me telephone contacts in case of emergency during my climb.

I returned to the hotel by taxi in time to meet Lorenz Zapanta from Trail Adventours, and Vincent, my guide for the climb. Vincent was a slightly built Filipino of 26, unmarried, living at home with his parents, a working brother, and sister at school.

We arranged for me to set off with Vincent the following morning at 4.00am. Vincent's English was limited, but, with the porter Michael, he was a ball of laughs in Filipino.

Day 3 Friday 23 November

I was in the lobby by 4 a.m. as requested and met Vincent, already waiting. We boarded a taxi to take us to the bus station with the idea of taking a public bus to Digos, a town 60 kilometres along the coast to the west. When the taxi driver offered to take us all the way to Digos, I quickly agreed a price. It was a big mistake — in the pre-dawn darkness, he set off at breakneck speed, with no seatbelts in the rear; he arrived triumphantly after 55 minutes at the Digos transport centre. I found I was having multiple extra heart-beats which I had not had for weeks. We waited half an hour for our porter, Michael, in his 20s, to join us; in the meantime, we observed the increasing traffic of motor bikes, motorbike three-wheel taxis, and brightly coloured jeepneys.

A woman across the square shouted and waved her arms in a demented way; all nonsense, confirmed Vincent. A group of women clustered at a nearby doorway and rushed into the doctor's office when it opened at 6 a.m. Once Michael had arrived, the three of us and our three backpacks piled onto a motor bike with side-car and made for the nearest restaurant for breakfast; we passed two invitingly new and smart Jollibee's, a Filipino chain of fast-food restaurants — but both were closed. In the very dingy place which was open, I had an excellent bowl of congee; but the hole-in-the-ground toilet was grubby and there was no running water. Next stop was a grocery store into which Vincent disappeared with a shopping list of provisions for the trip. I sat outside with Michael, watching as customers were checked by a guard at the entrance to the shop and their purchase receipts verified by another guard at the exit. Large wicker baskets of small, local, damaged bananas were placed between the two doors for people to scavenge through for free. After the purchases were completed, the backpacks became even bulkier; I watched as they were tied onto a motor bike. Then I realised with horror that I was expected to ride on the bike, behind the driver with Vincent behind me and Michael sitting on the fuel tank in front of the driver — none of us with crash helmets. I held on very tightly as we climbed up from Digos into the foothills on good roads, through the next town, Kidapawan; and then on increasingly rough dirt tracks up into the hills, until we reached the end of the road, marked by a small shack. This was the transport interchange where vegetable produce, carried on horseback from the farms, was transferred onto bikes to go to market.

At 9.00 a.m., after a day's worth of experiences, we started the trek. For the first hour, we walked along muddy paths at the side of fields where healthy-looking cabbages and carrots were being grown. We passed two simple wooden farm houses, one attractively surrounded by Arum lilies. Then we were into the lush rainforest, up stream beds or inching along their banks, over fallen logs, stepping carefully to avoid tree roots. We went through pools left by recent rains, through forest glades thronged with orange flowers, below first-growth trees hung with mosses and orchids not yet in bloom; all the time we were climbing. My ski sticks were not much help for support, given the softness of the ground.

With a brief stop for a lunch sandwich, we reached our target campsite at around 2,000 metres, Godi-Godi, at 2.20 p.m., on schedule; the camp site was a wide stretch of level ground overhung by huge trees, fringed by bushes, and a stream running down at one side. We were the only group there, which was delightful. Michael reported that, in March and April, the popular climbing season when it was dry but hot, there could be 1,000 people camped there. I lay down to rest in the tent that Vincent and Michael put up for me. I was very tired after the strenuous climb, but had to get up again after an hour because of leg cramps; they settled after I took calcium and salt tablets and did stretching and massage. Supper was a large bowl of rice, eggs and tuna fish, washed down by mineral water.

By 7.00 p.m., it was dark and we all retired to sleep.

Day 4. Saturday 24th November

I slept badly because of the hard ground and the chill in the air, and was happy to get up at 5 a.m. for a bowl of hot congee. At 7 a.m., we left camp to climb through more forest, thinning out to scrub, then opening out onto a mountainside of granite rock boulders, a daunting prospect — one false move could mean a twisted ankle or worse. Vincent threaded a way through this jumble of rock guided by stones placed on boulders at short intervals. I found my tough gardening gloves indispensable here to protect my hands from the rocks that I had to grip in scrambling up the slope. At this altitude, above 2,500 metres, my progress was slow, two minute's rest every ten yards or so; but I was stimulated by a view of the volcano crater rim towering above. The route skirted upwind of a volcanic vent gushing sulphurous steam — the occasional whiff of it burnt my throat. Vincent and Michael were happy to slow down later on during this stage because of a scattering of blueberry bushes; they fruited profusely despite their desperate location.

We paused to rest again and had some food in a sandy bowl at the foot of the final wall, facing a near vertical scramble to the crest of the crater. Clouds had been building up all morning; by the time we had reached the crater rim and looked out over the lake, we were in the clouds and had limited visibility. We climbed to the adjacent peak on our left, then descended back to where we reached the crater rim and plunged down on the lakeward side. We skirted the lake to the right to reach a lush green, grassy valley nestled in between several peaks, including Mt. Davao and Mt. Kidapawan. There was dispute over which was higher, so we climbed them both. At the valley campsite, we came across other climbers, a group of 10 friendly Filipinos who insisted having their picture taken with me. I was delighted to find a clump of thistles in bloom, a long way from Scotland.

From the crater rim, I could look down 1,500 feet to Lake Venado, our campsite for the night, in a valley surrounded by forest. Climbing down the hummocky grass slope was easy compared with what had gone before. It was not long before we came near to the treeline, so lay down on the grass to enjoy the view in a moment of sunshine before surrendering more of the altitude so painfully gained during the last two days. The lake was dumbbell-shaped about half a mile long, with a gentle shoreline fringed by grass and marshland with bulrushes. The soft soil had been extensively snouted by wild boar. There was no outgoing river, so the size of the lake depended on the amount of recent rain. I found a profuse patch of lilies, a contrast to the forest of huge trees bearded with mosses.

There was no wildlife to be seen apart from small birds. The very big monkey-eating eagle was not to be seen, nor any monkeys. On the positive side, there were no mosquitoes or leeches. Crickets beeping at night were not loud enough to keep me awake. We pitched camp by 4.00 p.m. on the far side of the lake from the Filipinos we had met up the mountain. Just as Michael was preparing supper, it started to rain, a heavy rain that had no trouble penetrating my tent, wetting everything not in waterproof wrapping. Once the rain had stopped, we had our supper — marinated chicken nuggets and rice, followed by handfuls of raisins I had brought from Hong Kong. Clean water came from a nearby stream, but I took the precaution of putting a chlorine tablet in each bottle to sterilise the water. This was a damp ending to a splendid day in which I had achieved my ambition to climb Mount Apo.

Day 5. Sunday 25 November

I woke at dawn after a surprisingly good night's sleep despite wet bedding. The clothes that I was to wear in the morning I took into the sleeping bag to try and dry out. After a quick breakfast, we set out at 7.00 a.m. on paths made even wetter by the rain on the night before and the morning mist. The trail was very steep, made possible at several points by sturdy wooden ladders or hanging ropes. There were more fallen trees, and a point where a landslide had obliterated the track. Every time Vincent called a halt for a rest, I knew there was a particularly difficult stretch to negotiate. By this time my legs were getting tired, so I was particularly careful in working my way down the muddy, root-terraced banks. Reaching the valley floor, we followed the Marble River downstream, having to cross it six times. We forded it the first four times, the water up to our knees; Michael had to steady me where the current was very swift. We dried out our shoes and socks expecting the fifth crossing place to be bridged; it was, but so crudely that we chose to wade across instead; and had to dry our boots again. The sixth crossing bridge had recently been built; it was a strong construction of massive bamboo trunks, so we walked over on it.

Nearing 3.00 p.m., we climbed out of the valley, past another hot, spraying geyser and onto the road just below Agco Lake hot springs resort. We had been scheduled to spend the night at Agco, relax and enjoy the hot springs, but all the cabins were full and I did not fancy another night in my non-waterproof tent;

also the place had the look of a really cheap resort. My suggestion that we call an end to the trip and head back home was greeted enthusiastically by Vincent and Michael. A short negotiation followed with a rotund Filipino who appeared to control the local transport; this resulted in the hire of another motor bike "taxi". This ride down to Kidapawan in Cotobato Province was marginally less scary than the last ride—down better roads but interrupted by a rainstorm. At the city transport hub, we transferred to a coach for the three-hour trip via Digos, where I said farewell to Michael, and on to Davao. Michael's wage was PhP500 per day (HK$100/day). I was so impressed with him that I gave him an extra PhP500—which he was initially reluctant to accept.

My room at Casa Leticia was vacant so I stopped there and said my farewells to Vincent. I spent the next hour unpacking my wet gear, hanging it up, selecting the dry clothes to wear and having a most welcome shower. I was not hungry, so for supper had a cup of hot milk and sugar and finished the raisins I had brought with me. I took a capsule of my anticoagulant; I had stopped it during the climb in case of accidents. I went to sleep happy with the successful completion of the trip up Mount Apo; I was happy that my body had come through unscathed, and happy to be returning home soon.

Day 6 Monday 22 November
I was up at 7.00 a.m., legs and back stiff and requiring stretching exercises. I had a leisurely breakfast reading The Star newspaper and gained an insight of the Filipino nation. It was three years since the Ampatuan massacre. It had occurred on the morning of 23 November 2009 and was also known as the Maguindanao massacre. Ampatuan was the town where the mass graves were found. The victims were on their way to file a certificate of

candidacy for Esmael Mangudadatu, when they were kidnapped and brutally killed. Mangudadatu was challenging the mayor of Datu Unsay, Andal Ampatuan, Jr. son of the incumbent Maguindanao governor, in the forthcoming gubernatorial election for that district; it was part of the national elections in 2010. The 58 people killed included Mangudadatu's wife, his two sisters, journalists, lawyers, aides, and motorists who were witnesses or mistakenly identified as part of the convoy. There were 91 suspects still hiding in the forest and marshland at the edge of Cotobato province.

Different Moslem factions were still killing each other. The Communists were engaged in an extortion racket with the local bus company; they were alleged to behind two roadside bombs that killed several people. Five thousand guns in one province were unaccounted for, their licences having not been renewed.

Police in another province had ordered 25 Apache helicopters to cope with the expected violence during the upcoming elections; a couple of candidates had already been shot.

The recent crash of a two-engine light passenger plane and the cover-up of the accident report findings had lain bare the incompetence and corruption of the airline industry administration; PAL was denied a certificate to fly to Europe because of non-compliance with regulations.

A Reproductive Health Bill reached a critical point; it was criticised by a bishop of the Catholic Church and supported by national surveys that showed that more than 70 per cent of Catholics wanted it to be passed.

25 years after Marcos was deposed, his billions of dollars of loot had still to be traced.

I bought two picture post-cards to send to our two sons and went down to the Central Post Office to post them. I lunched at the Apo View Hotel, a gloomy room looking out onto a decent garden; the buffet was less good than those of the other hotels I had sampled. In the afternoon I rested. The last triumph of the day was working out how to use the set-top box control to get Australian TV activated. A gratifyingly long sports programme told me that Rory McIlroy had won the season-ending tournament in Dubai with an astonishing five birdies over the last five holes; that neophyte South African batsman Francois du Plessis had scored an unbeaten 110 to deny Australia victory in the second Test Match; and that Sebastian Vittel, the 23-year-old German driver, had won the F1 World Championship for the third time.

At 10.00 p.m., I met Lawrenz Zapanta, owner of the trekking agency, for a debriefing. He suggested that I should climb Mt. Pulac, the second highest mountain in the Philippines, and the highest in Luzon. I told him I would think about it.

Day 7 Tuesday 27 November

My flight from Davao to Manila was not till 2.30 p.m., but I was in a taxi at noon. It was just as well, because there was a huge traffic jam on the main road out of town caused by a crash in which a container lorry had blocked two lanes of a four-lane highway. The two lanes of traffic leading out of town became three lanes and then four, allowing the oncoming traffic only the hard-shoulder of the road. Of course, the four lanes then had to whittle back to one lane to pass the accident. The rest of the journey was uneventful. I was home by 10.00 p.m. on a misty, cold, night, but with a very warm welcome, as always.

Epilogue: two days after I left Mindanao, the island was hit by a devastating typhoon; it left over 1,500 dead and 250,000 homeless.

SRI LANKA
Mt Pedro Pidurutalagala (Straw-laden Rock)
Height: 2,524 metres (8,281ft)
Date: January 1, 2002

A New Year visit to Sri Lanka was an opportunity both to climb its highest mountain and for Judith and me to have a family holiday, with our elder son and his family. It turned out to be one of my easiest ascents. Just as well: the previous year I had undergone a second heart operation to stop atrial fibrillation.

Our son Andrew, his wife Beverley and their teenage children, Kate and Robbie, had flown out from Scotland to join Judith and me for Christmas in Hong Kong. On Boxing Day, we all flew from Hong Kong to Colombo for a family tour of Sri Lanka. It was five years since its civil war had ended with the defeat of the Tamil Tigers. We left home at 5 a.m. and had a four hour stopover at Kuala Lumpur; this was followed by a three-hour delay because of the late arrival of our connecting flight to Colombo. We arrived at 8 p.m., to be met by the tour director, a Toyota van and driver Sampath. So began the toughest part of the journey. For the next three hours, it was a white-knuckle ride as we were driven through heavy traffic on the two-way road; it was single lanes with few passing places, winding through villages, plantations and forest. The Kings of the Road were clearly the bus drivers who fearlessly charged down oncoming vehicles; the likeliest victims were the myriad three-wheeled, motorcycle-engine-powered Tuk-tuks. We were more than grateful to reach our destination, the Green Paradise Resort, check in and go to bed.

Friday, December 27

In daylight, we could now see that the route from the Resort to the nearest town, Dambulla, was along the barrage containing a vast lake, or 'tank', Kandalama Reservoir, at one point the road dipping down across the flood overflow slipway. In the wet season, guests would have to wait till the water subsided or walk across the footbridge to be picked up on the other side. From Dambulla, we drove north for another half hour to reach Sigiriya. This was a huge granite core of a volcano with a flat top 660 feet high; it had once been a fortress built by King Kashyapa in the 5th century. When the King was overthrown, it became a Buddhist monastery until the 14th Century, and was then abandoned. To reach it, we paid a US$25 fee at a ticket booth near the museum. We then crossed the road and a wide moat surrounding the foundation remnants of the town and gardens at the base of the rock. A bathing pool was presided over by a large white Egret.

The way up the mountain was by a series of flights of steps and a metal spiral ladder attached to the side of the near-vertical rock face. At the bottom, Judith decided that she would prefer to stroll round the gardens, rather than join the solid line of visitors inching their way up the rock. After the first flight of steps, Kate collapsed with a hypotensive episode; she revived only after drinks of water, a banana and a spell lying down in the shade. To her great credit, she struggled on till she reached the top.

The first flights of stairs were followed by an iron spiral staircase winding up to the cave of Sigiriya Damsels; the cave walls were covered with magnificent paintings of palace female attendants painted in the 5th Century. Descending the stair, we walked along a channel cut into the face of the rock, with a highly polished Mirror Wall on our left built for the King, covered with graffiti from the 8th century. More stairs led up to a plateau about 50 yards in diameter. Two huge lion paws of stone guarded the last zigzag flights of metal stairs to the summit of the Lion Rock, Sigiriya. The summit had been fashioned into a series of terraces by excavating rock and building up sun-baked mud brick walls. A large reservoir supplied water, and a place for weary visitors to sit and bathe their feet. Outlines of the many buildings were marked by low brick and stone walls. The views over the surrounding countryside were magnificent — wooded planes punctuated by other granite volcanic cores such as the one we were on. Sigiriya lived up to its reputation as a unique and fascinating destination. Carefully descending the steep stairs, we re-joined Judith at the Museum and inspected the well-laid out exhibits.

The next site was Polonnaruwa, the great capital city of Sri Lanka from the 12th to 13th centuries; it stretched for miles to the left of the road. We entered the area at a river running from the lake, again paying an entry fee of US$25. The first site we walked around was the Palace, 31 x 13 metres in size, with elephant carvings and lions guarding the steps to the audience hall. Not until we were in the museum could we realise the magnificence of a building that had been seven stories high, all made of wood apart from the ground floor. Nearby was an ornate bathing pool with crocodile mouths to spout water. A short distance away was the Quadrangle, containing many different structures including the Hatadage, which at one time had held the Buddha Tooth Relic. The Vatadage was a round structure, its walls richly decorated with animal sculptures and the central shrine having four seated Buddhas. The Gal Potha, a single granite stone 9 metres long, 1.5 wide and 66 centimetres deep carried an inscription 1,000 years old; it had been dragged from a site 100 kilometres away. To get to the Potgul Vihara, an ancient library, we had to carefully evade a herd of cows. At one corner stood an impressive six-storey high ziggurat-like stepped structure of unknown purpose.

The last site we examined was Gal Vihara, 900 years old, a rock wall from which had been carved four Buddha images; three were sitting, and one was peacefully sleeping, 14 metres long — all magnificent carvings. At each temple throughout the day, we had to take off our shoes and walk on sometimes painfully uneven ground; it was a serious disincentive to joining the faith.

Saturday, December 28

We had another early start, to get to Anuradhapura, capital of Sri Lanka from the 4th to the 11th century; it was three hours north of our resort. The roads were better on this route but the traffic was severe, with heavily-laden trucks, charging busses and the ubiquitous Tuk-tuks darting in and out of the stream. Despite the chaos on the roads, we did not see a single accident all week. The surrounding countryside was flat, with rice paddies and coconut trees.

First stop was a museum, housed in a large colonial style building, 1937, and painted white; it used to be a District Office.

From the museum, we walked to a huge 120-foot-high stupa made of brick, Jetavanarama; when it was built in the 3rd century, it was the third tallest building in the world after the Pyramids at Giza. We walked round the stupa, barefoot of course, admiring the stone sculpture, and keeping clear of the monkeys; the original plaster coating had long gone, exposing the brick. Nearby was a second stupa only slightly smaller. In between was wooded parkland with throngs of white-clad Buddhist pilgrims praying at the shrines and walking among the myriad ruins, usually a stone base with granite pillars in place to hold up a now vanished upper floor.

In the afternoon we walked to another huge stupa Ruwanweli,140 BC; it was clothed in white plaster, just as the other stupas must have looked like centuries ago, surrounded by a wall of elephants standing shoulder to shoulder. We were passed by a band of colourfully dressed musicians leading a large procession of devotees dressed in white and waving the Sri Lankan flag. Instead of following them round the stupa, we walked down the ceremonial path to the holiest site on the island — the living descendent of the Sri Maha Bohdi, a Bo tree under which the Gautama achieved enlightenment in India. The cutting was brought from India 2,300 years earlier. The tree grew out of a central raised square temple surrounded by an enclosing wall of stone through which other fully grown off-shoots from the tree appeared; it reminded me of Ta Prom in Siem Reap, Cambodia. Stalls sold flowers and wax candles, offerings to the temple.

Sunday, December 29

This was another long day with an early start. We were sad to leave the beautiful resort. First stop was near Dambulla itself; we visited a cave complex excavated into another granite outcrop, 525 feet high. This was an overtly touristy place with a large, gilded face at the entrance, large model elephants, and a row of life-sized statues of saffron-robed monks circling the front of the rock. Steep stairs led up the rock to a ledge at the back of which a long line of caves had been dug in the 1st century BCE; each cave held images of many Buddhas, kings, and deities and the walls and roofs were all covered with paintings rich in gold and red and yellow colours. From the rock, we could see to the east the Siriya rock we had climbed and, to the south, the mountains to which we were now heading.

Back in the bus, we travelled through lush rain forest with plantations of banana, coconut palms and rice fields with newly planted green shoots standing in water. As we climbed up the valley, we were joined by the single track railway that runs from Colombo past Kandy and Nuwara Eliya to Badulla, a spectacular 10-hour journey. We stopped at a Spice Garden where a guide showed us around the impressive array of trees and bushes and herbs from which spices are derived. We then had a chance to buy some of the products, offering cures for anything from diabetes, obesity, smoking and various skin complaints. We ate a healthy and well spiced lunch at the dining hall guarded by two large wooden elephants.

The route south into the mountains became even more tortuous, as the valley narrowed. The road surface was excellent and well-marked, though drivers did not often take note of the double white lines, gaily passing on blind corners; Sampath was a careful driver, thank goodness. We drove through several small villages—rows of dilapidated shop-houses crowding either side of the road. At last, we crested a final ridge and drove down into the bowl in which Kandy lies at an altitude of 1,500ft. It was the last capital of an independent Sri Lankan kingdom, the Southern Indian king being ousted by Singhalese nobles and deported to India by Britain in 1815. We stayed at the magnificent five-star Mahaweli Reach Hotel. We only had time to check in before departing for the YMBA hall for a cultural show. We joined a packed audience to watch a colourful display of native dances backed by energetic drummers. The finale was a fire-walking display outside in the courtyard.

After the show, we went down to the lake in the centre of town. We walked round the eastern side, past the historic 160-year-old Queens Hotel, and past the temple of the Buddha's Tooth opened in 1595, housed in what used to be the royal palace. The tooth was brought to Sri Lanka in the 300s AD and held as a symbol of power by each king, wherever his capital might be. On the edge of the lake stood a handsome stone structure, the bath house built for the Queen. A flower market for temple offerings, even late in the evening, was a blaze with lights. In 1807, the farmers, who objected to King Rajasinha's order that their fields be turned into a lake, were tied to stakes in the lake and executed.

Monday, December 30

We travelled part of the way down the road to Colombo to visit the Pinnewala elephant refuge. We spent a fascinating hour watching a herd of 30 elephants being bathed in a wide but shallow river. There were no mature males — plenty of adult females and a group of four youngsters trumpeting noisily and romping about as youngsters do. We were able to watch safely from the balcony of a restaurant, but within reach for Kate and Robbie to feed bananas to the elephants. We were in one of the shops lining the narrow road from the river when the elephants came charging back after their bathe, within touching distance.

Tuesday, December 31

We started the day with a massive breakfast at the Mahaweli Hotel, because we were headed further into the mountains to stay for a night at a self-catering house in Nuwara Eliya, our Base Camp for the attempt on Mt Pedro. First stop was at a food store to buy essentials for our home stay. We stopped again at the western edge of Kandy, at the Botanical Gardens originating in 1371 and developed by Kew Gardens from 1843. The 147 acres of undulating gardens were enclosed by a loop of the river. The orchid house had a wonderful display; we left Robbie to paint flowers there, while we walked around the spectacular avenues of trees. We admired the enormous teak trees, intrigued by the appropriately-named 'Cannon Ball' tree planted by King George IV and Queen Mary in 1906, and enjoyed the flower garden and the large open lawns.

Nawara Eliya is at 6,122 feet, a hill resort developed by the British in the 1800s. We had rented a house for the night, with two staff. As the daylight faded, so did all the electric lights in the valley. Our host located a store of candles and matches; we gathered round the sitting-room table and played "Go Fish", a card game new to me, Scrabble and Whist, all by candlelight. Cooking was on gas; by the time the lights came on again, we were eating an excellent vegetarian curry prepared by our host. We were told the electricity only went off two to three times a year. The other good news was that there was plenty of hot water because of efficient solar water heaters. We toasted the New Year at midnight Hong Kong time — a uniquely memorable New Year!

On New Year's Day we breakfasted well. Afterwards, Sampath drove Andrew, Kate, Robbie and me to the base of Mt Pedro; the Lonely Planet reported a walking trail there that would take us up about four kilometres towards the summit of Mount Pedro. The trail was blocked by a bar gate. We found our way back to the main road up to the peak and the Army checkpoint there. To our surprise and delight, once we had filled in identification details, we were allowed to continue driving up a bumpy metalled road. Notices at the side of the road warned of the danger of leopards – the reason why no one was allowed to walk up the mountain. As we ascended higher, the thick forest gave way to stunted trees, and rhododendrons. At the top was an extensive establishment of radio, TV and air-craft navigation equipment maintained by the Air Force; a group of senior Air Force officers making an inspection passed us with smiles. We waited by a large bank of hydrangeas at the entrance while Sampath parked the van; then all went to the highest point. No pictures were allowed within the military perimeter, but we did take them once we were out of the perimeter gate. This was one of my easier summit conquests.

That day Sampath drove us the 97 miles back down the mountains and on to Negombo, a beach resort near Colombo airport. We had two days to enjoy ourselves at the resort. We went sailing in an outrigger boat, schnorkelling and visiting a seabird reserve, before we departed for our separate destinations, 10,000 miles apart. Two days later a tropical cyclone hit the island.

The trip went as planned thanks to Andrew's attention to detail. The extended family unit got on very well together. The deal was that Judith and I paid for the trip but Andrew was responsible for detailed planning in consultation with us, and supervised the day to day expenditures during the trip. This worked very well. He remarked that he always assumed this role on his own family holidays. It meant that Judith and I could relax and enjoy the trip. I only had a carry-on suitcase and bought nothing. Judith had a check-in suitcase and bought lovely summer clothing to fill it to capacity; her carry-on case had her mini-Vio computer and associated electric wires, Blackberry and I-Pod. Mementoes of the trip were a small elephant stone carving with a baby elephant inside, and a small stone reproduction of a moonstone, and of course, countless photographs.

CYPRUS
Mount Olympus, Chionistra
Height: 1,952 m., 6,401 ft.
Date: December 5, 1995, Aged 60

We were in Cyprus because Judith was speaking at a WHO meeting on cardio-vascular disease. Base camp was The Forum Intercontinental Hotel, Nicosia, on the Greek side of the border with Cyprus. I had one day to make my ascent of the island's highest mountain.

09.15 am. My transport arrived, an ancient Mercedes limousine with a capacity for seven, on hire for the day at the extravagant cost of 65 Cypriot pounds, about 70 Sterling; driver, Andreas, was a small, round, cheerful Greek Cypriot.

The road he took led across the plain in a south-west direction, just south of the border with the Turkish occupied zone.

Farming country, it was parched, brown, at the end of the dry season, fields were ploughed ready for sowing and the rains. Some fields of potatoes were being harvested; fruit trees were laden with oranges, lemons and olives.

There were small villages, much new building, but one more ancient town, Peristeron, with a 10th century five-domed Orthodox church, and nearby a mosque, now unused.

After 45 minutes we took a right fork off the main road, at the start of the foothills, and climbed up the Marathasa valley following the Strakhos river on a winding road, bordered with firs and fruit trees and terraces of grape vines. The few villages were a jumble of red-tiled roofs clinging to the sides of the valleys. Kalopanayiotis, Moutoulas and Pedhoulas (3,600ft) were particularly scenic, the latter being dominated by the silver domes of the Archangel Michael Church.

First stop was Mount Kykkos, 4,000 ft., the burial site of Archbishop Makarios III, first President of the Republic of Cyprus.

From the car park a short road led up to the summit crowned by a place of worship, the Throni, commanding spectacular views over the Troodos Mountains.

The tomb itself was along the ridge from the Throni, a simple, rough-hewn stone crypt, with a photograph of Makarios in front of the stone plinth covered with a black marble grave stone. The two soldiers on guard did not object to photographs being taken. The whole area inspired a feeling of dignity and of a peace that Makarios himself must have had little experience of during his lifetime.

Just down the mountain was the Kykkos Monastery, the biggest and richest monastery in Cyprus, founded 1092; burned down five times, most recently by the Turks in 1821; occupied by the Gordon Highlanders in 1956 during the EOKA conflict while they tried to capture Colonel Grivas who was reported to have sheltered there.

It was a handsome stone structure, many buildings on different levels, linked by cloisters and stairways.

Cloisters were hung with religious paintings, icons, the main chapel being lavishly adorned with frescoes, icons and gold-plated chandeliers and screens, the whole of a sumptuous splendour overpowering to my Protestant background.

We lunched at the nearby tourist restaurant, now virtually empty in the off-season, perched on the edge of the ridge with a view across to Mt Olympus at whose summit the first wispy clouds were beginning to gather in an otherwise cloudless sky.

Outside, surrounding the restaurant car-park were the usual string of tourist stalls selling mementoes, religious and otherwise, post-cards, locally produced dried fruit and nuts, and liquor.

Each stall-holder would entice customers by offering a nip of a clear liquid. Andreas happily accepted a couple of nips prior to buying a couple of bottles of the stuff.

I would have been even more alarmed at the time if I had known that this was the local hooch, a grape spirit, 90 percent proof, Zivania

From Kykkos it was a half hour drive, through Prodromos at 4.600 ft. the highest village in Cyprus, to Mt. Olympus. Turning off the road to Troodos village we ascended a smaller road through pine forest with snow on the ground and children sledging.

The ascent had turned out to be even less taxing than that of Doi Inthenon in Thailand in that the car park this time was actually on the summit. To one side was the inevitable array of electronic communications masts, but in other directions an attractive wintry scene of snow, Black Pines (Pinus nigra) and dry-brown bracken.

A LOVE OF MOUNTAINS

In the distance I could see to the North, a sunlit coast; to the East, the plains leading to Nicosia, and beyond to the hills in the Turkish sector; and to the West and South, ranges of the Troodos Mountains.

Cheated of my day's exercise I opted to go on one of the nature trails marked on my guide book, the Caledonian Trail.

The trail started just down from the Troodos hill resort at the head of the Kryos Potamos river valley, beside the summer Presidential Residence.

It led down a delightful, wooded valley for two kilometres, crossing and recrossing a clear stream, with fish in the pools, as far as a waterfall. The trail was well named. It could easily have been in Scotland. The climb back was steep enough to make me happy to see my limousine again, and Andreas asleep in the driver's seat.

The drive down from the mountains passed an immense open-cast asbestos mine, Amiandos.

Heading north, Kekopetria was the first considerable town we came to, at the junction of two rivers, a popular hill resort. The old town, perched on the narrow ridge between the rivers was medieval; a narrow stone-cobbled street overhung by terraced houses, ground floor walls of stone, upper walls of sun-dried mud bricks surfaced with mud and straw, wooden balconies with hanging baskets of flowers, tile roofs.

Andreas then introduced me to his friend who owned The Mill Restaurant, a spectacular four storey old mill house built into the side of the narrow valley. Uniquely the water power was provided by a vertical fall of water that turned a horizontally rotating mill wheel on a vertical drive shaft.

From Kakopetria we were quickly back on the plains and back to Nicosia by 16.30 in a brilliant sunset.

It had been an interesting day scenically, but discomforting to hear the recent history from the Cypriot angle with Colonel Grivas the elusive hero and the British soldiers as the bad guys. One side's "terrorists" are always the other side's "freedom fighters".

GUERNSEY, CHANNEL ISLANDS

La Villiaze, Forest
Height: 98m (321 Ft.)
Date: Dec. 1995

Judith and I flew into Guernsey airport from Heathrow, en route from sunny Cyprus, with the idea of acclimatising gently for a few days in the milder climate of the Channel Islands before travelling further north to Yorkshire.

Surprise, surprise — we stepped out of the plane into the teeth of a winter gale and had to hold onto each other to reach the terminal building.

Next day the wind had only abated slightly and low scudding clouds promised more rain.

Despite the elements, our hosts Bill and Marjorie Lane took us along the coast to the North-East cliffs, in search of the highest point on the island.

After a half hour drive and a short cliff-top walk we reached a spectacular headland with a huge Martello Tower at the crest of the ridge.

Satisfied with our conquest we returned to the home of our hosts and spent the next few days with them in glorious sunshine.

Later, I wrote to the Guernsey authorities to confirm the highest point: to be told we had reached it when we landed at the airport!

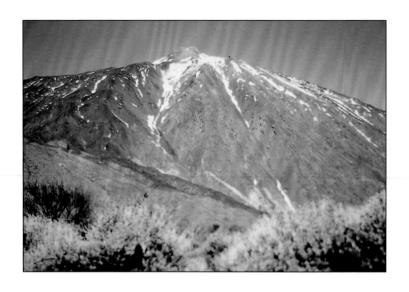

SPAIN

Pico del Teide, Spain
Height: 3,718m (12,199ft)
Date: Sunday 28th February, 1999

The Spanish Canary Islands were our destination. Its highest mountain is an extinct volcano; the islands are part of the extension of the Atlas range of North Africa. An added incentive was to join Judith at The Second European Conference on Tobacco or Health at Las Palmas on Gran Canaria.

The day after the conference, we set off from our "base camp", the venerable and luxurious Hotel Santa Catalina in Las Palmas, in time to catch the 8.00 a.m. jetfoil ferry to Tenerife. Once we were clear of the harbour, we headed west round the northern tip of the island into a big swell, with white horses riding down on us. Half an hour later, we welcomed the first hazy view of Tenerife, even though it was covered in low cloud; it looked grey, mountainous and uninviting. It was not until we were in the lee of the island that the sea quietened and we could coast into the port of Santa Cruz, an hour and 20 minutes from departure. A city of 200,000 people, Santa Cruz spreads up from the shoreline into the hills that make up most of the island.

We hired a small Opel two-door saloon from an office on the pier, filled up with petrol, and set off with a guide map to work our way out of the city. We drove along the curving avenue of the Rambin del General Franco, then took a right turn when we reached the main highway, TF5. It was raining hard, so we missed the turning to the most direct route to the mountain along the spine of the island. We began to feel this was not going to be a good day. We carried on down the main highway onto the west coast, which was in sunshine, as far as La Oratavo; there we took the C821, a tortuous road that wound its way inland up into the mountains.

The countryside on the west coast had been agricultural, with small fields carpeting the hillside. We saw some productive fields, but the area was largely taken over by holiday homes and little villages of colourful cottages. The road snaked its way through this area and up into the rain and clouds again at the tree-line. Higher still and we were through the clouds and above the trees and into the Parque Nacional de las Canadas del Teide. We could now see the snowy peak of the mountain.

We drove through fields of fresh-looking larval flows, up to 2,250 metres and the base station of the cable car that could take us to the top in eight minutes. We had been told that the hiking trails had been closed because of snow. We did not see any gondolas going up or down the cable to the summit and soon found out why — the lift was closed because of the gale-force winds. There was nothing to do but have a snack lunch at the cable-car station and start back. First, however, we went two miles south to look at the Roques de Garcia, a series of huge eroded larval rocks inside the crater. We drove back along the spine of the island, along route C824. Once we had left the snow and rockscape of the crater area, we were back into forests of pine, with spectacular views down to the eastern coastal plain. We were back at the harbour in time to catch the 3.00 p.m. ferry back to Gran Canaria.

It had been a rushed and ultimately disappointing trip, but interesting enough to have been worthwhile.

GERMANY
Zugspitze
Height: 2964 metres, (9,725 feet)
Date: 25th June, 2000

Judith and I had flown from Hong Kong to Zurich, Judith to attend a conference in Berlin, myself to go on to the UK.

We had opted to give ourselves a few days to have a look at the Bavarian Alps, and Liechtenstein so had hired a car at Zurich and driven from the airport through Swiss, Austrian and German territory to reach Grainau a gorgeous Bavarian town.

It turned out to be an excellent choice. The Hotel am Badersee was delightfully situated at the edge of a crystal-clear, spring-fed lake, surrounded by forest and looking up to the Zugspitze range. Our room, 376, was one of the best ones in the house.

The cloud on the mountains had now thickened, and it had started to rain so we were happy to have an early night.

Sunday 25th June

The morning was grey with cloud and rain. At midday it had cleared somewhat so we drove up the road to the Eibsee cog-railway station, Bayer Zugspitzbahn. Walking from the parked car to the station I was caught unexpectedly by a sneeze. This precipitated a severe pain in my lower back which was the start of a bad few days. We rode the train up the mountain, initially enjoying spectacular views, but quickly plunging into a tunnel from which we did not emerge until we had reached the terminus, 45 minutes later, at Zugspitze-Platt.

We were now in cloud, with a fine snow being driven by a freezing wind. The terminal restaurant was closed, so we boarded the cable-car gondola on the Gletscherbahn to take us a further short distance to the summit. There we found a considerable group of buildings, and an observation platform from which we could just make out the summit marker, at 2964 metres, 9725 feet, the highest in Germany.

We stayed at the summit long enough to have a hot plate of soup in a pleasantly warm restaurant. I sneezed repeatedly at the sudden change in temperature—terrified that the back pain would be made worse.

We came down on the Eibseeseilbahn cable-car in a spectacular 10-minute ride and walked back to the car.

The rest of the day I spent lying down in bed. That evening we had a serious discussion regarding our options; whether Judith should accompany me to London from the nearest airport, Munich; call the SOS emergency rescue casivac service; check into the nearest hospital. All of it depressing. Judith was scheduled to be in Berlin on 29th, so there was little time to play with.

Monday 26th June

It had been a bad night, with spasms of severe pains in my back whenever I moved to roll over or get up. There was no sciatic involvement.

Judith drove me down the valley to Garmisch-Partenkirchen to see an orthopedic doctor. He had a thriving clinic and was very professional. He gave me 5 minutes infra-red treatment, a gesture really, and prescribed Voltaren, an NSAID, and a muscle relaxant related to Valium.

We walked gently around the city, wide streets, largely new buildings, its large size making us happy to be staying at Grainau. We sat down at an open-air restaurant, too many smokers inside, and had coffee and raspberry cake.

I spent the rest of the day in bed but did manage to get downstairs for dinner. The Maitre'D turned out to be a chatty man from Manchester.

Tuesday 27th June

I slept better on the firmer couch than the bed, feeling less pain in the back once the morning stiffness had eased.

We walked round the Badersee, watching the large trout in the clear water, the ducks paddling above them, and woodpeckers and crows in the forest.

For the first time the mountains were clear of cloud, and I felt confident enough in my back to proceed with the trip as planned.

I was determined to do Zugspitze justice, so after breakfast we drove to the cable car station at Eibsee and went to the top again. This time the views were spectacular. Below us was the green valley of the Loisach river that we had just come from, while in every other direction were the serried ranks of jagged rocky peaks of the alps. Well worth the return trip, even at DM78 for half an hour at the top.

Walking round the summit building we discovered that part of it was Austrian, with their own cable car route to the west, and their own eagle insignia on view. The ladder leading the few remaining feet to the actual summit had broken and the route was blocked to climbers. We were as high as we could go.

By 10.45am we had packed up and left the hotel en route for Liechtenstein.

LIECHTENSTEIN
Grauspitz
Height: 2,599m (8,527ft.)
Date: 27 June, 2000

From Grainau in Bavaria Judith drove the dramatic route through the Austrian mountains, Fernpass, Nassereith, St. Anton tunnel, Arlberg tunnel—11 kilometres that seemed to go on forever, stopping for a snack after the tunnel, and then on to Bludenz at the entrance to the Rhine valley, and Felkirch where we left the main highway for the road to Liechtenstein.

4pm, tea-time, so we stopped at the Parkhotel Sonnenhof above the capital, Vaduz, a very smooth establishment perched on the hillside overlooking the city, with attractive gardens, and a fountain beside which we sat and had lemon tea and elegant little biscuits. The room cost was 350 to 430 Swiss Francs per night. Altogether delightful but not where we wanted in the mountains.

We drove on up the hill, past the Prince's Schloss, through Triesen from which there were fine views across the Rhine valley to the Mountains of Switzerland, and on up to Malbun.

This was the place, a storybook-typical alpine valley, with lush pastures in a wide basin, leading up to a ridge flecked with patches of snow, and mellow cowbells sounding a constant background tintinnabulation.

We checked in at the Hotel Gorfion, at three floors high above any other house in the village. We were received by the very large and jovial manageress, speaking excellent English, and her young blonde assistant who was pleasant but not very bright.

The cable-car from the village to the crest of the ridge was not running, being between the skiing and summer holiday seasons, so we took a walk up the floor of the valley. We enjoyed the amazing profusion of flowers, the stream, the cows with their different bell-tones, and the sunlit views down the valley, a soothing antidote to our long drive in.

Afterwards we sat outside drinking wine, and apfelsaft, (apple juice) as the sun went down.

That evening we dined comfortably, with families and children and dogs at nearby tables, and debated whether to spend all the next day enjoying Malbun or make for Zurich the following evening to be on hand to catch flights early the following morning.

Wednesday 28th June.

We breakfasted well and picked up buns and cheese and fruit for a picnic lunch. It started to rain lightly as we set off to climb to the ridge. The rain continued off and on as we climbed, unpleasant, but Judith in particular was determined to get to the top.

It was a 400m. climb up rough roads to Sareiserjoch at 2,000m. Up there the wind was really cold, and we very soon started to get chilled. The view was shrouded in rain, so we started back down as soon as I had taken some photos. Happily, on the way down, the sun came out briefly and the colours of the valley came to life, rich greens of the pasture and firs, whites, yellows, pinks and purples of the flowers, and browns of the cattle and roof-tops far below.

I noted that Grauspitz, at 2,599m the highest in the country was still shrouded in mist, on a ridge further to the west of Malbun, up the valley from Steg, and not to be climbed today.

We had just sat down on the hillside to eat our picnic lunch when more rain swept up the valley, so decided there was no point in staying in Malbun.

By noon we were on the road, down the mountain to Vaduz, across the river Rhine, and down its west bank to St Gallen in heavy rain, and then west to Zurich. We had trouble getting an hotel room, ending up in a very expensive one at the Hilton.

After checking in we drove to the airport to hand back the car and confirm flights. Then returned to bathe luxuriously, change into clean clothes and treat ourselves to a 'Gala Californian Buffet'.

Judith, who had been using every available moment to attend to work items on her computer, spent this evening 'talking' to work colleagues in Brazil.

SOUTH AFRICA
The Drakensbergs, KwaZulu-Natal Province
1996

My second African journey began on Sunday 18 August 1996. I left Hong Kong after a fond farewell from Judith, who would follow a week later. We planned to meet in Cape Town after she had finished the conference she was to attend there. My Cathay Pacific flight went overnight directly to Johannesburg, The plane was packed, with 90 per cent of the passengers Chinese. I was in seat 68A, the last row in steerage, with a small Chinese man beside me. We were surrounded by 30 very large youngsters; a High School rugby team from New Zealand, who were accompanied by a number of equally large minders. They seemed impervious to cold, only wearing T-shirts and shorts. I thought to myself: "Thank goodness for non-smoking flights!" Even right at the back the air quality was good: the only disadvantage was that the film screen was a long way away. The captain of the flight was Warwick Guy, a golfing companion from Clearwater Bay Golf Club.

Monday 19th August

At 5.25 a.m. local time, we arrived in Johannesburg. As the plane was descending, still in the dark, we could distinguish the lights of the suburbs. There were very tall lighting masts and orange halogen lights; areas with no individual street lights were, I assumed shanty towns. Other areas had garlands of lights along every street – for a wealthier class of resident. Jan Smuts Airport was clean and smart, with efficient staff of all colours. I saw many Dunhill and Camel cigarette adverts and photographed them for Judith's collection.

At 7.30 a.m., I caught a flight with Air Link for Pietermaritzburg, capital of KwaZulu-Natal province. The one-hour flight was initially over flat farming country, then was parallel to the Drakensberg mountains. There was cloud cover up to approximately 2,500 metres of the Berg escarpment; the snow-covered peaks of the Lesotho highlands were shining in the sunshine. In July, there had been the heaviest snow fall for 40 years; some of the passes were reportedly still closed. The airport was one tarmac strip on a small field overlooking the city; it was pleasantly situated in a valley, surrounded by hills. The terminal building was a single room to handle arrivals and departures, with a small Air Link office. Much to my surprise, the Food and Beverage manager of the Hilton, the best hotel in town, came to pick me up at the airport. It transpired that the hotel was situated on Hilton Hill; it had nothing to do with the international hotel chain, and, because it was not peak season, was not fully staffed. My misgivings were put to rest by a first sight of the hotel – a beautiful Tudor-style mansion set in extensive gardens.

I slept from 2 p.m. to 4 p.m,, had a short walk and was back in time to meet Gavin Raubenheimer of Peak High Mountaineering, and Robin Gardner, who would be my guide on the trek starting the next morning. Both were very pleasant, organised and experienced in the Drakensbergs—Gavin the "Rock Spider", Robin more the hiker. Both worked full-time with the Natal Forestry Commission and did mountain guiding in their spare time. Gavin looked to be in his mid-thirties, tall, thin, very fit and rather serious. Robin was stockier, around 40 and more outgoing.

Tuesday 20 August
At 6 a.m., I was woken by my alarm clock after a fair night's sleep. I enjoyed a lavish breakfast buffet of fresh fruit and cereals. At 7 a.m., Gavin arrived with a sleeping bag and a large back pack; he judged mine too small. The rest of my climbing gear I had brought with me. At 7.30, I checked out, while Robin waited with his car at the front door. It was all a rush; I left my camera in the bedroom, with my other gear, to be picked up on my return from the mountains. The hotel was situated just off National Highway, N3; Robin drove north, skirting Pietermaritzburg and Howick, through pleasantly rolling agricultural country. We saw rows of trees, firs and acacias—they had been badly damaged by the heavy snow. After 160 kilometres of excellent roads, we branched off west on dirt roads through KwaZulu-Natal tribal homeland areas; we went past rondaavals, native round houses, and up the Injasuti river valley to "Solitude", the Injasuti Park Headquarters.

The Headquarters were situated at the junction of the Delmhlwazini (Old Woman) and Injasuti rivers, at the base of the Little Berg escarpment. They were laid out in a wide circle of cabins round a lawn and shade trees. Each cabin had electricity and its own cooking and bathroom facilities. We checked in at the Park office giving details of the route, times, personnel and our degrees of experience.

At 10.15, we started walking along a well-marked trail, in cool weather with low cloud on the hills. My pack was about 15 kilos and Robin's rather more. Our first sighting of game was of a troop of baboons. After half an hour walking gently up the north bank of the Injasuti River, we came to a crossing point—and disaster. Robin crossed safely leaping from boulder to boulder. I followed but the unaccustomed weight of my pack threw me off balance. I pitched off a large rock in the middle of the river and fell downstream head first onto a submerged rock, rolling over onto my side. I was dazed and held down by the weight of my pack in about a foot of rushing water. Robin dropped his pack, jumped into the water, helped me to my feet and to the bank. I was streaming blood externally from a laceration and internally from my nostrils, from a broken nose. We controlled the bleeding with cold compresses and first-aid dressings. I emptied the water out of my boots, and we continued the trek to avoid chilling further in my soaked clothing. The trail led up a grassy valley buttressed by sandstone cliffs with a few trees—Cabbage trees, Proteas, Fern Trees and Tree Fuchsias; there was no sign of game.

We successfully made a second crossing of the Injasuti; Robin made a second trip to carry my pack. We crossed over shortly before Battle Cave, the site of famous Bushmen wall paintings, onto the grassy south bank of the Marble Baths River. It runs in a narrow valley with dramatic sculpted cliffs overhanging the north bank, thickly covered by natural podocarp forest. The path climbed more steeply up onto the more open valley between the Little Berg and the Berg itself. At 1.30 p.m., we stopped at Marble Bath Cave, a platform under a sandstone rock overhang; at an elevation of about 1,700 metres, it was large enough to sleep comfortably about 10 people. The view was spectacular, looking north over grass-covered hills and west up the valley to Leslie's pass, around 3,000 metres at the summit; that was our planned route up to the high plateau.

Robin cooked hot soup on a propane gas heater—no fires are allowed in the park. I changed into dry clothes, slipped into my sleeping bag to try and get warm, and mopped the blood still seeping from my nose. By the time we had eaten, the cloud had come down, rain was falling outside the cave, and snow was falling further up the valley. The prospect of another two to three hours "boulder hopping" to pitch a tent on an exposed mountainside at 2,000 metres did not appeal. So we spent the remainder of the day sheltering; we put off plans for the following day until the morning.

Wednesday 21 August

I awoke to a fine clear morning after a long cold night. I had been warm enough with a silver-coated polystyrene under-blanket and sleeping bag inside my German thermal bag, and wearing all my clothes. Breakfast was coffee, muesli and chocolate biscuits. Since we had lost much of one day because of yesterday's accident, it was impossible to reach Mafadi peak and get back to Park Headquarters in three days, as indicated in our trek plan.

I was also keen to get medical attention for my facial lacerations.

We spent the morning climbing to the crest of the ridge above the cave, to an altitude of around 2,500 metres, from where we had a panoramic view of the Drakensbergs. In the far north, we could see Cathkin Peak, Monk's Cowl and Champagne Castle; nearer were the peaks of The Old Woman Grinding Corn and The Ape; ahead of us Leslie's Pass and on its left the sheer cliffs of Injasuti Buttress, the Injasuti Triplets standing out from the cliffs; The Red Wall, Trojan's Wall. Mafadi was out of sight behind the Injasuti Buttress. On a mountainside across the Marble Bath Valley to the north, we could make out the light brown shapes of grazing Cape Eland, and, on the ridge to the south, a large troop of Chacma baboons slowly foraging up the slope.

In the air, Robin identified an Orange-throated Longclaw, a White-necked Raven and a Cape Vulture. Reluctantly we started down back to the cave, the first cloud already beginning to gather on the mountain tops. In our absence, a baboon had foraged through our camp looking for food—but had left unsatisfied. By 1400, we were back at Park Headquarters signing off; I felt conspicuous with a bloody dressing over my nose. The only excitement on the way was a Striped Skaapsteker snake which slithered across the path just in front of Robin. The bird life in the valley included Black Crows, Cape Weavers, Hadeda Ibis and a Secretary Bird—the last not commonly seen.

Two hours later we were back at Hilton village seeing Robin's doctor, Dr Matthews. He was a tall, distinguished-looking man with grey hair and a very British accent; he told me that he had spent his whole life in Natal. On examination, he confirmed that I had broken my nose. His nurse cleaned the wound, applied Steri-strip plasters and gave a tetanus toxoid injection. When she asked the doctor what to charge, he replied "Nothing. Dog does not eat dog, you know". There was no room at the Hilton Hotel, so Robin drove me 20 kilometres back to Howick and the Fern Hill Hotel. After a long bath and a huge buffet dinner, I felt very much better. A concerned Gavin came round afterwards to see how I was and confirm arrangements for the next climbing project. And so I went to bed, exhausted, at 21.00.

Thursday 22 August

I slept poorly but made up for it with a large buffet breakfast. The hotel was good value at 260 Rand Bed & Breakfast, equivalent to HK$142. Mid-morning Robin picked me up and drove me to Howick, named after Hawick in the Scottish borders; it was an attractive village more English than Scottish. We saw its waterfall, a spectacular drop of 95 metres over a basalt outcrop; and thence to the Hilton Hotel, where a room was now available. In the afternoon, I walked to the Hilton shopping centre "The Quarry" and then for about half an hour through a high-class residential district. Houses were for sale. A large modern mansion with four bedrooms, swimming pool, tennis court and large garden was going for HK$1 million — startlingly cheap compared to Hong Kong. The shopping centre was a very new complex of single storey buildings with roofs a pleasant shade of green. It was built on a cliff overlooking a disused stone quarry that was now partly filled with water and home to a family of ducks. The whole atmosphere was very English; nearly all of the people were white, with only a single black man struggling to make the bank cash dispenser work. He had my sympathy. It was only two years since the first general election in which blacks were able to vote, in April 1994; it ended the apartheid system established in 1948. The second hand shops were full of 19th century furniture and the Tea Shoppe was full of fascinating Victoriana. I bought three post cards: a view of the Drakensbergs for my son Andrew, Zulu royalty for my son Richard, and one of three topless Zulu beauties to scandalise David Burns, my best man and very proper lawyer friend in Edinburgh. The first two cards arrived swiftly, but the last took months to get to David; it arrived long after I had written it off as having been impounded by the Ethics Police! Robin had told me that Dr. Matthews was a keen fly fisher, so I bought a collection of trout flies for him and dropped them off at his clinic. I dined in my room in front of the television, then read a book on the mountains until I was ready to sleep at 2100. I was still very tired and frustrated that I was not myself up on the mountains.

Friday 23 August
I had a better night's sleep. The bedroom was a large ground-floor room at the end of the east wing; it looked out past bougainvillaea onto an array of exotic trees set in wide lawns. The garden is famously on show every year. In mid-winter it was full of colour — daffodils, half a dozen varieties of azalea, aloes and a rose garden. I spent the morning reading a book on the Drakensberg area and extensive notes on the fauna and flora compiled by Robin.

From the book I learned that the original inhabitants were the Bushmen (San or Khoi San), hunter gatherers who arrived about 8,000 years ago; they were known as "Hottentots" by the early Dutch settlers. At the end of the 17th century, the first wave of Bantu arrived from the north. Pastoralists, they gradually displaced the Bushmen from the planes and Natal midlands to the highland areas, where they lived in the caves scattered along the sandstone cliffs of the Berg. By the beginning of the 19th century, they were limited to the High Berg and the Lesotho plateau.

In 1812, Shaka and his Zulu warriors invaded from the north driving the Bantu into the hills and in turn forcing the Bushmen further into the highlands. In 1837, the first Boer Voortreckers arrived; they found few inhabitants left after the Zulu conquest.

They took over wide areas of the Natal midlands to graze their cattle and sheep; and hunted for game in the Little Berg. This depleted the stocks relied on by the Bushmen, particularly in the winter when the High Berg and Lesotho plateau were too cold for game. Having no concept of animals "belonging" to anyone, the Bushmen raided the Boer livestock. To control the problem, the settlers established Bantu reserves along the foot of the Drakensbergs to act as a buffer between themselves and the Bushmen. Even so, by 1840, the Voortreckers declared the Bushmen to be "vermin".

Remnants of the race were absorbed into the Basotho tribes of Lesotho or by the Bantu. The nearest living related race is the Bushmen of the Kalahari. The Bushman way of life survives in the cave paintings, depicting hunting scenes and battles with the Bantu. The last Bushman was shot in 1860. He was an artist; around his waist were strung 10 antelope horns containing different pigments for his paints.

LESOTHO 1996
Thebana Ntlenyana
The Highest Mountain in Southern Africa
Height: 3,482 metres (11,425 feet)
Date: 1996

My next objective during the same visit to Africa was Thebana Ntlenyana (Beautiful Little Mountain) in Lesotho. A survey in 1951 first identified it for certain as the highest mountain in southern Africa. Lesotho is an independent country of two million people, landlocked and entirely surrounded by South Africa. It has a border with KwaZulu-Natal, where I was staying.

Saturday 24 August 1996
I was up at 5.45 a.m., ready for Gavin to pick me up an hour later for the 120-km drive to Sani at the foot of the pass leading into Lesotho. From Hilton, we turned south and west through hill

country much like the Scottish borders — forests of plantation firs and eucalypts with stands of yellow or black acacia. The latter thrive in this area and are grown commercially for the tannin in the bark used in the leather trade; local people use the wood for their fires.

Further on we passed through the farming country of middle KwaZulu-Natal — rolling plains, winter-brown, plenty of water and trees bare-leaved deciduous. We stopped at Enderbery for coffee at a bakery and passed through Himeville; both were one-street villages of retirement homes and farm stores. The two villages were founded by rival families; after years of feuding, they managed to become friends. To prove that friendship, they planted an avenue of trees along the several miles between their villages; it was still standing. Out of Himeville, we drove onto dirt roads heading through native areas up the Mkhomazana river valley and closing in on the Drakensberg.

At 9 a.m., we were at Sani Pass Tours, a vehicle repair outfit and bunk house for trekkers, and base for the Land Rovers used to ascend the Berg escarpment to Sani Pass. The cost was Rand 200 for a round trip. It was run by Arthur & Son. Arthur was a larger-than-life English South African whose favourite amusement was to take passengers half way up the escarpment, then swerve off the road towards the abyss, only to halt at the edge. Once they had stopped screaming, the passengers had a chance to admire the view. We had to wait an hour for latecomers; by the end of the day, this turned out to be precious time wasted. There was no option, since only four-wheel-drive vehicles were allowed on the Pass.

Finally, we set off in a convoy of three Land Rovers. Arthur led with Gavin, me and four others in an open-top one; it was chilly but gave the best visibility. First stop was a mile along the road at the Sani Pass Hotel; it was an attractive group of thatched cabins and a four-star hotel offering riding, golf, trekking and fishing. A barrier half a mile further on marked the South African border post with Lesotho. There was panic amongst the latecomers, who had not brought passports. Somehow Arthur managed to smuggle them through by mixing them with the 20 other passengers. Over the next six kilometres, we climbed 1,000 metres up a gravel road, which wound up the increasingly precipitous gradient, the corners punctuated by wrecked vehicles. Blocked by snow drifts, the road had been closed until the week before. Snow was still piled high on either side of the road near the summit.

The scenery was spectacular. On the right were The Twelve Apostles of the Phinong Buttress and the High Berg cliffs glistening with icefalls; on the left, the towering Sekong Buttress: behind and above were Hodgson's Peaks named after the leader of an army unit hunting for Bushmen who was accidentally shot by one of his own men. Perched precariously at the summit of the pass, at an elevation of 3,000 metres, was Sani Pass Hostel, a huddle of wooden frame shacks offering food and shelter to hikers. When the snowstorm had struck a month earlier, it had trapped a dozen hikers at the hostel. The crew of the rescue helicopter who came for them had a tough time because they found the victims all rolling drunk.

To get to the hostel, we first had to pass the Basotho customs post and again have our passports checked. Nearby was a Basotho village, primitive round stone dwellings with thatched roofs without chimneys; a few native people were wrapped in blankets and knitted woollen caps—unsurprisingly like the highland Nepalese, given the similar climate. Behind stretched a wide plane devoid of trees, wet with running water in sunlit areas, icy in the shade and a scattering of horses—a different world from the valley from which we had come.

Arthur dropped off the rest of the party at the hostel and took Gavin and me about 10 km across the plane to a ridge nearer to our goal, Thebana Ntlenyana , the highest peak in southern Africa. From the ridge, we could see right across the brown plane of Sani flats to the Hodgson's Peaks to the south-east marking the edge of the Berg. In all other directions were snow-covered mountains, rounded, rolling away to the horizon, sparkling in the sunshine. By now it was midday and we had a lot of walking to do; difficult walking too, as we quickly found out.

The snow had only a thin crust on it, so every few steps we plunged in up to our thighs. Gavin fared worse than me, as he was heavier and carried a load of 22 kilograms compared to my eight. Even so he was faster than me, being half my age and used to the altitude. In Hong Kong, my own training had of necessity been near sea level. We ploughed on, taking advantage of rock outcrops for easier walking, pausing briefly to drink and eat snacks. We crossed the first ridge, then a wide valley and down a north-facing muddy slope awash with snow-melt water. Then it was up a long slope of deeper snow to a point about one kilometre from the summit.

Here we dumped our packs over the crest of the ridge, on the southern slope away from the wind. It was now 5 p.m. and would be dark in another hour; but the peak was now visible, accessible either by following the ridge round a wide arc to the east and then north, or by traversing straight across the intervening shallow valley where the snow would be deeper but the distance much shorter.

We opted for the direct route, moving more quickly without packs, and enjoyed a spectacular sunset. The climb up the last ridge, stone-covered and swept bare of snow by the wind, was a struggle against fatigue and the gathering dusk. This was offset by the exhilaration of finally reaching the summit cairn.

We paused long enough only to take photographs and to place a stone on the cairn.

The trek back to the camp by moonlight had a surreal quality; the temptation to prolong the enjoyment of the moment was modified by the difficulty of keeping balance through the deep snow on rubbery legs, and the imperative of getting back to make camp. Setting up our small two-man tent was hampered by the strong and freezing wind; by the time we had stowed all the gear inside and settled into our sleeping bags, we were chilled, and impatient to have the snow melt in the pan for our first hot drink since early that morning. Gavin also cooked a pasta and chicken dish though I had little appetite for it — but canned peaches went down well. I lay back to sleep, hopefully that I did not to have to get up for a toilet call.

Sunday 25 August
I slept fitfully on hard and uneven ground with the wind whipping at the tent, but warm enough. Only my boots and gaiters were out of the sleeping bag; they were frozen solid by morning. For breakfast, we had tea, muesli and an apple; camp packed and on our way by 8 a.m. It was a fine morning but still with a high wind; it brought a bank of clouds from the north-west that had Gavin anxious to get going. We retraced the first part of the route then swung south across a long snowfield. Regrettably, the overnight freeze had not been enough to create a weight-bearing crust on the snow, so we were again ploughing through the drifts.

There was little evidence of wildlife apart from sheep and horse droppings, little holes in the snow made by a small burrowing animal, and the carcass of a horse; this was evidence of the severity of a winter that had led to the loss of a number of herd boys and much Basotho livestock. At noon, we reached the crest of a ridge and again could see Sani Flats from a point much to the east of where we had started the trek. A long slope lead down the mountainside to a herdsman's shelter of stone and thatch set in a walled corral for sheep. Here we rested in the warmth of the midday sun and out of the wind. While waiting for a brew of tea, Gavin had me take pictures of him in winter hiking gear provided by a firm that sponsored him. This was a mistake — Gavin realised too late that we were scheduled to meet Arthur and his Land-Rover at around 2 p.m. and it was nearly that time already, with about three kilometres to go. Arthur could not wait long for us because the border post closed at 4 p.m. The Sani Pass Hostel was too far to walk to before dark, and, apart from the tent, the only other shelter was a flea-ridden native stone house.

We set off at speed, but I could not keep up with Gavin's long-legged stride through another belt of snow as we climbed over a shoulder of mountain towards the flat ground. So he hoisted my pack onto his own in a remarkable exhibition of strength and stamina. Once clear of the snow on the Flats, we made better speed over frozen ground covered by a thin layer of mud and running water. By now it was 2.30 and the road was visible about one kilometre away, with a Land Rover heading out of sight!

Slogging on at top speed, we came to the Sani River swollen with melted snow. To go downstream to the only bridge at a Basotho village would take another hour. We had to cross. Steadying each other against the rush of water reaching up to our thighs, we inched our way across and climbed the far bank, just in time to see another Land Rover. A final dash of 200 metres and we were there, with a jovial and relieved Arthur happy to have spotted us on his final run past. The drive to the Sani Pass Hostel was a joy, even with soaking clothes in the back of an open vehicle. At the hostel, we had time to have a much needed drink, warm ourselves at the fire and sign in on the climbing log book, before the long run down the escarpment back to the warmth of the valley, and Gavin's car.

After grateful farewells to Arthur, we poured the water out of our boots, wrung out socks and set off for Pietermaritzburg. We reached there at 6.30 p.m. with only a break for coffee at Underberg. The view back was memorable for the wonderful evening light, hazy through the smoke of grass fires, a contrast to the stark beauty of the sunset the evening before. Back at the Hilton Hotel, I luxuriated in a long bath, ate a great steak dinner, washed out some of my muddy climbing gear, and retired to a real bed.

I was thrilled to have reached the highest point in Southern Africa. In retrospect, I would have liked to have spent another day on the climb. Snow-free, as it is most of the year, it would have been an easy trek; with deep snow, the effort at altitude was severe. I was impressed by Gavin, his expertise, strength and love of mountaineering.

SOUTH AFRICA
Table Mountain
Height: 1,084m (3,558ft)
Date: August 1996

I flew the 800 miles from Durban to Cape Town where I met Judith, who had finished an anti-tobacco conference. She was staying with our friend Krisela Steyn who worked for the South African Medical Research Council. She had arranged for me to climb Table Mountain with a group headed by a friend of hers, the President of the Mountain Club of South Africa founded in 1891.

The next morning, I was picked-up by him. We met the other three members at the cable car terminus car park — Graham, Mark and Lyn, a 72- year-old psychiatrist. We had an easy climb up a long flight of stone steps as far as the first rock face, a fixed chain that marked the start of the Kastells Poort route. Lyn managed to haul himself up this route with some difficulty; but I opted for the offer of a gentler route, the "India-Venster", in the company of Jeff and Graham. Mark went up the chain to accompany Lyn, arranging to meet us further up where the routes joined. The route up the north face became progressively steeper till we reached a rock chimney where we had to take off our rucksacks and scramble. We stopped here for a rest and waited for the other pair to join us, which they did before long. They descended by the route we had climbed, accompanied by Graham who had a luncheon engagement in the city.

Jeff and I had gone only a short distance further when we caught up with three other climbers who were lost. Two men, a Dutchman and an Australian, had persuaded their tour leader to take them up, although she herself had never been up before. Jeff was happy to take them under his wing and we continued together. Progress was now along narrow grassy ledges between huge boulders gradually working our way up and around the west shoulder of the mountain; the vertical drop on our right became ever deeper. As we neared the summit table and the going got easier, Jeff typically led us up a steeper and "more interesting " route. Finally, we were on the summit; it was indeed a very flat "table", rocky with Fynbos shrubs but no rock hyrax to see. These rabbit-like animals have padded feet like elephants and are allegedly related to them.

We sat on rocks at the edge of the cliffs looking out over Cape Town, False Bay and Robbens Island. We congratulated ourselves on having a clear day with little wind –– this was a rarity, I learnt.

Jeff took us down the "Diagonal" route, across the table and down a defile between two of the "Twelve Apostles" on the western side, with spectacular views over Camps Bay. There was much colour in the Fynbos, flowering proteas of different varieties, heathers, and a couple of Yellow Breasted Sun-birds. The last part of the trip was a half-hour walk along a contour path back around the west shoulder of the mountain to the car. Jeff dropped me off at Krisela's, exhausted, at 16.00 to find only Krisela's son Dirk Steyn at home.

I was shortly followed in by an elated Judith and Krisela — they had also climbed to the top of Table Mountain, on the easier Platteklip route, a wonderful surprise! That evening we had a celebratory dinner at the home of Krisela and her son. We watched Judith performing brilliantly on "Focus", South Africa T.V.'s most prestigious current affairs talk show.

What a big day! I had no problems with altitude, as I had on Mount Kinabalu, but it was much more dangerous. Looking up at the cliffs from the contour route, I found it difficult to believe that I had been at such places on the ascent.

KENYA
MT KENYA, Point Lenana
Height: 4,985 metres (16,355 feet)
Date: February 1998

In February 1998, I returned to Africa for the first time since 1996. My objective was to climb two major peaks. The first was Mount Kenya's Point Lenana, the trekker's summit. Mount Kenya has two other peaks, rocky spires requiring technical rock-climbing skills. Batian, at 5,199 meters (17,057 feet), is the highest in Kenya and the second highest in Africa, and Nelion 5,188 meters (17,021 feet).

The second was Mount Kilimanjaro, in Tanzania, the country which borders Kenya to the south. This is the highest mountain in Africa, at 5,895 metres (19,341 feet). To climb Kilimanjaro is the ambition of every global mountaineer; it is one of The Seven, the highest mountain on each of the seven continents. Each year they attract climbers from all over the world. But I thought long and hard before deciding to go. Both were higher than any mountain I had climbed before. Two years ago my climbing had come to a halt after I had undergone spinal surgery for sciatica, but I had been building back strength by hiking in the hills of Hong Kong. It was time, aged 63, to test my recovery and give a boost to my ego.

Monday February 2, 1998

I got up at 5.30 a.m., the worst time, and left loving arms, a warm bed, comfortable home, regular routines and full domestic support—all to satisfy an ambition to climb mountains in East Africa. I flew from Hong Kong, arriving late at Dubai Airport because of head winds. The flight to Nairobi was already boarding. Armed with an Express Transit document, I quickly reached the departure lounge, concerned about the luggage, my large rucksack and a suitcase with all my climbing gear. I asked a ground steward about the luggage; he assured me it would be on the connecting flight, but I was not convinced. I was on an Emirates Airbus 340, with only two engines. I recalled a recent remark by a senior Cathay captain of 747s: "Fly with only two engines? I am too old for that game!"

My baggage had travelled with me! Much relieved, I collected it and stepped outside to meet a driver arranged by Let's Go Travel. He spoke good English, and drove me carefully the 15 kilometers into town, to the Norfolk Hotel. The hotel was built in 1904, when the railhead at Nairobi had just been completed, connecting it to the coast at Mombasa. Since then, it had been Nairobi's premier hotel; it had hosted so many of the British nobility that it came to be called The House of Lords. The front entrance was presided over by an imposing top-hatted doorman; it led directly off the road and into a small foyer — not at all imposing. The reception area led into a large, enclosed garden with flowering shrubs, mature thorn and palm trees. On each side were two-story buildings, with one side looking like old coach houses.

Behind this square was a second rank of buildings. On the left was a sports area with a weights room and aerobic exercise room and ground floor restaurant overlooking a swimming pool; and, straight ahead, a further row of bedrooms overlooking a more private garden and fountain. To the right of the entrance was the Lord Delamere Terrace, partly covered but mostly open-air, leading to the bar of the same name at the far end and the main Lord Delamere restaurant on its left. The bar had two large paintings on the far wall. One was of the original Nairobi railway station with a mass of people in Victorian dress meeting a train: the other was a view of the front of the Norfolk showing the terrace overlooking a tree-lined country road. The dining room also had a large painting across the far wall — a scene of huntsmen and hounds in a village square in front of two inns, The Blue Boar and The White Swan. It reminded me of Helmsley in the Vale of York. I found out later that Lord Delamere was an early settler who sank all his money into farming at the start of the 20th Century and ultimately made good. A flamboyant character, he was known to have on occasion fired his pistol at the hunting scene in the dining room. The pock marks were reportedly still visible in the plaster.

I slept well, waking (on Tuesday) at 5.00 a.m. and opened curtains, to be up at dawn in line with trekking practice. I still had a mild headache from the night before, possibly caused by the altitude, now 5,000 feet. I felt better after a large buffet breakfast at the Lord Delamere restaurant. I noted a brilliantly coloured sun-bird feeding at the hibiscus outside my bedroom window.

I had booked to stay in Nairobi for four nights to get over jet-lag, begin acclimatization and complete organization of my treks with the travel agent, Let's Go Travel. After breakfast, I walked down to the travel agent at Standard Street, about fifteen minutes away. Previously, I had asked at Reception if it was safe to walk in town; I was told that it was safe in daylight as long as you did not go into "the lanes".

My first impression of Nairobi was not good. Pavements were broken and roads severely pot-holed; there were fine new multi-story buildings, but the majority were old and run down, particularly the central area dominated by Asian stores in dilapidated two-story blocks. There were plenty of cars, mostly small sedans, some motorbikes and no cyclists. There were many men hanging around street corners and very few white people. At Let's Go Travel, I confirmed the itinerary and paid the balance of expenses for the Kilimanjaro climb. The office was reassuringly large and equipped with desk-top video monitors and competent-looking people. Next stop was the British High Commission on Upper Hill Road, where I registered in case of accidents. To get there, I had to walk down Uhuru Highway and up Haile Selassie Avenue, on the muddy border of the roads with no pavements and flanked by open sewers. I felt distinctly uneasy at this point going through a treed area; no-one else walking there was remotely well dressed. Consciously, I was dressed in sports shirt and slacks with no camera, backpack or other items worth stealing. I was relieved to get back to the hotel. It was getting hot. The humidity was low, so walking was comfortable. I enjoyed a long swim in the heated pool and then lunched at the poolside restaurant reading The Daily Nation'; it had been recommended by the hotel newsvendor as an independent publication.

Items from newspaper:

- Tribal warfare in the Rift Valley; sixty people had been killed in clashes between the Kikuyu and the supporters of President Daniel Arap Moi who had recently been re-elected, aged74, for a fifth term of reportedly corrupt rule."
- "One wretched man had been tossed into a river where his assailants watched him being eaten by a crocodile."
- "A bridge on the Nairobi to Mombasa main highway had been washed out by floods, so traffic was at a standstill."
- "Hyacinth weed was widespread on Lake Victoria and had blocked the harbour and stopped the fishing."
- "The recent heavy rains, attributed to El Nino, had led to much flooding, disruption of clean water supplies and much standing water. This had brought an epidemic of Rift Valley fever, resulting in many deaths."
- "In Kisii in the northeast, ninety people had died of malaria in one week, 1,500 had been treated but medication had run out."
- "Typhoid and cholera were spreading."
- On a lighter note: "a wedding was disrupted when a snake crawled up the trouser leg of one of the guests. After much careful manoeuvring, it was brought out and killed."

What sort of a place had I come to?

After a short siesta, I left the hotel again, turning right this time, up Harry Thuku Road for 10 minutes, to the National

Museum. As might be expected, it had a very strong exhibit of palaeontology, the work of the Leakey family and others at Olduvai Gorge and at Lake Turkana. There was also a large collection of native artifacts and art. In addition, there was a fascinating collection of 400 oil paintings of natives in tribal dress, done by Joy Adamson, author of *Born Free* about raising a lion cub named Elsa. Clearly she was a talented artist as well as a protector of lions. She had also chronicled the birds and flowers of East Africa. There was an exhaustive collection of snakes — horrifying. I was sorry I had gone in, and declined to see the snake farm next door. Back at the hotel, I called Judith, a five-hour time difference to Hong Kong, and reported that all was well. I had a room service supper of soup, bread rolls and coffee; I read my *Lonely Planet* book on 'Trekking in East Africa' and later watched BBC World Service on television.

I slept poorly, being awakened by mosquitoes. I put on the Vape-mat. The mosquito netting on the windows appeared intact. At 4.00 a.m., a muezzin called to prayers for half an hour. My alarm sounded at 6.00 a.m., just as dawn was breaking. I had breakfast at 7.30 a.m. with *The Nation* — no more tribal bloodshed, but cholera and malaria still bad; a peaceful demonstration in town the day before had been broken up by police wielding batons.

I walked for twenty-five minutes down to the Tanzanian Trade Commission to get a visa. After collecting the application form, I found that I would need photographs and other documents, so I took a taxi back to the hotel. The driver had a sign on his dashboard, 'I put my trust in God'; as I got out, I complimented him on it, and suggested that he would also do well to put his trust in good breaks. Actually, he drove well and the car was in good shape. I walked back downtown again, handed in my completed forms and was advised that they would be ready the next day for a fee of $55. On the way back to the hotel, I called at a couple of shops reputed to sell climbing gear. Atul's was a large muddled Indian tailor's, which offered a book of camping gear items for hire. Colpro on Kimathi Street was another large Indian shop selling cheap clothing, and safari gear of the approved 'African Bush Look'; I had seen American tourists rigged out in it as they made their way from the hotel to waiting 'African Adventure' mini-buses and four-wheel drive vehicles — I believe they were called 'zebroids'.

As on the previous day, I had a long swim and then lunch on the poolside terrace. I almost completed the crossword in *The Nation*, syndicated from the *Daily Telegraph* or *Guardian*, I should not wonder. I discovered that I had forgotten to pack a razor — lots of blades, but no holder. I had been thinking of growing a beard, anyway, so here was the chance. Having had my exercise in the morning, I spent the afternoon relaxing, then dressed to go down to the Delamere Terrace for supper. I chose a pizza; it was much too large to finish. I watched African Nations Football Cup on television; the quality of the play was poor.

Thursday February 5
I slept well until 5.00 a.m., and no mosquitoes. I did my stretching exercises. After breakfast, I walked down to the Tanzanian office, a bare and poorly furnished half-floor in a fairly new but cheap-looking building, and picked up my passport with visa. Back at the Norfolk, the tour desk lady established that I could get a round of golf at The Royal Nairobi Golf Course. I changed in a flash into shorts and sports shirt. I had brought a golf glove and my shoes could pass as golfing ones, although they were only for hill-walking. The taxi ride only took 10 minutes. David, the driver, spoke good English and was happy to tell me that he was self-taught, having had only had one year of schooling. He

had been taught to drive in the Army; he promised to come and pick me up at 2.00 p.m. For Kenya shillings (Ksh) 1,800 (about HK$300), I paid the green fee, hired a set of clubs, bought three golf-balls and a bag of tees, and hired a caddy.

The course was pleasant parkland, but just recovering from the severely heavy rains which had caused partial flooding. I played quite well but could not get the pace of the very slow greens. The caddy was helpful, with a smattering of English; he had played golf himself for 10 years but was not permitted to play in any competitions and so did not have a handicap. At the far end of the course was a high stone wall with barbed wire on top; it kept at bay the residents of a vast shanty town whose tin roofs I could make out on the other side. The remarkable thing about the round was that it only took two and a half hours, despite the second nine holes being played behind a three-ball. In Hong Kong, it would have taken an hour longer.

David picked me up as scheduled, even though I had already paid him for the trip out — a remarkable confirmation of my faith in human nature.

I had a late poolside lunch, with "The Nation". I learnt that the Army had thrown a Bailey bridge across the Tana river, so that traffic to and from Mombasa was moving again, slowly. The bus companies were complaining that, because the roads were so bad, the repair bills for their buses were enormous. Raiders were coming down from Uganda and devastating villages in the north-west.

I took my first Diamox tablet, 250 mgm (acetazolamide) to reduce chances of mountain sickness; and my second weekly Lariam, anti-malaria. At 6.00 p.m., I had an energetic swim. By then the sun was off the water and it was cool getting out. While showering afterwards, I experienced the sudden onset of severe tingling, amounting to a vibration, in my hands; this was a recognised side-effect of the Diamox. It was unpleasant. Back in my room, I packed in readiness for my pick-up the next morning; I found myself ridiculously tense at the prospect of finally going to the mountain. At the same time, I was pleased to be leaving Nairobi. Supper was a bowl of soup and a glass of milk in the room.

Friday February 6

I had a poor night's sleep, with worries about the climb crowding in. I rose at 6.00 a.m. to wash and do stretching exercises. I took breakfast at 7.30 a.m. with my companion "The Nation". There were the usual stories of cattle rustling.

The day before several hundred students at Kenyatta University had staged a sit-down protest blocking the main road North, at Thika, to protest against the killing of a student in the recent ethnic violence. When they failed to disperse, the chancellor closed down indefinitely the whole university of 8,000 students. There was another incident in town which I must only have just missed. A street battle developed when 30 Askaris (police) tried to clear a street of hawkers. Two Askaris were taken to hospital with head injuries, while the remainder "beat the children indiscriminately".

I was ready when the driver, Joseph, came to pick me up at 9.00 a.m. for the drive to Naro Moru River Lodge, hopefully a more peaceful location. He had come down the evening before to collect stores for the hotel. I was his only passenger in the mini-van. The route led north through a heavily settled rolling plane, through Thika, with a number of unhappy looking students waiting for lifts home; an immense pineapple farm owned by Del Monte; coffee plantations; over the Thana river which had caused so much flood damage; and to a restaurant/native handicrafts shop/ rest-room area at about the half way mark in the three- hour, 200-kilometre journey.

There I caught up with three Abercrombie and Kent tourist minibuses carrying ex-Norfolk Hotel guests to Sweetwater's camp and a Lonhro Hotel, to view game. More unexpectedly, I saw two truckloads of British Army soldiers. Joseph told me that there was a British Army base at Nanyuki near to Mount Kenya where groups came for jungle training.

The first half of the trip had been along a fine double-carriageway. The road deteriorated as it climbed into the foothills, in a valley between the Aberdare Range on the west and Mount Kenya. The rich, red, volcanic soil was heavily farmed, growing coffee, tea, maize, pineapple, papaya, passion-fruit and commercial flowers for export. The road then climbed up the Sagana River valley to the plateau land at about 2,000 metres, from which the Mount Kenya range arises. We were running alongside a narrow-gauge railway that extends from Nanyuki to Nairobi and thence the coast. Only about two trains run each day, carrying farm produce only to Nairobi.

Naro Moru village consisted of a huddle of tin-roof shacks, market stalls, a railway loading siding and a road checkpoint where carriers have to pay a tax on movement of produce. Off the main road to the left, a dirt track led for a mile or so across the open plain, then suddenly dropped down into the narrow Naro Moru river valley, heavily forested, and into the Lodge grounds, my Base Camp. To the right of the driveway, at the top of the bank was the main dining room and bar, arched round a swimming pool and looking out towards Mount Kenya itself. At the foot of the drive, flanked by tennis courts and a squash court, was a small reception area and the mountain equipment store, adorned with photographs of all the famous people who had stayed there. Flower-bordered walkways led down from Reception to around 30 chalets scattered along the left bank of the river.

Another larger building contained a bar, games room, and dining and conference rooms. Once I had settled in, I was introduced to my mountain guide, William, who checked and approved of my gear; in addition, he recommended a sleeping mat of sponge rubber since I would be camping in a tent for the first three nights. He could not remember the number of times he had climbed the mountain, seemed highly competent, and reassured me that there would be three porters—one to carry my gear, one to carry some of his and the tent, and one to carry food. I was so taken with the location that I called the travel agents and advised them that I would stay at the Lodge on my descent from the climb rather than travel back to Nairobi that same day. Just as the sun set, the clouds over the mountain lifted; the gentle contours of the lower slopes gave way at the centre to dramatic rock pinnacles, streaked with snow, much more exciting. I was beginning to feel good about the climb.

Saturday February 7

I was awake before sunrise and went out with the cameras to catch views of the peak as the sun came up. Our expected departure at 10.00 a.m. was put off until the afternoon because the four-wheel-drive transport was being used elsewhere. I spent the morning happily sitting on the balcony of my chalet watching the many birds. At 2.00 p.m., we were finally loaded with luggage and three healthy looking young porters—but the engine refused to start. A few well-directed blows from William with a rock on the battery lead connections solved the problem. We had various stops, one at Naro Moru village, one at a filling station to buy paraffin, again to buy fruit from a vendor sitting under a tree by the roadside, and, finally, as we crossed the Earth's Equator, for me to take pictures. After about 40 kilometres, and through Nanyuki, we turned off the main road onto a muddy track that led to the Sirimon Gate of the Mount Kenya Country Park. Here we registered and paid park fees, so much per day for each person. At the Sirimon Gate, we passed a number of trekkers and their porters and drove on up through the rain forest for a further couple of kilometers on a very bumpy gravel road, making up time for our late start.

At last it was time to start walking. William and I set off at an easy pace leaving the porters to sort out the loads, carried in canvas bags on their backs, or in baskets on their heads. I was not unhappy to leave the transport. The old man at the wheel was an atrocious driver and lurched into every pothole. We climbed a gentle track for two hours through the rain forest; William named all the birds we saw, exotic names such as Crimson Cheeked Bee-eater, Golden Winged Sun-bird, White Headed Wood Hoopoe, Streaked Sedata, Scaly Francolin, and Regal Sunbird.

Breaking out onto the open heath land, we saw Old Moses Camp only a couple of kilometers away on the crest of a ridge, at 3,400 metres. The camp consisted of a long wooden bunkhouse, with tables and benches in the front eating area and doors leading off to the rear to four dormitory rooms with two-tier bunk beds. At one end was the kitchen area where food was prepared over wood fires. There were another two smaller huts for porters, a running cold water supply from a pipe leading from a stream further up the hill, and a couple of "long drop" toilets, holes in the floor leading to a septic tank. The bunk houses were run by Mountain Rock Hotel and were already occupied by two trekking groups. My tent was pitched a short distance away—a colder, harder but quieter option. I had supper by candlelight—soup, bread rolls, chicken and potatoes with beans and carrots and fruit salad. It was more than I could eat.

Sunday February 8

I slept poorly, finding the ground hard despite the sleeping mat and being cold despite wearing trousers, T-shirt, and sweater inside my sleeping bag, itself inside a wind and waterproof outer covering. I was happy to get up at dawn, 6.00 a.m., to pack up my gear before breakfast at 7.00 a.m.– fruit, cornflakes with powdered milk, fried egg with bacon, sausage, and tomato, three slices of bread, and coffee. The excessive amount of food continued throughout the trip despite my protestations. I gathered that what I did not eat was happily finished off by the porters. An hour later, we were on the trail, the sun now warm, and myself comfortable in a T-shirt and trousers. William and I leap-frogged with the porters as we climbed a gentle incline up to 4,000 metres, just short of The Barrow, a rock formation; from there, we angled down into the Liki North River valley to make camp at noon at about 3,800 metres.

We saw wild game on the trail—a distant herd of buffalo, a couple of small antelopes, Dik-Dik, and a number of Auger Buzzards. At the camp, there were many Rock Hyrax, small rabbit-like animals tame enough to come to the hut for scraps of food. Liki North Hut was a small structure raised on stilts situated on the flood plain just 20 yards from the river. It was about 20 feet long by 10 wide, the rear portion having a sleeping platform about four feet off the ground, and the front area a metal-covered shelf on the right for cooking and a single bench down the left wall. It was reported to be 30 years old and looked it. The corrugated iron roof was rusty and the same material had been used to patch up holes in the wooden walls, the floor and one of the two windows. Lunch was soup, sandwiches, peas, beans, bread and tea.

I went back to the tent to rest. It had clouded over and become cold. Soon afterwards it began to rain heavily, and continued to do so till 5.00 p.m. Tea and biscuits were brought to the tent at 4.00 p.m. After the rain stopped, I went for a short walk and enjoyed the rich green of the grasses on the valley floor; huge boulders that had rolled down from the ridge above in previous years, covered with colourful lichens, yellow, orange and red and grey; the solitary ancient tree groundsel across the river; the Hyraxes always with a lookout on the nearest rock; and the tiny mice scurrying along their trails through the grasses. There were caves at the bases of some of the rock outcrops but William said the area had never supported a population like the Bushmen of the Drakensbergs. We could just see the tips of the main peaks behind the western rim of the valley.

Supper at 6.00 p.m. in the relative warmth of the hut consisted of cream of mushroom soup, fried pork chops with three vegetables, and dessert of pineapple, passion fruit and tree tomato; the latter was scooped out of a hard shell like the passion fruit but tasted different — sharp but pleasant. There was concern about Edward, one of the porters. He had mislaid his knife which he had treasured for four years; he set off back down the trail to look for it. He walked all the way back to Old Moses Camp without finding it and did not return till after dark. By 7.00 p.m., I was in my sleeping bag again, with thicker clothes on, thermal long sleeved vest and trousers, ski trousers and a sweater, and using my quilted North Face jacket as a pillow. The long nights were tedious, but they did pass in a mixture of sleep and half-wakeful drowsing. I was pleased with progress so far — a gentle climb, fine weather in the mornings when we were walking, and no hint of altitude sickness. The daily Diamox might be helping and perhaps more so the gradual rate of ascent. I had opted to take one more day than usual to climb, to give myself the best chance of enjoying it free from difficulties.

Monday February 9

It was a very cold night despite my extra clothing. The outer skin of the tent was frozen when I got up at 6.00 a.m. The inner layer was not. I packed up my rucksack; it was not easy in a one-man tent with a maximum height of about three feet. William had prepared the same breakfast as yesterday, which I ate in the Hut while the porters lay in. They would get up later when the sun hit the valley floor and wait for it to thaw out my tent before they packed it.

At 7.40 a.m., William and I started the day's trek. First there was a long climb up the west side of the valley, then over the top of the ridge and down into the Mackinder Valley, at the head of which was the Shipton Camp. In 1929 Eric Shipton was the first person to climb Mt Kenya's Nelion Peak, and went on to become a famous Himalayan climber. We set off in shadow, with me wearing multiple layers. Within half an hour, we had climbed into the sunshine and I was stripping off garments down to what I had worn the day before. It was a stiff climb up wet stream beds, made fascinating by the forest of Giant Lobelia and Tree Groundsel and Teleki Lobelia. Malachite sunbirds were everywhere singing from perches on the Groundsel, in a frenzy of courtship displays. Working our way up the Mackinder valley, we were on the eastern bank of the Liki River, with the great red rock buttresses of Terere and Sendeo on our left, and, at the head of the valley on the right, the twin peaks of Nelion and Batian, with Point Lenana coming into view on their left.

We stopped for a chat with one of a group of young American students who were on an "Outward-bound" type of adventure. They had come over the top of the ridge from the Mackinder valley that morning and were camped by the riverside. One was paddling around barefoot in the boggy grass wearing thin jeans and T-shirt—chilling to look at. Further up, we crossed the river and climbed the western edge of the valley, past Shipton's Cave, and sat on the rocks above it until we could see the porters catching us up. It was midday and clouding over, already cooler; but we only had another kilometre to go before we came to the camp. It was set on the last piece of flat ground before the scree, glaciers and rock faces of the main peaks, a spectacular sight as mist swirled round the crags. The camp was similar to Old Moses and was also run by Mountain Rock Hotel. For Ksh 800, I could have had a bed inside the bunk-house but felt that would be a cop-out; so I helped put up my tent for a third night. After lunch and a rest, I explored the area, particularly the route which we would take at 4.00 a.m. the next morning. Finally, I felt confident that I could make it to the top.

The only other group at the camp was of four Germans, ages 59 to 70, who had spent two nights at Old Moses camp to acclimatise. They were friendly but did not speak much English, so our communication was limited. Our mutual word was "Jambo",' a Swahili word of greeting. After dark, a weary young American, Eric, flopped in having walked all the way from the Sirimon Park Gate with one porter. He was on a short break from his work with an aid agency in Burundi. He was circumspect in his comments but was clearly not impressed by the quality of some of the United Nations staff there. His aim had been to make the climb in two days, but he was already suffering from mild altitude sickness and exhaustion and so decided to go down again the next day; it was a wise decision. I did not see him again.

Tuesday, February 10
I had sorted out my gear for the climb before going to sleep ready for the early start. I had simply slept in all my clothes, including my boots. I had been warm enough but had been disturbed by nasal congestion, a response to the cold dry air. Also, excessive

gas had made me appreciate why airline passengers are not fed beans! I was woken by William at 3.30 a.m. and packed up my bedding before going to the bunkhouse for cornflakes, hot milk, bread and jam and coffee. The other group had already departed at 2.30 a.m. The porters would be up later to pack up the tent and carry the equipment round the south circular path to meet us that afternoon at Mackinder's Hut in the Teleki Valley. At 4.00 a.m., we set off in bright moonlight that made our torches almost unnecessary. I had lent William my spare torch because his own had broken; I used my head-mounted one. Our route took us straight up the scree below the Gregory Glacier and then turned left onto the ridge above Harris Tarn. We were climbing on snowdrifts on the North face of the peak, crusted over with frost which made for faster progress than later in the day. The reflection from my headlight beam was of a myriad of diamonds. Conditions were perfect—clear sky and no wind. The sky was lightening and, by sunrise, we were just below Point Lenana. Shouts of "JAMBO" from the German group told us they had just reached the top. We waited for them to clear the summit before we scrambled up the last rock step to get there ourselves.

From Point Lenana, 4,985 metres, we could look across the ridge joining the heads of the Gregory and Lewis Glaciers, and up to the sheer rock face of Nelion, 5,188 metres, with Batian, 5,199 metres, hidden behind it from this angle. The top of Lenana was marked by a cross and a tribute to the memory of a climber who had died on the mountain.

We had only been there for 15 minutes when the cloud swept up the valley obscuring the view. So we started down. William took me very carefully down the frozen scree overlying the border of the Lewis Glacier. He told me that only the previous week a climber had slipped onto the glacier and hurtled down into the "Curling Pond", a deep pool below the snout of the glacier. His body was hooked out from the bottom four days later.

Below the glacier, we stopped for a rest and cup of tea at the Austrian Hut, the base for people intent on doing serious technical rock climbing on the main peaks. We now traversed along the broad south-west ridge, with the Hobley Valley falling away on the left. On the right the Lewis Tarn at the head of the Teleki Valley lay between us and a huge rock buttress, Point John, linked to a smaller but still impressive "Midget Peak". William pointed out the Diamond Glacier in the Diamond Couloir, a favourite route for climbers to access the summits. He told me that, at this time of year, there was little snow or ice on this side of the mountain, whereas there would be in the autumn when the sun would be more on the north face. Despite being on the Equator, the tilt of the earth did make this difference.

There followed a long walk down a scree slope, already thawed out by the sunshine. This led to the Mackinder Hut on the east side of the valley, at 4,200 metres, where we arrived at 9.00 a.m. This bunk house was run by the Naro Moru Lodge; it was a substantial stone-built structure with internal lay-out similar to the others, with beds for 80 or so. At last I was to have a bunk indoors with a mattress. There was no electricity or heating. There had been charcoal stoves at one time; but they were not now used because they dried out the air and reduced further the oxygen, causing discomfort to the climbers.

After a snack of biscuits and tea, I rested on the luxury of a mattress. At 12.30 p.m., I was given too much lunch as usual, and retired again to sleep because by now it was raining and cold. Later, when the rain cleared, I went for a nature ramble round the campsite. Tree Groundsels dominated between the massive boulders. The boulders themselves were colourful with mosses of all shades from green to yellow to a rich dark chocolate. Lichens competed for brilliance with various shades of orange. Carpets of small pinkish purple flowers, cardinis kensiensis, and even tinier yellow flowers added colour to the lush green grass. The Hyrax here again kept a watchful eye from the tops of boulders. They had a loud high-pitched call that is almost like the scream of an eagle. By evening, the flat land round the Hut was filled with tents. The Naro Moru route was the most popular because it was the shortest.

The communal living area inside the Hut was a great place to meet people. Gabby was an unusual character, a middle-aged Englishman. A surveyor in Zambia for several years, he loved Africa and had already done a trip from Cairo to Cape Town by public transport. He had been three weeks in Kenya on this trip living on the cheap in hostels. He had arrived at Mackinder's with a single, unqualified guide, and a supply of food which seemed to consist of a loaf of bread and a bag of ground nuts. He had struggled to reach the camp from the Park entrance yesterday, carrying his own pack, and gave up the idea of trying for Point Lenana. He went up as far as the American Hut, 4,300 metres, during the afternoon, and was caught in the rain and sleet.

He seemed to exist by scrounging handouts. I gave him my remaining high calorie trail-bars, and he had bowls of soup passed out from the kitchen by the sympathetic warden of the camp. He seemed to be dogged by ill-fortune. On his first day in Nairobi, he was drenched in a storm: on the second day, he fell into a storm drain: and, on the third, he was mugged by two Africans in broad daylight at the intersection of Uhuru Highway and Kenyatta Avenue, two of the main roads in Nairobi.

Richard, an experienced rock climber, had arrived at Nairobi from London three days before and come straight up to Mackinder's with his climbing partner from U.K. who had arrived a week earlier. Yesterday they had reached Point Lenana, each carrying 20 kilos of equipment and aiming to climb Nelion and Batian. The speed of ascent had been too quick for Richard, and they were forced to come down to Mackinder's because of his altitude sickness. On that day, they had opted for a "half-day" climb up the rock spire called "The Midget". All went well until, on the way down, their abseiling ropes became tangled and could not be released. They spent the next five hours trying to free the ropes or work out another way down; at the same time, they were drenched by rain and sleet. Finally, they cut one rope and came down on fixed ropes, leaving their brand-new ropes on the rock.

Wednesday February 11

A warm and comfortable night was disturbed by people snoring. At 6.00 a.m., I was roused by William and packed my gear. I breakfasted at 6.30 a.m., declining bacon, eggs and sausage. William came with me and the porters for the first two kilometres, before turning back to take up duties as camp warden for the next week. I gave him a tip of Ksh 2,000, about HK$340. He had been excellent and I commented as much on the exit report with the Naro Moru Lodge.

The 10-kilometre route from Mackinder's to the Park Gate started off as a pleasant stroll down the Teleki valley. We then crossed over the Naro Moru River and worked our way up the west bank, through forests of tree groundsel and lobelia to start with and then, at the top of the ridge, heathland where heather was predominant, erica arborea. Happily, here I could see the mature plants, whereas, on the Sirimon route, a fire two years before had burned them off. Then I came to the so-called "vertical bog", a long slope down of clumps of tussock grass separated by rocky watercourses or, more frequently, areas of mud. It was tiring and unpleasant walking but at least I was going downhill and could afford to give a cheerful "Jambo" to those struggling up. Giant groundsel senecio, having broad leaves with pale undersides, and outcrops of larva rock relieved the monotony. It was misty enough already to obscure views of the peaks behind us and the plains below.

At that point, I was joined by Gabby and his guide. He proceeded to amaze the porters by breakfasting off docken stems. At around 3,200 metres, we entered woodland. I saw two plants of the uncommon Mackinder's Lilly, a brilliant red flower. Lower down we passed through an area of bamboo, and trees of ever-increasing size — East African yellow wood podocarps, and African pencil cedar or Juniper, festooned with mosses and Usnea, appropriately called "old man's beard". At the Meteorological Station, we came at last to a serviceable road, and shortly after to the Meteorological Station Camp at 3,050 metres where I was happy to see our Land Rover waiting for us. I tipped the porters Ksh 800 each, possibly above the norm; they had been cheerful and reliable.

I was glad to see that the driver was a different one from the one on the way in. He agreed to take extra passengers, so Gabby and his guide Nicholas piled into the back with the luggage. This would save them another 29-kilometre walk to his hostel. But it did mean that we were **very** overloaded, with eight passengers and their baggage. However, the driver brought us down very expertly, even out of a huge water-filled pool in the muddy road, that required him to use the 4-W-D and much rocking backwards and forwards. We passed a number of groups walking up the trail — good luck to them. By the time we came to Naro Moru Lodge, I was the only passenger. I was happy and relieved to be back in comfortable surroundings and warmth after the extremes of temperature up on the mountain. I retrieved my suitcase containing all my clean clothes from the store, and, at last, cast off my very dirty clothes and enjoyed the long shower that I had been fantasising about for days. With ten day's growth of beard, I still looked distinctly scruffy. I thought I might as well continue with it to give it a chance of improving.

Sammy, the head of mountaineering, checked the letter prepared by William certifying that I had reached Point Lenana, and set about preparing a certificate to commemorate the achievement. I was the only person in for lunch and celebrated with a glass of soda. As usual, I had not had any alcohol for some weeks while training for the trip. The afternoon I spent on the verandah writing up my diary. It was cloudy with rain on the hills and no view of the peaks. I had been so lucky with the weather. In January, Richard's climbing partner had been with a group who reached within 200 yards of the summit of Point Lenana but had to turn back because the snow on the north ridge was too deep. At 7.30 p.m., there were 20 4WD vehicles in the car park and the dining room was packed with families. It was the AGM of a Danish aid organisation. I found the last free table and sat down to enjoy the buffet provided, including delicious freshwater fish, on which I complemented the chef and the manager, much to their pleasure. I was in bed by 9.00 p.m., tired and happy.

Thursday February 12
I was up at 7.00 a.m. after a good night's sleep despite being chilled in my silk pyjamas—silk because they took up minimal space when packed. There was no sunrise spectacular that morning; it had rained heavily during the night, judging by the height of the river. The dining room at breakfast was full of the Danish group. After eating. I collected the vital "achievement certificate" from the front desk and my safe deposit envelope from the manager. At 9.15 a.m., I was on the road again with the

same driver, Joseph, who had brought me from Nairobi. I was leaving with some regret — the Lodge was a most attractive spot.

The roads were in atrocious condition after the rain, massive potholes filled with water. In fact, there was a local saying that, if you see a vehicle being driven in a straight line, the driver must be drunk! There was little traffic until 11.00 a.m. when we came close to Nairobi; there were diesel-engine lorries belching out black smoke, and "'mutatus" (minivans), loaded to the gills with people hanging out of the back door. The housing varied from little hovels made from branches and grass around Mt Kenya and wooden board shacks with corrugated iron roofs around Naro Moru to modern homes around Nairobi. The most common advertisement seemed to be for "Sportsman" cigarettes.

The Norfolk Hotel was seething with newly arrived tour groups headed by pushy group leaders. My room was not ready; I sat on the terrace drinking excellent coffee and catching up on the news in "The Nation". Life, or rather death, went on much as before; malaria deaths in the north-east had reached 1,500, with 50 dying every day. Robbers were sentenced to death, or if they got out of jail, were lynched by fellow villagers. Tribal killings appear to have been inspired by activists of President Moi's KANU party (Kenyan African National Union), as a way to solidify the votes of the pro-government faction, the Kametusa, made up of the Kalenjin, Maasai, Turkana and Samburu; who were ranged against the numerically stronger Kikuyu. The killers appeared to have had the help of the army and police.

On a more positive note, the paper reported Kenya's first trans-cutaneous angioplasty, a procedure to open a blocked coronary artery. Previously, patients had been sent to South Africa, if they had the money.

Finally, in my room, I did a large wash of my muddy climbing gear, saving many hundreds of dollars. I skipped lunch and supper as a reaction to all the eating I had forced myself to do on the mountain. I went to bed delighted that everything had gone according to plan on the climb—I had been quite easily up to it physically and I could reasonably hope to be successful on my next target—Mount Kilimanjaro.

TANZANIA
Mt Kilimanjaro
Height: 5,895 meters (19,341 feet)
Date: February 1998

My second objective in this visit to East Africa was to climb Mt Kilimanjaro, the highest peak in Africa. I knew that this would be a more difficult and dangerous climb than scaling Mount Kenya. I was ready for it, physically and psychologically.

On February 13, I was resting in the Norfolk Hotel, Nairobi, after the successful ascent of Point Lenana on Mt Kenya and preparing for an attempt on Mt Kilimanjaro. It had rained in the night and continued in the morning — so much for their 'dry season'. Everything is blamed on El Nino. I walked fast and tried to look fierce, to discourage muggers. I paid the extra $100 to make up the shortfall in the price I had originally been quoted for the Norfolk Hotel, $130 per day instead of the $150 I was actually charged.

I bought more torch batteries for the climb and boiled sweets. Picture postcards were all of animals; there were no decent ones of Mt Kenya. Kenyatta Avenue had deteriorated even further — huge potholes filled with water. Back at the hotel, I wrote postcards and sent them off to the boys and Granny Longstaff, Judith's mother. Then I had a long swim and lunched by the poolside. In the afternoon, I completed my clothes wash. I had dinner on the terrace, surrounded by animal safari groups and local people. I could not wait to return to the mountains and re-join the trekking fraternity.

I was up at 6.30 a.m. after a good sleep. Before breakfast, I went out of the front entrance and a hundred yards down the road to the left to confirm that the Davanu Shuttle, my transport to Tanzania for the next day, did depart from that point. Again it was a dull morning with a light rain. I had my daily swim and lunch at the poolside, and then retired for a siesta.

Sitting at the Lord Delamere Bar and drinking a lime soda, I overheard a tour operator making the best of unfavourable circumstances; he reassured his thirty or so clients that none of his clientele had been mugged, but "'just in case", they should not wear jewellery or expensive watches or take taxis after dark. On seeing game, he had to tell them that, because of the rains, the animals were not conveniently grouped around water holes and that roads in various areas were impassable, so the schedule had been changed. He did not mention the tribal warfare and epidemic of Rift Valley Fever in the Rift Valley. If he had, his clients would probably all have gone straight home. I dined on the terrace again, watching the world go by: groups of really well-dressed people coming for a reception in the hotel, tour groups leaving for the airport, taxi drivers lounging across the road beside their cars — some traditional London taxis but mostly Japanese sedans.

Sunday 15 February. I was awake at 6.00 a.m. and ready for the room service breakfast that arrived promptly half an hour later. At 7.15 a.m., I was the first to arrive at the Davanu Shuttle bus, a large luxury coach. It was scheduled to leave at 7.30 a.m. but did not get going until 8.40 a.m., largely because of late arrivals. When we did leave, it was a pleasant ride, air-conditioned with reclining seats and a VCR film of African wildlife on the TV monitor.

The road was a double carriageway past the 'industrial estate' and as far as the airport, it was a single highway with wide sloping shoulders to cope with heavy rains. The sealed surface was reasonable apart from the occasional flood-damaged sections. As we travelled south, the wide-open plains of grass, scattered with thorn trees and ant-hills, gradually gave way to rolling foothills as we neared the border. The only wildlife were cattle and donkeys watched by Maasai herdsmen with red cloaks and long staffs.

On the outskirts of Namanga, we paused briefly at a native crafts-cum- restaurant-cum-toilet. We stopped at the Kenyan side of the border crossing, where we had departure cards checked and passports stamped. One hundred yards further on, we stopped again at the Tanzanian immigration post to have visas checked and stamped; both offices were housed in dilapidated shacks. The surrounding area lined on each side by stalls selling food, drink and curios. Elderly native women in colourful clothing and festooned with jewellery clamoured for attention to sell their trinkets. Large holes in their earlobes showed where decorative ornaments at least two inches across could be inserted. I was reminded of the paintings of native women by Joy Adamson on display at the Nairobi Museum.

The vehicle parks contained dozens of container trucks and heavy lorries waiting for customs inspection. For a main border post, the facilities were not impressive. The road to the regional capital Arusha was narrower and in poor condition — I winced as container trucks hurtled past within inches of our coach.

In Arusha, we stopped at the five-star Novotel Mount Meru Hotel. About 20 of us transferred to a smaller Davanu bus that left one hour later for the two-hour trip to Moshi, capital of the Kilimanjaro region on the lower slopes of the mountain. Arusha is the center for safari groups going west to the crater highlands, Serengeti National Parks, Ngorongoro Crater conservation area, and for trekkers on Mt Meru immediately to the north. We travelled east on an excellent highway, upgraded three years earlier; across more plains with Maasai herdsmen and their cattle, goats and donkeys and kraals of round grass-thatch dwellings. Further on, villages became more frequent, surrounded by fields of corn, coffee and bananas. The village stores invariably had a brilliant paint job featuring OMO washing powder. In Kenya, it was Persil that seemed to be the big seller.

In Moshi, we dropped off people at various locations, including two young Swedes I had been chatting with; they were also going climbing the next day.

Finally, I was deposited at the Mountain View Hotel, a farther four kilometers to the south. The hotel was an unattractive two-story building in a small garden just off the main highway. On the gate, a sign read 'Shah Tours. Mountain View Hotel. The Start of Your Kilimanjaro Climb'.

Although the mountain was not visible from the hotel, it did indeed seem to cater only for climbers. The floors were bare of any carpets, wisely so no doubt with the heavy traffic in muddy boots. My double room was large with an ensuite bathroom and usual Maasai height shower (the men all seem to be over six foot

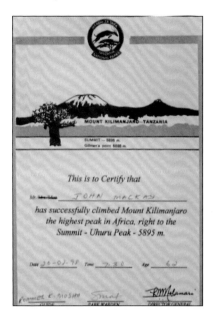

tall) and mosquito-netting over the window. I had no complaints. At 7.00 p.m., supper was served on the first floor under the stars; it was fine but a little too close to nature with bats, humming-bird hawk moths and numerous other flying insects whirling around the table. The only other guests were two Australian medical students; they had just come down from a successful climb of the mountain. They were on their way home from an elective at the teaching hospital in Accra, capital of Ghana; they said it made Nairobi look like the height of civilisation. That evening I had a thorough briefing on the climb from a young representative of Shah Tours — things to take, what to wear, and what to tip the guide and porters. The only addition to my kit I felt worthwhile was a second ski-stick, which I hired for $3.

Monday February 16
On Monday, after breakfast on the balcony, I deposited my

valuables in the hotel safe-deposit and my suitcase of non-climbing gear in the luggage storeroom. At 8.00 a.m., a Shah Tours minivan picked me up, with a tour guide to handle administration, and Rommel, the mountain guide for the trip; he was looking very smart in a suit and tie. We travelled due east on the main road for twenty kilometers at about 1,000 meters altitude. At this point, we left the Dar es Salaam Road where it turned south. Shortly afterwards, we reached Himo, a small market town and climbing base. There we turned left and climbed a further twenty kilometers on a tarred road up through the foothills of Kilimanjaro through a heavily farmed area. The occasional small tourist hotel appeared in the gaps between the lush vegetation.

At the Marangu Gate (1,980 meters), we signed in, and the tour representative paid the dues, so much per person per day. The large car park already had a number of transports parked in it, either disgorging trekkers or waiting to pick them up. Porters were lounging around waiting for their loads. Opposite the Park Office was a shop selling an assortment of food, t-shirts, postcards and climbing gear. I bought bars of chocolate for emergency rations. My mountain guide Rommel found one of our porters, Cerea, and loaded him up with my gear. There was enough spare room in my rucksack for Cerea to add his own gear, wrapped in a large polythene bag. The two of us set off through the high wooden archway, flanked on one side by a plaque to the memory of Hans Meyer, a German geographer who was the first recorded person to reach the summit of the mountain in October 1889.

On the other side was a notice warning what to do and not to do while climbing. The plan was for Rommel to wait to organize the other two porters and catch us up on the trail. I realized his name was not so surprising when I remembered that the region had been part of German East Africa between 1890 and 1918.

Administration was granted to Britain in 1920 after the Treaty of Versailles. It became a republic in 1961 and in 1964 with Zanzibar, became Tanzania.

Coming down the road were villagers carrying sheaves of grass on their heads for thatching, or great bundles of branches for cooking. Later came porters with loads of camping equipment in rattan baskets, canvas bags or even tin trunks; all were balanced effortlessly on their heads despite the uneven and slippery footing.

The day had begun with bright sunshine and only enough cloud to obscure the upper part of the mountain. As we started walking, however, there were light showers, gradually deteriorating into a persistent downpour with thunder overhead. The unsealed road quickly became a river and, when the road gave way to a footpath, walking became even more unpleasant. We were climbing up tree-root ladders against cataracts of water or squelching our way round muddy pools. At that point, I was amused by the irony of a notice telling me not to throw away lighted cigarettes that might start forest fires. Later the path became a narrow, eroded, defile between thick walls of jungle; the choice was between trying to keep a footing on the slippery clay banks or to walk up the stream rushing down the base of the cleft.

As the weather deteriorated, I hurried on ahead of the porter, intent on getting to the shelter of the Mandara camp, at 2,700 meters, seven kilometers and about five hours and 700 meters above the Park Gate. My t-shirt and shorts were quickly soaked despite my 'waterproof' jacket; my waterproof trousers were with the porter. But, as long as I kept moving, I was warm enough.

At 2.00 p.m., I reached the camp and checked in without guide or porter, to the surprise of the warden. I had a four

bunk A-shaped cabin to myself; each bunk had a mattress and cover and a pillow. I crouched down in my wet clothes trying to maintain body heat and ate my picnic lunch. I felt tired and discouraged by the terrible weather. Things began to look up when Cerea arrived about half an hour later with my rucksack containing dry clothes. They improved further when he looked in later to tell me that tea and biscuits were waiting for me in the mess hall. Cerea must have had a hard time in the conditions, even with the use of the ski stick that I had lent him. The canvas sack holding my sleeping bag was not waterproof, so the foot of the bag was sodden. Nevertheless I was warm and comfortably resting in it when Rommel arrived two hours later with the porters carrying food. Supper at 6.00 p.m. consisted of soup, stewed meat, roast potatoes, vegetables, noodles and fresh fruit. There was more than I could eat. I chatted with a couple of German climbers. Other climbers were a group of eighteen Germans, two Swedes, two Americans and four Frenchmen. At 8.00 p.m., I headed gratefully to bed, having learned two lessons—have truly waterproof gear and make sure everything is packed inside plastic bags.

Tuesday. I slept well, enjoying the comfort of a cabin more than that of a tent, especially having the room to myself. The clothes that I had hung up were still sopping wet, but the boots and jacket that Rommel had taken to put in front of the fire were now dry—great. The next day the sole of one boot came off. The boots had been too close to the stove during the night and the glue had melted. Rommel retrieved the situation that night by finding someone who cobbled the sole back on again, not an easy job; I gave him an appropriate tip. The boots are still in use twenty years later.

Breakfast was a feast of porridge, eggs, bacon, sliced cucumber, bread, jam, honey or peanut butter and tea. At 8.30 a.m., Rommel and I set off for the trek to the Horombo Camp, at 3,700 meters and eleven kilometres away; it was a climb of 1,000 meters scheduled to take five to seven hours. It was fine to start with, but before long the sky began to cloud over. The rain forest quickly gave way to an area of giant heathers, and we were up on the heathland, which had been burnt off last spring. Grasses and flowers were well established again among the blackened stems of the bushes. The trail was drier than the previous day, except for a few stretches of boggy ground where streams came down. At the half-way point, we stopped briefly for a snack. Finally, after four and a half hours of steady walking, we rounded a shoulder of hill and saw the camp dimly through the mist, just ten minutes away across yet another stream. I had just time to register with the warden and get myself to cabin number three when the rain started. Good timing and worth the push to get to the camp early, before the majority of the trekkers. No sooner had I unpacked and spread my belongings around the same four-bunk sized cabin as at Mandara, when I had to tidy up again; a young Japanese man arrived, exhausted, having climbed to Gillman's Point at dawn that day. He reported that there was deep snow at the top, sufficient for the guides to stop climbers from going on to Uhuru Peak. Shortly afterwards, the two Swedish brothers arrived from Mandara. The trip was the 30th birthday present for the elder one; the younger one was a professional photographer and had masses of gear.

Wednesday. I slept well and breakfasted at a leisurely 8.15 a.m., having opted to spend a day at Horombo to acclimatize. The other three had left early—the Japanese to go on down the mountain and the brothers to continue climbing. In the bright sunshine of the early morning, I had my first clear view of Kibo, the main dome of the volcano, just poking above the shoulder of mountain to the west, and of Mawenzi, the mass of rock towering more closely over the camp. The sunshine lasted until 9.30 a.m., then the mist rolled in, leaving my clothes still wet from the day before.. At that moment, I felt that high-altitude climbing was an overrated pastime and involved too much discomfort. I had assumed that the porters would be enjoying a day off—but no, they had to go about six kilometers down the hill again to fetch more fuel for cooking. All cooking was done over communal wood stoves in cook huts that belched smoke most of the day. This was nether ecologically desirable nor sustainable, since the large number of people trekking on the mountain were all given three cooked meals a day. It could well be that some of the heathland fires were started deliberately to provide firewood. In my report at the end of the trip, I suggested that fuel in the form of paraffin should be carried in, as on Mt Kenya.

My old SLR Pentax camera had not performed well in the cold on the last climb, so I was only carrying the Pentax automatic this time. Half of one film was lost when the battery ran down and some shots were not working for reasons unknown. I kept my fingers crossed that some decent pictures would come out. At 10.00 a.m., Rommel and I set off on a short walk up the mountainside above the camp, along the old trail to the summit as far as the Zebra Rock at 4,000 meters; this was an outcrop of larva stained with vertical white streaks. This was as close as we came to Mawenzi; it was wreathed in swirling clouds, which denied me a good picture. At 1.00 p.m., we were back at Horombo, just half an hour before the rain started again. We had left the large German group at the Zebra rock; no doubt they would be caught in the rain. After lunch, three large Germans came in—not English-speaking, so not good company for me. I dozed most of the afternoon, before going to supper just before sundown. The mess-hut was very crowded, mostly with Germans; however, I sat next to a 33-year-old American, Randy from Chicago, a triathlete who was very chatty. He had enjoyed the climb so far and talked of going back to climb Mt McKinley and Aconcagua, the highest mountains in North and South America. Standing outside the mess hall to watch the sunset, I saw a porter coming back from a cookhouse with a serving spoon. As he reached the steps to the mess hall, he appeared to notice that it was still dirty, paused for a moment, and licked it clean before going in to do the serving.

Lights were out by 8.00 p.m. Solar-powered batteries provided enough of a glow. The next day, The Germans were up at 6.30 a.m., lights on and packing without any reference to me. As it happened, I also had to be on the road and so was packed and ready for breakfast half an hour later. Personal hygiene was taken care of by a wet face cloth wiped over the face and brushing the teeth.

Thursday. At 8.00 a.m., I was on the trail with Cerea to Kibo Hut, 1,000 meters higher at 4,700 meter and a distance of 10 kilometers. We climbed for the first hour or so in a north westerly direction through heath, until we came to a stream marking the last water supply point. Here porters filled up containers to supply the next camp-site. The track now swung north onto the almost flat saddle area between Mawenzi and Kibo—an arctic desert of gravel and rock. The mist had by now come down and a cold wind made more clothing essential.

At this point, ghostly figures started appearing out of the mist—trekkers and porters on their way down the mountain. The Swedish brothers appeared to have made it to Gillman's Point with great difficulty because their boots were designed for walking, not climbing; they had continually slipped in the snow, and their cold weather gear was inadequate. "The worst day of my life", said the younger brother. However, he was ecstatic about the sunrise pictures he had taken. They wished me well. I also chatted with a grey-haired Scandinavian couple. He had reached Uhuru Peak and she Gillman's Point—both were very happy with their success.

The low point in my day came in the middle of this mist and cold; I began to feel hypoglycaemic and had to stop for boiled sweets and a drink. Thereafter, I proceeded more slowly. Soon after, the mist momentarily cleared and I could see Kibo peak and the camp huts at the foot of the dome about forty-five minutes away. The last part of the trek was up a steeper slope, past huge boulders and larva outcrops. On top of one of these was perched what in the mist looked like a vulture; in fact, it was a collared raven, a large scavenger. Appropriate, I thought, that it should be waiting to feed on trekkers as they succumbed to fatigue.

We reached Kibo Camp at 11.30 a.m., in excellent time, better than average. The advantage of arriving early at the next camp, apart from missing the afternoon rain, was that I could choose my bunk in the dormitory. Kibo was a cold bleak place with nothing to do but rest in the warmth of my sleeping bag and get

up for meals. Its bunkhouse was made of stone. A passage from one end led down the centre of the building, with dormitories leading off on each side; there were five rooms, with six to ten two-tier bunks in each and a central table and benches. At the far end of the passage was the eating area, with long wooden tables, benches and an iron stove — but no heating. The toilet block, three 'long drops', was about thirty yards away. There was no running water. The warden sold beer and soft drinks, all carried up by porters. I did not ask the price. I was astonished at the number of climbers still puffing cigarettes. In late afternoon, snow started to fall and persisted into the night. I wondered how this would affect the climb the next day.

Supper at 5.00 p.m. was spaghetti and chicken meat sauce, very tasty, washed down with boiled water. I had stopped drinking tea and coffee as being too gastritic. The large German group was down to fourteen. A separate group of Germans sharing the same dormitory with me could speak some English and were friendly. The early meal was so that we could all rest before the call at 11.30 p.m. to get ready for the summit climb. Rommel told me later that the guides chatted until midnight rather than sleep. I went to bed dressed in climbing gear, thermal trousers and long-sleeved vest with a rollneck, a sweater, and a fresh pair of thick socks. I felt very dirty after so many days without a shower and I looked forward to the next one. The rest of my clothing and my boots were in the sleeping bag with me, warm and dry.

At 11.30 p.m., the wake-up call came when I was already dressing; I put on my quilted ski trousers, waterproof Gortex trousers, North Face jacket, and boots.

Friday 20 Feb 1998. Sweet tea and biscuits helped to wake me. A toilet call, and then I was ready to climb. In my small backpack, I had a bottle of sweetened water, spare batteries for the torch, snow goggles, boiled sweets, bars of chocolate and spare rolls of film. My camera was hung round my neck to keep it warm.

Rommel brought a large bottle of water and put it in his backpack. At 00.45 a.m., we started climbing on a clear starry night with a half-moon giving some light to the snow-covered landscape. Looking up, I could see the bulk of Kibo in white, with outcrops of rock showing as sinister black masses. Rommel led at a very slow pace, small steps barely one in front of the other. It was frustrating to start with but, as the slope steepened, the pace continued the same, and was fast enough. Above and behind us were little wavering strings of lights as other climbing groups made their way upwards, zig-zagging through the snow, aiming for the gaps between the rock buttresses. I had a headlight torch and Rommel a hand-held one, although the moonlight was almost bright enough for us to do without either. Much of the time we progressed on the light from my torch alone. We stopped three times for a rest, to eat sweets and to drink water. Despite this and our slow pace, we passed two groups of climbers.

As we went higher, the slopes became steeper and the soft, new, powder snow lying on a layer of crusted snow became very slippery. Rommel had difficulty in keeping his footing and was grateful to take my second ski-stick. At this altitude, I had to stop to catch my breath after every traverse.

We caught up with another group of three climbers and their guide who was leading them hesitantly, I thought, between two snow hillocks.

Suddenly we were at the crater rim! Past the hillocks, the ground fell away to a dark abyss. No wonder the guide was going slowly. It was 6.00 a.m. and the first streaks of light were beginning to appear between clouds on the eastern horizon. This was Gillman's Point, 5,680 metres. We congratulated each other and took photographs. I sat down thankfully to relax and drink my sweetened water.

As soon as it was light, I followed Rommel starting to make a trail round the rim of the crater to Uhuru Peak, 5,896 meter, 200 meters higher and on the opposite side of the crater. The overnight snowfall and drifting snow had obliterated the previous day's trail. Rommel had to edge his way forward uncertainly between the rock face on his left and the edge of the precipitous slope falling away to the floor of the crater far below.

This was the only part of the climb where I felt at all nervous. Gradually, we worked our way round, the width of the rim becoming wider as we went. I stopped at frequent intervals to take pictures as the spectacular dawn colours outlined the rocky peaks of Mawenzi in dramatic yellow-to-orange shafts of light; they bathed the snowscape in colour and left the plains far below still in darkness. Further round the rim, we came to immense ice cliffs, layer upon layer of snow and ice decorated with a cascade of icicles — beautiful and amazing. Rommel led at a steady pace; I kept up with him as best I could, determined not to have to give way to the following group. The last 200 yards were up a gentle, wide snowfield. At last, at 7.30 a.m., we reached Uhuru (Freedom) Peak, at 5,896 meters, (19,345 feet), the highest point in Africa!

There was much shaking of hands, hugs, and congratulations and taking of photographs among Rommel, myself, the three Germans and their guide who had followed us to the summit. It was marked by a flagpole. The plaque had a quote from Julius Nyerere, first President of Tanzania from 1964 to 1985, and a tin box with a logbook on which people could sign their names. But they were not to be seen — possibly buried under the snow.

I took photographs in all directions, north to a faint Mt Meru, east across the crater to Mawenzi, west across the summit snow field to the ice cliff, and south down the track we had made.

At 8.00 a.m., with much reluctance, we set off down the way we had come, now easy to follow, passing about ten others on their way to the summit, including a small, determined German lady and her guide — the only two from the large group to make it. By the time we had arrived back at Gillman's Point, at 8.30 a.m., the mist had already swirled in to blot out the view across the crater. The descent was more fun than the ascent. Rommel descended by sliding down the first 400 meters of steep snow on his backside. I slid part of the way but became wary of the rocky outcrops becoming exposed by the melting snow; so I ran down the fine gravel scree at the center of the slope. At 5,182 meters, we passed the Hans Meyer cave where a number of the large German group were resting glumly, having reached their limit, now on their way down.

By 11.30 a.m., we were back at Kibo Hut being greeted by smiling porters bearing cups of orange juice. What a great idea! Rommel was particularly pleased with himself at having guided 'Papa John' to the summit and, I suspect, at having been the first to the summit that day. Two Germans gave me compliments that I am happy to remember. "You have a very good climbing rhythm." "I wish I will be as fit as you when I am your age." I was 63.

In retrospect, I was overdressed for the climb, too hot with the effort of going up, and too hot in the sun coming down. I might have been better off with a thinner fleece jacket and a waterproof in case of rain. By the time I had sat down at Kibo Hut, fatigue began to catch up and the chill inside the hut made me happy to get into my sleeping bag for a rest. Half an hour later, a bowl of hot soup and hot water helped to restore inner warmth and energy.

At noon we set off again, this time to walk the ten kilometres back to the Horombo Camp. Again, I had the experience of walking through the mist and passing ghostly figures coming the other way. Very happily this time, it was me on the way down. I could not help but think of the trekkers straining to get to Kibo as lambs on their way to slaughter. At the Saddle, I was passed at speed by a one-wheel stretcher being controlled by five young men; they were taking a woman with an injured leg down the mountain. Another man who had developed a fever was also being helped down by his friends. This did not reassure those on their way up. I passed a cheery "Jambo" to all and sundry, including two large British groups being managed by Shah Tours. At 3.00 p.m., I reached Horombo, having taken the last few kilometers slowly and carefully because of fatigue and the belief that this was the most likely time to take a fall.

I was directed to hut 13; a young Englishman was already in residence and disconcertingly honest in his regret that he was not going to have the hut to himself as he had at Mandara the previous night. He should have tried three German non-linguists for size. My first action after unpacking was to wash my feet and

change into clean socks and shoes—it's vital to keep the feet in good condition. The rest of me no doubt smelt abominably. I rested in my sleeping bag until 5.00 p.m. when I got up for a supper I had chosen myself in preference to yet another mega-meal; this was Weetabix, hot water, powdered milk and sugar, with an orange to follow. An Australian family trio opposite regretted that they had not done likewise, as they struggled with a heaped tray of food. And so to bed at 6.00 p.m.

What an unforgettable day, one of the most memorable of my climbing career! To put Kilimanjaro's 5,896 metres in context—Mont Blanc is 4,810 meters and Everest Base Camp is 5,300 meters.

Saturday. At 6.30 a.m., I was up to admire a most beautiful sunrise, at breakfast half an hour later, and ready at 8.00 a.m. for the long walk of eighteen kilometers down to the Park Gate. Before leaving Horombo, I lined up the porters and guide for a group photograph. Cerea and I set off together, leaving the others to finish their packing and to join us later. After the first hour, the mist came in as usual; it gave us only glimpses of sunshine thereafter. This was all right because it kept the temperature down. At this point, Rommel joined me and instructed Cerea to go on ahead to gather fuel for cooking lunch at Mandara Camp. Just before reaching the camp, I saw a Colobus monkey swinging through the trees, a striking sight with black body and flowing white fur on its arms. At 11.00 a.m., we reached Mandara camp. I had a bowl of soup and boiled water and declined anything more substantial. Half an hour later, by the time we were ready to set off on the last leg of the descent, it was raining. The first and narrowest part of the track was slippery on the wet clay. Here I fell without injury, and saw a porter fall for the first time on the trip. Lower down the trail, the water run-off had built up to the extent that we were paddling down the small river that we had walked up six days before. We reached the Marangu Gate at 1.30 p.m., wet but happy, and signed out at the warden's office. Rommel and the warden filled in and signed a certificate to authenticate my success. I noted in the logbook that there were very few 60-year-olds recorded as having reached the summit. From a nearby kiosk, I bought postcards to send to the family. It was now time to say goodbye to the team. I thanked them all very sincerely and handed out the maximum suggested tips –$50 for Rommel and $10 to each of the porters.

The Shah Tours transport was waiting, so I loaded my gear and we were away. I gave a lift to another climber and his guide who were with Shah Tours but had not booked transport. Back at the Mountain View Hotel, I handed in my borrowed ski stick, retrieved my suitcase and safe-deposit envelope, and spent the next hour in the shower room washing mud off my boots and clothing. I avoided looking at myself in the mirror for as long as I could. When eventually I did, I looked incredibly scruffy.

The long shower that I had been looking forward to for a week was well worth the wait. I washed my hair three times –great to be clean. The only physical effect of the climb was a tenderness in the calves, which was gone in a day, and not even a blister. Supper was at 7.30 p.m., a good meal spoiled by myriad insects attracted to the lights on the roof top. There were three groups of German climbers, and one English father and son. I was happy to pass on experiences and encouragement. There was an element of me that was itching to pass on the comment of the Zambezi White Water Rafting boatman, "It's not as bad as you think. It is worse!"

Sunday February 22

I was awakened at 4.00 a.m. by the muezzin calling the faithful to prayer. My shower at a more reasonable hour was upset by the sprinkler cone falling off the Maasai-level outlet. Before breakfast, I walked up the country road running past the hotel towards the mountain hoping to get a view of the peak from the plains; but there was already too much cloud over the high ground. I passed numbers of women going to a fresh water supply point in a field. They did not respond to "Jambo" and were shy of having their picture taken. Some small children in ragged and dirty clothing going to school were chattier in limited English. All wanted pens. They called me 'teacher' — presumably they had experience of white schoolteachers. The small fields were growing crops of maize, corn, sunflowers, bananas and cassava. Breakfast was on the roof, now happily free of insects. The waiter was attentive, had good English and was worth his tip. Back in the bedroom, I realized that, despite having scraped my shoes on the grill at the front entrance, I still had a layer of clay packed onto the soles of my shoes. I spent the next half hour cleaning it off, and then had another shower, as much to clean the floor as to wash myself.

At 10.30 a.m., I left for the 10-minute ride to the Davanu Shuttle terminal in Moshi. Arriving there, I checked that my booking was in the record, and then had forty minutes to wait. I sat down outside in the sun, ignoring a gaggle of hopeful men trying to sell lethal-looking spears and knives in decorated scabbards. Two Norwegians sitting next to me had also been climbing over the same days as myself. They had been most unfortunate in that the expensive mountain equipment they had carefully bought for the trip had all been lost by British Airways on the transfer from Heathrow to Gatwick so they had hired very inferior equipment in Moshi. They had opted to climb on the Macchame route, using tents. It sounded more interesting, with cliffs and glaciers, and more wildlife, including buffalo and leopards. They responded to my story about the raven at Kibo by telling me how one morning they woke up to find the tent under snow and four ravens waiting hungrily outside the tent.

When it left Moshi, the Davanu bus was packed full of people and loaded with luggage on the roof. The diesel engine was not up to the task, so we progressed very slowly uphill. Downhill was faster but no sooner had we built up some speed than we had to slow for a village speedbump or a police checkpoint; there were several, often commanded by women. The road skirted round the south and west sides of Mount Meru (4,550 metres), another extinct volcano but still with an ash dome visible in the center of the crater. It looked an interesting two- to three-day climb. We reached the Novotel Meru Hotel at Arusha at 1.15 p.m., shortly followed by the luxury coach from Nairobi. I watched carefully as the luggage was transferred, then chose a seat on the right side to be out of the afternoon sun and to have a view of the mountains. I had a snack lunch before we set off on time, with the bus half full, retracing the route to the border past the coffee plantations, the wide plains with Maasai herds and Mount Meru, by now wreathed in clouds. The road was worse than last time because of heavy flooding. The crossing at Namanga was even more congested with container trucks than it had been last time.

Half an hour into Kenya, we had our comfort stop at another native crafts shop and restaurant, and met yet another squad of British soldiers coming back from an exercise. Not long after this, in the middle of the plains, the coach stopped. The driver had noticed the engine overheating. On inspection, he found a leak in the hosepipe of the water-cooling system: there was no spare. The driver and his mechanic tried to mock up a replacement without success. Passengers tried to help, took pictures, chatted and drank beer. Young men with their long staffs came over from a distant village and drifted off again. The sun started to set and I had visions of us spending the night there in the wilderness, surrounded by lions and Maasai moran (warriors) with long spears. Eventually the driver found a spare inner tyre and cut it into strips which he wound tightly round the broken pipe, effecting a partial repair. He and his mechanic then disappeared into the bush with large plastic cans to look for water, successfully. Once the water tank had been filled, we set off again at a much-reduced rate. In the evening light, I could see grazing herds of springbok and bush-buck. We stopped twice more to fill up with water, finally stopping at a garage thirty kilometres from Nairobi, where we transferred onto a relief bus.

One of the passengers had spent an anxious afternoon, having a flight to catch that night; he was dropped off at the airport with just enough time to spare. I thanked my lucky stars that I had postponed my departure till the following day. Otherwise, I would certainly have missed my flight. The coach reached the Norfolk Hotel at 8.30 p.m. I checked in, tired and dusty, had a shower and changed into my smartest clothes for dinner on the terrace. I was too tired for the celebratory meal that I had planned.

Instead, I had a bowl of soup and a glass of milk — disappointing, no doubt, for the waiter, whom I imagined was expecting the bearded gentleman to order a pint of beer and a large steak. Back in my room, I briefly watched the continuing debate that would lead to the disastrous invasion of Iraq; then I switched to an excellent British soccer cup tie between Manchester United and Barnsley — it ended in a draw 1-1.

At 7.30 a.m. on Monday, 23rd February, I was up for a large breakfast, and then went to the Let's Go Travel office to thank them for their good offices and to collect the booking voucher for the Norfolk, costing $150 as opposed to $230, the standard rate. Check-out time was 11.00 a.m. and I was not due at the airport until 5;30 p.m. So I left my baggage under guard of the doorman in the hall and retired to my favourite spot, the poolside restaurant, to write up my diary, read 'The Daly Nation' and a book recommended to me, titled *White Mischief*.

The pool area, on the deck below me, was busy with a 'mother and child swimming morning', just as the United Services Recreation Club in Hong Kong in years gone by when it was an all-white institution. There were two moments of drama inherent in this sort of event.

One two-year-old red-haired boy, standing at the edge of the pool at the shallow end, carefully took off his flotation device and jumped in. He went straight under despite flailing arms. Seconds later a woman shrieked, leapt out of her deck chair and plunged in to the rescue. She handed the child over to the grateful mother who had been standing in the pool watching her other offspring. She collapsed back onto her deck-chair, reaching for a cigarette to calm her shattered nerves. In the second episode, a mother was trying to entice her one-and-a-half-year-old into the pool at the shallow end when he suddenly squatted down with a rather preoccupied look on his face. Recognising the symptoms, the mother jumped out of the pool, gathered the infant into her arms in a face down position and rushed with him to the nanny who was waiting, poised, with the necessary nappy.

Back to 'The Nation'—still much news of the tragic and bizarre:

In the Mount Kenya National Park, rangers reported a 600-acre plantation of bhang (hemp) a narcotic, guarded by gunmen.

Two nuns had been attacked and severely injured by robbers who had made off with money collected to build a new chapel.

A man was killed when he was hit by a pulpit stand, in a battle between rival factions of the Nyeri Bondeni African Independent Pentecostal Church of East Africa. Four others were critically injured in the battle between the supporters of two rival self-appointed archbishops.

In the Northeast, people were still dying at a rate of 20 per day from cholera, typhoid and malaria brought on by the recent flooding.

Once the pool had cleared, I went down for my swim. I had lunch at the poolside, then lay down very comfortably on a deck chair to read 'White Mischief' about Kenya in 1941, when at least a section of the white settler population led a life of privileges and great licentiousness. Quote: "Are you married, or do you live in Kenya?"

I was obliged to leave this pleasant spot to catch my plane. The taxi to the airport, $20, took forty minutes through busy traffic. Checking-in went smoothly and I settled down in Emirates First Class lounge until my flight was called. We took off after dark, so there was no last view of Mt Kenya. At Dubai, there was a six-hour wait for my flight to Hong Kong, which I passed comfortably enough stretched out on a cushioned settee. Twice there were calls for flights to London. I thought wistfully of going to meet the rest of the family in England, but my luggage was already booked through to the Hong Kong flight, so there was no turning around. The flight to Hong Kong was uneventful, arriving at 7.30 p.m. on a cold grey, misty evening.

In three weeks, I had done everything I had set out to do. I felt enormous satisfaction, particularly as I had great doubts as to the wisdom of going to Kenya at all, and how I would perform at a higher altitude than I had attempted before. During my brief visit I had learned a great deal about Kenya, and had met many interesting people, and enjoyed again the companionship of mountain people.

Now for the next one.

MOROCCO
Toubkal
Height: 4,167 metres (13,672 feet)
Date: 2001

In the spring of 2001, my objective was the highest mountain in
north Africa, in Morocco, Jebel Toubkal, at 4,167 metres or 13,672
feet. It was my first expedition to a country in North Africa. It
was a solo expedition. Judith and I were staying at a friend's flat
in London: she left for a conference in Geneva, while I headed for
Morocco. I flew from Heathrow. The weather was clear en route;
I had a good view of snow-streaked mountains in northern
Spain, and of Gibraltar. It is extraordinary that it is still not part
of Spain—the inhabitants voted against it. The plane crossed the
green Rif mountains, before flying down the African coast to land

at Casablanca, surrounded by flat coastal plains, heavily farmed. I watched the sunset at 7 p.m. before taking off for Marrakesh. When we landed there 30 minutes later, it was dark.

The airport building was newish, barn-like with a high white ceiling; immigration was smooth, the luggage arrived swiftly and customs inspection was perfunctory. I changed £200 into 3,215 Dirhams. Outside, in the ill-lit car park, I took a taxi, for 80 dirhams despite the Lonely Planet estimate of 50. This was not the time to haggle — no airport bus was in sight. The driver was helpful, in response to my request for a "deuxieme classe hotel"; he took me to a backpackers' hangout in the medina, the old town, which was happily full. We went on to a better establishment, Hotel Islane, strategically placed on the main road opposite the Koutoubia Mosque on Ave. Mohammed V. The receptionist was suspicious and demanded money up front — 300 dirhams. The driver had given me the figure of 2,000 Dirhams a night as the cost of the major hotels and Riads, a traditional Moroccan house or palace with interior courtyard. The room was large and clean, with shower, television and telephone; the only negative was that there was no plug for the basin.

There was a roof-garden bar, and a restaurant offering a fine-looking buffet of mysterious dishes. But I was not hungry; I bought a bottle of Sprite and went for a walk outside. The pavement was very wide, flanked on one side by cafes and bars and on the other by noisy traffic, cars, taxis, buses, motor-cycles and horse-drawn carriages. Over it all towered the steeple of the mosque, floodlit — an unmistakable landmark. Tired, I was back in my room by 11 p.m. local time.

Saturday 28th April
I slept well and was up at 7 a.m. Breakfast was fruit juice, a basket of different breads, butter, apricot jam and coffee. I checked out

at 8 a.m. and was advised that no room was available for my return. I had learnt from Lonely Planet that the cheapest way to get into the mountains was to share a taxi to Asmi, a market town in the foot-hills, and then transfer to a truck to negotiate the rough road up the valley to my destination, Imlil. With luck, the whole trip might take two hours.

A Petit Taxi took me from the hotel to a concourse outside the city walls, a "transport hub" in a field; an obliging young man introduced me to the driver of a large Mercedes "Grand Taxi" that was about to depart for Asmi. I objected that it was already full, with one passenger in front and three veiled women in the back. No problem—I squeezed into the back seat and yet another person joined the passenger in front. For the first 20 minutes, we travelled along a dry, flat plane, the roadside lined with eucalypts, cacti, and olive trees; for the next 40 minutes, we climbed up a narrow valley. The hillside looked very friable; there was much afforestation. The little amount of water in the river suggested reassuringly that the melting of the snow had finished.

At Asmi market, all the others left the taxi. When I enquired about Imlil, the driver offered to take me for only another 150 dirhams. This was good value because the next hour was on a winding, poor quality, road that had been completely washed away at one point; so he had to drive along the stony bed of the river. Imlil turned out to be a small village of a single street, a few small restaurants, and shops, situated on the left bank of the river; it was surrounded by trees and guarded on both sides by towering mountains of bare, rocky, red soil. A rough track led further uphill, through olive groves, to my destination, The Kasbah du Toubkal.

I had struck lucky, thanks to Lonely Planet. The Kasbah had been the summer residence of a Caif, a chieftain, who

had ultimately abandoned it. It had been bought by a British group, who had restored it using entirely Berber methods of construction and materials. There were only two double rooms with en suite bathrooms — and I had one of them. In fact, I was the only guest. At Easter, it had been packed to the rafters with school parties, 65 people, mostly in dormitory-type rooms, some in a tent in the garden. The hotel had been used as the location of a "monastery" in a film about the Dalai Lama called "Kundan", directed by Martin Scorsese. I could see why; the surroundings look like Tibet.

I was introduced to Mohammed, who was to be my guide for the ascent of Jebel Toubkal. He spoke good English and French, and reassured me that there was virtually no snow on the mountains. It had not snowed since December. So much for the trekking organisations to whom I had spoken in London, and Lonely Planet; they all advised that, at the end of April, it would be a "winter ascent" requiring crampons and ice-axes. Following their advice, I had bought a new pair of heavy boots suitable for crampons, crampons, and an ice axe.

Seated at a low table, I lunched in style on the roof terrace, on a carpeted platform. Salad was followed by a spicy tomato omelette, with bread, coffee and water. In the afternoon, I walked back down to Imlil, then up a valley to the west, past terraces of fruit trees, with vegetables growing underneath. On the hillside opposite was a Berber village. It was a straggle of mud-brick and stone dwellings, two- or three-storied, livestock on the ground floor, with a tall minaret marking the mosque. It was hot in the sun when out of the wind. I returned to the Kasbah for tea, a strong sweet mint tea, the staple local drink. By now I had two fellow travellers, from Scotland; they were middle-aged women, married to army officers, who had taken a week off domestic duties and family ties for an exotic holiday in Morocco. They had been planning their itinerary for months. They presented themselves to hotel staff as "cousins", so that there would be no misconceptions about their sharing a room together.

We chatted on the roof till sundown, and it became suddenly cold. We dined together in an area curtained off from the central courtyard. In summer, the courtyard was open to the sky; in winter, it was covered with a Berber tent. Berbers are the original inhabitants of Morocco and north Africa, as opposed to the Arabs who had migrated from the Middle East. It was still cold so a paraffin heater was produced. I was wearing a woollen Jalapa, the local garment, shapeless like a collapsed tent, very warm. Naturally, there was too much to eat — soup, couscous with vegetables and mutton; tasty bread in large, flat, loaves, brought in a wide, round, woven-rush basket covered with a high conical lid; melon and coffee. I was in bed by 9 p.m., leaving the others chatting with members of the staff.

Sunday 29th April

I slept only fitfully after 2 a.m. perhaps because of the altitude effect — 1,800 metres. I was warm and comfortable. It was another beautiful morning, with a cloudless sky; it was a delight to have breakfast on the roof terrace — orange juice, boiled egg, bread, honey and weak tea.

At 8.15 a.m., Judy, the more active of the two ladies, and I set off on a walk up the valley to the east, past the 400-year old hamlet of Tamaret, to the pass above, Tizi du Tamartert, 2,279 metres. It was a gentle climb of two and a half hours up and the same coming down on the road. The lower part of the valley was intensively farmed, with walnut, cherry and apple trees, and cereal grains and vegetables. I noted irises growing in the fields, very pretty but a surprising feature. Later I was told that the bulbs are ground down to make a flour to flavour the Berber baking. There was little water in the river since the snow-melt in March. I was wearing-in my newly-bought climbing boots, comfortable but heavy. Judy was faster uphill in her light trekking boots. Above the fields, there were plantations of pine trees, above the tree line, rocky hillside with a minimal amount of feed for the herds of goats and sheep. Shepherds followed the flocks, shouting or throwing stones to chivvy them on. One objected to us taking photographs, but a small boy carrying a lamb was happy to pose.

From the pass, I could look down on a deep valley similar to that of the Imane River, with its narrow ribbon of greenery close to the water, and arid mountainside above. At the pass, there was a stone refuge and soft drink stall with an attendant Berber man. We had plenty of water and so did not need to buy anything. On our way back, I was concerned to see that the wind had now swung round to the west and was bringing the first clouds I had seen in three days. By the time we reached

the hotel, a cold mist was beginning to sweep up the valley. I showered and changed and took lunch on the roof in my Jalaba; the same meal as yesterday but with a desert of sliced oranges dusted with nutmeg—tasty. I spent the afternoon lying on the roof terrace carpets reading, and watching the clouds build up over the mountains, imagining heavy falls of snow by morning, as at Kilimanjaro. Later, over mint tea, Mohammed reassured me there would not be a problem. He had been guiding for over 10 years; in his mid-thirties, he looked fit. Originally from this area, his father, a local government official, had sent him to study law in Marrakesh. He had not finished the course; he preferred life in the hills. That evening's dinner was equally large, highly spiced with salt, pepper and cumin. I went early to bed, hoping for a good rest before the climb tomorrow.

Monday 30th April

I was up at 6 a.m. and could not see across the valley because of mist. At breakfast, on the terrace, the mist was becoming slightly thinner. We set off at 9 a.m. — Mohammed, a mule and the muleteer/cook called Omar, and myself. The mule was unnamed; the custom of the Berbers was to name only horses and dogs, not other animals. Omar was in his twenties and looking for a wife. He had a high-pitched voice but was bearded — clearly not a glandular condition. A trail led steeply up from the Kasbah to a road, high above a deep defile where the river had cut through the left flank of a glacial moraine. Across the river was Aroumd, a well-to-do Berber village judging from the number of TV satellite dishes on the flat roofs of the stone houses.

Above the defile, the valley widened out, a mass of stones. Before 1995, the valley floor had been covered with fields; but that year the melting snow after a particularly hard winter caused a flood which had covered the fields with millions of tons of stones and gravel. The main factor that caused the flood was deforestation of the mountainsides. Since then, the government has given funding to plant fruit trees and build irrigation ditches. In 1997, it passed a law forbidding the villagers from cutting growing timber. The cedar forests were now beginning to recover. But I could see no chance for tree seedlings to thrive when goats and sheep were free to graze over the mountainside.

Even then in the spring, there was little greenery, and there would be searing heat and no rain for the next four to five months — a grim prospect. The cedars that were growing were stunted by the climate and altitude, and by the previous harvesting of branches. We walked across the valley of stones and up a rough track on the far side, greeting each descending group with a "Bonjour, ca va?" Mohammed and Omar knew nearly all the other guides, so the atmosphere was friendly. At Sidi Chamharouch, 2,310 metres, the mist was still with us, and it was cold. We had been climbing for two hours already. We stopped for mint tea and a plate of rice and vegetables and tinned sardines cooked by Omar; we sheltered in one of the dozen or so stone-built shops/tea-houses. Mohammed told me the stallholders all lived in Aroumd and came up for the day to cater for the trekkers and mountain climbers passing by. The focus of Sidi Chamharouch was the shrine of a sage and healer who used to live there; it was marked by a huge boulder painted white. He used the crystal-clear waters of the stream to cleanse the people of their illnesses. Apparently, strict Muslims disapproved of faith healing, believing that only God can heal. The shops were selling Berber artifacts, hand-woven woollen carpets, prayer mats, leather goods, jewellery, silver, ornately decorated daggers and crystals.

We climbed up from the village round a shoulder of mountain and were finally above the mist. All around were rocky mountain peaks with snow in the shadowed hollows. After two hours of gentle climbing, the valley widened out and, an hour later, we reached the Toubkal Refuge, at 3,106 metres. The building had been put up by the Club Alpine Francais (CAF). It was sturdy with thick stone walls, three dining areas and a kitchen on the ground floor, four dormitories holding continuous rows of two-tier bunks on the first floor, and toilet facilities in the basement. A solar energy array supplied electricity briefly in the evening. Cooking was done by bottled gas; the canisters being carried up by mules. A separate building housed the muleteers. Half a dozen tents were scattered across the valley.

After a stroll around the area, taking a look at the start of the climb for next morning, I went into the refuge for a rest; leather slippers were provided at the entrance. The bunks had mattresses and pillows, and I had the sleeping bag provided by the Kasbah; I was warm and comfortable despite an outside temperature of just above freezing. Supper at 6 p.m. consisted of soup, spaghetti and vegetables, bread and cheese, an orange and tea. I was in bed by 8 p.m. When the phone of the refuge warden rang, I was surprised and delighted to hear it play "Scotland the Brave". There was a great mixture of trekkers; French of course, Germans, a few Brits and a party of 22 Czechs. One group had brought hang-gliders so that they could float down from the summit—much the best way to go.

Monday 1st May

At 5.30 a.m., Mohammed woke me, just as it was getting light. He was keen to start before the sun came on to the western slopes on which we would be climbing. Breakfast was hot chocolate, bread and cheese and an orange. At 6.30 a.m., Mohammed and I started the climb. First, we had to cross the river, easily done at a place below a waterfall close to the refuge, then started the long slow climb up the scree and rock slopes. I carried a light day-pack containing two cameras (slide and film), chocolate, water, and a water/windproof jacket.

The first steep scree slope gave way to a band of rock and then a jumble of rocks; higher still, the valley opened out and was less steep but still rough going. I was feeling the altitude and had to stop frequently; Mohammed waited patiently to go on. The sun came up half an hour before we reached the ridge leading to the summit, but there was a cold wind to keep us cool. The first sight of the summit was across a gap revealing huge cliffs on the eastern face of the mountain. We had to detour round to the west to reach the summit. It was marked by a steel cone on four struts, covered in graffiti, as were some of the surrounding rocks. A few of the party from the Czech Republic had arrived first. We took photos of each other, and the view. There was dust haze, so the horizon was indistinct; even so I could see ranges of mountains receding to the east and west, the plains towards Marrakesh to the north and a tailing off of the mountains as the land fell away to the Sahara Desert in the south. From the edge of the summit plateau I could look down at Imlil. We paused for a rest and food in a shelter formed by a ring of rocks, warm out of the wind and in the sun.

On the way up, we had been passed by some of the Czechs; one had tossed aside an empty can of beer. Mohammed was disgusted, picked up the can, crushed it and handed it back to the man at the summit—to his discomfiture. The climb had taken three hours, within the Lonely Planet estimate. The climb down took another two hours, non-stop travel but slow because of the bad footing. Back at the refuge, I had something to eat with the others and the warden, rested for half an hour and then set off again for Imlil. The walk down was pleasant, in the sun. We stopped at Sidi Chamharouch for a drink. A woman was lying prostrate below the huge white rock wailing; she was trying to drive away evil spirits. One teenager looking after one of the stalls was very keen to sell me something—failing that, to buy my clothing. A good businessperson, he was bright and spoke English, French, Berber, and Arabic.

I stopped further down the track to take pictures of the cedar trees in the hope that I might get one accepted for the *Trees For Life* calendar. We met one English pair climbing up. I was astounded when one of them said: "You must be John". He had been staying at the Kasbah. By the time we reached Imlil, there were shadows on the western flanks of the mountains, reaching across the floor of the valley. Omar was paid 50 dirhams per day for the two-day trip and I gave him the recommended tip of 15 per cent, 15 dirhams. I did not know Mohammed's wage; I gave him 50 dirhams. I had paid 2,000 dirhams to the Discovery Company for the trip—it was worth it.

Tuesday 2nd May

I was awake early to pack my clothes for the trip back to Marrakesh. But no passport in my money pouch — Panic! The nearest British consul was in Casablanca; I could hardly get there and a passport renewal before the weekend and my flight to UK. In an unhappy mood, I breakfasted on the terrace and ran over the possibilities. When the Kasbah office opened. I had the manager, Abdou, call the hotel in Marrakesh, The Islane. The passport was there! What joy! I could only think that I had left it on the counter when I checked out. Much relieved, I walked down to the Kasbah office in Imlil, only to find that it was closed, and that the computer I wished to locate to send an e-mail was back at the Kasbah. Abdou switched on the machine and left me to stumble my way through the very unfamiliar French keyboard; the numerals were above the other symbols, and the letters were all in different sequence to those I had been used to. I sent the message to Judith that my climb had been successful, and I hoped to be back in UK on Friday, not Saturday as originally scheduled.

Luncheon on the terrace was enlivened by the presence of two French couples, just up for the day. They happily ate the last of my chocolate. At 3 p.m., I left the Kasbah and walked down to Imlil to the waiting taxi, as always, a large Mercedes. We stopped only once on the way down, to photograph a camel. The trip cost each of us 140 dirhams. First stop was the Asilane Hotel. The porter recognised me immediately and led me to the reception desk, and my passport. The whole story was more amazing than I had suspected. The driver of the "Petit Taxi" who had picked me up at the hotel had found the passport on the back seat of the car and delivered it back to the hotel! I gave the porter a 100-dirham tip and hoped he would share some of it with the taxi driver.

There was room in the hotel, so I booked for a further two nights. This room was smaller, with again no plug for the basin, and, disturbingly, no glass in the window from the bathroom into the hotel corridor, providing space for a thin and agile intruder. I checked with British Airways in Casablanca—I had a reservation for Saturday, but the Friday flight was full. I could only change my ticket at the airport. There was no British Airways office in town. What to do? I was keen to get back to my son Richard and his partner Kate, for the weekend; on the other hand, two days in Marrakesh could be very interesting. I had deliberately given myself an extra day in the mountains in case of bad weather. At sundown, I went out for a stroll turning left from the hotel, and again left off the Avenue Mohammed V. It was a short road with a small park on the right fronted by a long row of horse-drawn carriages, and, improbably, a Club Med compound on the left. This led right onto the Djemaa el Fna, the main square and centre of social life in the city.

Once I had worked my way through the chaotic traffic at the edge of the square and came to the heart of it, I found an exotic scene—crowds of people milling around, gathering in groups round street entertainers, groups of musicians and singers, storytellers, conjurors, fortune-tellers, and simple fair-ground games, such as trying to put a small ring held on a string from a fishing-rod over the wide neck of a bottle. To one side was a long double row of brightly lit food stands, with people sitting in front of them eating freshly-cooked meals prepared by immaculate-looking chefs in white hats and aprons. As an added attraction, many stalls had rows of skinned and dehorned sheep heads, enough to persuade anyone of the virtues of vegetarianism. I walked back to the hotel and enjoyed a vegetarian pizza and mineral water celebratory dinner on the roof garden overlooking the Koutoubia Mosque. I spent the next day exploring Marrakesh. The day after, I flew back to UK. It had been a great trip.

CHILE–EASTER ISLAND, RAPA NUI, ILHA DE PASCUA

Terevaka
Height: 580 metres
Date: August 31, 2005

In 2005, Judith and I visited one of the most remote and remarkable places on earth—Easter Island in the south-eastern Pacific Ocean. It is 3,500 kilometres off the west coast of Chile, the country to which it belongs. It is most famous for large standing stone statues, known as mo'ai, which were carved between 1100 and 1680 A.D. The indigenous inhabitants, of Polynesian origin, are called Rapa Nui. The first Europeans to reach Easter Island were Dutch explorers in April 1722. Chile annexed the territory in 1888. Our aim was to climb Tereveka, the highest point on Easter Island.

That year, after our summer holiday in U.K., Judith and I decided to return to Hong Kong via the southern hemisphere—Brazil, Chile (Easter Island), Tahiti, New Zealand and Australia. To reach Easter Island, we flew from the Chilean capital of Santiago de Chile. We flew on a new Boeing 767 of the state airline LAN, on the afternoon flight. The only disquieting aspect was the knowledge that we had to fly over 3,700 kilometers of open water, with only two engines to get us to one of the most isolated islands in the world. We both thought of Amelia Earhardt as darkness came and there was not a glimmer of light below. An American, she was the first female aviator to fly solo across the Atlantic, in June 1928. She disappeared on 2 July 1938 on a flight with a navigator over the central Pacific Ocean. So we were very relieved at 8 p.m. when we touched down on time at Easter Island, guided in by the advanced communications set up by the American NASA program, at a time when the landing strip was lengthened to take the Space Shuttle.

Easter Island, Rapa Nui, Isla de Pasqua, is an extraordinary and unique place. It was a place of mystery for everyone from the time the first western explorers found it in the 1720s. Now, after years of expert scrutiny, it is a place whose history is largely understood. But controversy continues as to how the great statues, the mo'ai, were moved from Ranu Raraku where they were quarried to various sites all around the coast. It is thought that many of the trees, palms, on the island were cut down to provide a base for the statues and the logs over which they could be rolled. During three days, we saw enough of the island to get a feel for its past years of prosperity, years of privation, and current return to prosperity. On 31 August, we could have joined a half-day tour to look at cave dwellings and more mo'ai. But we chose instead to ride horses to ascend to the highest point on the island, Mount Terevaka.

At 9.30 a.m., we were picked up in a battered four-wheel-drive car by Pantu, the owner of the horses. He drove us across to the far side of Hanga Roa, to Pikera Uri. There we and another tourist, a young woman from Germany, were introduced to our horses; we were assured that they were quiet. And so they turned out to be, requiring steady encouragement by Pantu's 22-year-old son to move faster than a slow walk. At first, we walked along country roads past patches of eucalypts, acacia and Indian Coral trees and abandoned fields covered by long grasses and scrub guava. This gave way to a larva field, waterlogged and tricky for the horses to navigate. Later we came out onto upland pastures, with cattle grazing on the thick grass. We passed Ahu Akivi, a group of seven restored mo'ai representing the first seven explorers who discovered and settled the island. Small hawks were the only birds to be seen.

Slowly we climbed the gentle slope of the volcano, finally reaching the summit at 580 metres and dismounted to admire the view stretching out in all directions. To the north and west there was the ocean; to the east was rolling grassland leading to the rounded peak of the volcano Poike; to the south was the bulk of the island, rolling countryside pock-marked with lesser volcanic cones and scattered clumps of eucalypt plantations; the capital, Hanga Roa, inconspicuous with its low buildings; and, in the far distance, the bulk of the third volcano, Rano Kau.

On the way back, we passed the crater-lake, Rano Aroi, fringed by totora reeds. From the summit, we had seen a curtain of rain approaching across the sea; we did indeed get drenched by soft warm rain as we rode cross-country through tussocks of long grass on the way back. Without hard hats, we were, as Judith put it, "only a stumble away from a quadriplegia". So we walked the horses all the way back; pack-animals, they were content to amble one behind the other. All the way down my thighs were very painful, so I was most grateful to finally reach base again at 3 p.m. and hardly able to stand for the first five minutes after dismounting. A nearby ahu overlooking Hanga Roa had been restored with five mo'ai re-erected; closer still was a single large mo'ai with his coral eyes replaced — something that never happened after a mo'ai had been toppled by an unfriendly village in historical times.

This was the only peak I 'summited' on horseback.

FRENCH POLYNESIA, TAHITI

Mount Aorai
Height: 2,006 metres
Date: September 7, 2005

From Chile, our next stop was the island of Tahiti and Papeete, capital of French Polynesia in the centre of the Pacific Ocean. The nearest large landmass is Australia, 6,300 kilometres away. Originally settled by Polynesians, it was annexed by France in 1880. My aim was to climb the highest mountain, Orohena, 2,237m (7,339ft).

We arrived at 1am local time, after an eight hour flight. Glasses of Pisco Sour, champagne, and red wine had helped me to sleep for three hours on the flight. Once settled into the Sheraton, just ten minutes from the airport, I slept again till 5.30am.

Breakfast was a delight, a large buffet choice eaten in the

restaurant on a pavilion built on stilts over the coral, with fish swimming underneath just waiting to be fed. Our room was a large suite on the ground floor, very quiet, looking straight out onto the sea.

Morning calls to 'Polynesian Adventures' established that no climbers were going up Orohena, the highest mountain because it was too dangerous in the wet weather.

The second highest, Aorai, was climbable but the guide would only take up groups, not individuals. The low cloud and rain made it impractical anyway on that day. This was disappointing news, but there was still much to enjoy.

In the afternoon we joined a bus tour of the island. The driver and guide was an islander who spoke English in a strange sing-song American accent that we found difficult to understand. '

We set off in bright sunshine which continued while we travelled clockwise round the island on the coast road from Pape'ete in the north-west, sea on our left and precipitous hills covered with dense vegetation on our right. We went into one valley where there were fruit trees of many varieties, and a spectacular waterfall. We were overtaken by heavy rain which persisted for the remainder of the trip, causing us to miss the botanical gardens. We did spend a fascinating hour at the Gauguin museum which gave a very full account of his life in the islands and his art, a constant search for the purity of primitive races. He abandoned Tahiti finding it too altered by French Colonials, ending his days in the Marquesas in 1903 aged 54.

The next day in the morning I walked the 25 minutes into the centre of the city along the Boulevard Pomare. The harbour was busy, dominated by a multi-layered cruise boat like a Christmas cake, towering over catamaran high speed ferries, freighters, French naval ships and pleasure yachts.

The streets too were thronged with shoppers and people just

sitting around.

I bought some picture post-cards, having some difficulty in finding ones without women in lascivious poses, wearing inviting smiles and scanty or non-existent clothing

The only unique local produce was the jewellery featuring black pearls.

At noon we were picked up by a taxi driver, Carl, a very chatty American — Tahitian with an Australian accent, who drove us through Pape'ete and up a narrow winding road through rainforest till we reached our luncheon venue, Le Belvedere, reputed the best restaurant in Tahiti.

The restaurant, at 600m., was nearly a third of the way up the trail to the top of Mount Aorai, 2,006m., a trail I hoped to follow later in the week.

We had a splendid meal of salad, Beef Bourgogne, and a mound of French fries, (Carl had to help us out with the beef and fries), followed by taro ice-cream and coffee.

The view of Pape'ete was intermittently obscured by the low cloud. A disappointment to find that the dry season was just over, and spring rains had begun.

On the way down the hill Carl offered to accompany me three days later to the top of the hill, something he had never done himself.

I retired to bed felling excessively tired and with a sore throat.

3rd September
We had booked a day tour of Moorea. A catamaran ferry took us smoothly across the 10 nautical mile strait to the island. A spectacular scene of jagged volcanic spires clothed with dense vegetation and ringed by pristine beaches. A waiting hire car and driver drove us past the Sofitel beach resort, separate cabins spread out on stilts above crystal clear waters, past Cook Bay

visited by Captain Cook in 1777, and up to the Belvedere Lookout where we watched at the finishing post the Tahiti Motor sports Hill-climb race.

We lunched well and rested on a beach in the afternoon. The trip back to Papeete was against the wind, with seas breaking over the top deck.

Back at the Sheraton hotel we ate supper in the room, and watched the US Open tennis on TV, only French players of course, Mary Pierce, Amelie Mouresmo, and their male counterparts.

The news channel in English, CNN, was 90% about Hurricane Katrina and the devastation in the gulf states.

Not feeling well.

4th September
We spent the day in the hotel, myself resting in bed with flu symptoms, and Judith on her computer.

I called Carl to postpone the following day's climb from Monday to Wednesday.

On TV we watched more French progress at the US Open Tennis, more news of the Katrina disaster, and found a third avenue for TV enjoyment. Judith found a channel dedicated to American Westerns. We watched exciting, and by no means simplistic films of the era of John Wayne, Henry Fonda, Robert Taylor, and others.

5th September
Another rest day, feeling a little better but with no energy to do more than walk around the grounds of the hotel and spend ten minutes on a step machine in the gym.

I watched more tennis, and Judith worked on her books, and in the evening we both watched Westerns

6th September

Despite not feeling 100% well we went on another day trip, to Bora Bora. To get there, 40 miles from Tahiti we flew west past Moorea, stopping first at Huahine, a double island with a coral reef surrounding it, with Bora Bora only a few miles further on. From the air Bora Bora looked very inviting, a small island with a dramatic central volcanic core, Mt Otemanu 727m, surrounded by a coral reef studded with islands, or 'motu', and enclosing a lagoon.

The airstrip was on the most northerly of the reef islands. From there we rode to the main island on a large catamaran ferry: some hotels had their own craft picking up passengers.

At the Viatape boat dock we were met by a minivan to take us round the coast to the Novotel Bora Bora Beach Hotel on the south coast. It was a delightful spot but we did not have long to enjoy it. We only had time for a quick bite of lunch before we were collected to join a lagoon trip, even having to abandon two enormous ice-creams, which, if we had finished them would surely have made us ill.

Another minibus nearly full of holidaymakers was waiting for us at the entrance of the hotel . With them we drove further round the coast to a jetty, boarded another boat and were ferried out to a motu where there was a marine park. Our guide here was a great character, a Frenchman fluent in at least three languages apart from his own, including English and Japanese.

Once we had changed into swimming gear he gave us schnorkel masks and led is into a series of pens where we watched him feed the fish. In the first pen were turtles; then Jack fish and small sharks, Lemon, White tip and Black tip; then tropical reef fish of many brilliant colours and varieties; finally we drifted down the length of the largest enclosure while he fed stingrays, puffer fish, and sharks, 14 of the latter, the biggest being a couple of 7ft. long Lemon sharks. It was somewhat nerve-wracking when the big ones cruised close by. Our guide had reassured us they were completely safe, in daylight.

After our swim we had fruit and drinks in a beach cabana, where he demonstrated how to fold the rectangle of cloth that he wore instead of a bathing suit, a form of dhoti; and how the ladies could make it into a wrap-around garment.

He then drove us at breakneck speed back to the ferry pier so that we could catch our plane back to Tahiti.

It was a great day, and brought home the fact that when people come to French Polynesia, Tahiti is just the transit spot before they get to the real beach-holiday places in the out-islands.

Back at the Sheraton we had a quiet meal in our room and caught up with the tennis and a Western.

7th September

Carl Emery picked me up in his taxi from the Sheraton Hotel at 6.30 a.m. and drove me through heavy traffic in Pape'ete, the capital, to Le Belvedere, the mountain lodge; it was the first step of our climb up Mt. Aorai, the second highest mountain in Tahiti. At 7.15 a.m., we started from Le Belvedere in fine weather, along the well-marked trail, but steep; this required fixed ropes at places to assist when tree roots and branches were not to hand. We worked our way up through the rainforest along the crest of a steep sided ridge, with deep valleys falling away on either side that gave spectacular views of other ridges.

By 9.45 a.m., we had reached the first refuge, at 1,400 metres, a corrugated–iron-roofed square building perched on a narrow ridge; it was big enough to sleep a dozen people on two-tiered metal shelves. Outside was a storage tank with clear fresh running water. On the way up, I had found the going difficult, my legs cramping in a way I had not experienced before; this was probably a consequence of my recent flu infection and being unfit after weeks of travelling. The next segment was even steeper, along a knife-edge ridge with more fixed ropes. Despite a rest at the first refuge, my legs cramped even more, slowing me right down. Carl was still in good shape and keen to go on.

At 11.15 a.m., at a height of 1,700 metres, clouds had swirled up from the valleys, so there was no point to go on just for the view. I would have loved to have reached the top but it was just not possible. To do the climb in one day, I would have had to be fully fit, and to have started climbing from the Belvedere at least an hour earlier. The normal advice is to climb to the first stage in the afternoon and make the final ascent first thing the next day before the cloud rolls in.

We were both disappointed. Carl might have made it to the top at his own speed; he was a fit, 47-year-old Australian and still played rugby. I was disappointed. I could have made it if I had been fit and had a second day to play with—but Judith and I had to leave for Australia early the next morning. At 2.45 p.m., we were back at the Belvedere. I was happy to reach it in one piece, and grateful to be driven back to base camp at the Sheraton Hotel. Overall, the outing was a disappointment—my compensation, in part, was the spectacular scenery

CUBA
Pico Turquino
Height: 1,974 metres (6,476 feet)
Date: November 2010

Judith and I had long wanted to visit Cuba. I had been interested ever since the revolution led by Fidel Castro in 1959. The final spur was an open invitation to come and stay from my cousin George Fleming, who lived there in the winters with his Cuban wife Madelaine. I was not to be disappointed. Havana is a unique city, even without the huge portraits of Fidel and Raul Castro; the time spent living with George in Santiago da Cuba gave us an insight into the way of life in a country that could be very prosperous if not for the USA embargo.

I remember George from Keith junior school—he was a blonde, wee toughie, not an academic student. He was sent to a preparatory school, Wester Elchies, up the Spey River valley;

from there, he went to Gordonstoun, near Lossiemouth. The school had a reputation for being an "Outward Bound" type of institution; it had suited Prince Philip, but not Prince Charles, and was the right place for George. On leaving school, George followed in the footsteps of so many Scots and emigrated to Canada. He joined the Hudson Bay Company and spent his first years with them in the Northern Territories on a fur-trading post. He enjoyed this so much that, when the next promotion meant a job in a city, he resigned. He leased a block of land of about 500 square miles, not far south of the Arctic Circle, and opened "Hatchet Lake Fishing Lodge". With the help of local Indians, he built log cabins on an island on the lake where float-planes could land. When he needed to build an air-strip for bigger planes, he drove a bulldozer cross-country over the snow and ice in late winter, from the nearest road-head hundreds of miles away — an epic journey.

In the 1980s, my family and I stayed there with George and his wife Lana for five days. It was a fabulous place, with comfortable cabins, great fishing and great food. But George's marriage with Lana broke up eventually when she had had enough of the outback. Their son Jeremy was a trained pharmacist working in Calgary.

In the winters, George used to run a ski-slope outside Calgary. He and his partners sold it to the city when it hosted the Winter Olympics in 1988. After that, he wintered in Cuba. He used to contribute to the plane-loads of medicines sent from Canada to Cuba: the USA had banned any supply of their medicines being sent. In 1999, he married Madelaine, a Cuban from a prosperous farm-owning family. They lived in an apartment in Santiago da Cuba, registered in her name because non-Cubans were not allowed to own property.

In 2010, we made our first visit, flying direct on 17th November from Gatwick to Havana on Virgin Atlantic. An elderly driver took us in his very elderly car, gently into the city of Havana 25 kilometers away, and deposited us on a narrow street, with a derelict building on one side and our hotel on the other. The Palacio O'Farrill had recently been restored to its former glory; it was the three-storey former townhouse of a rich Irish sugar trader. Huge entry wooden doors, large enough to let in a coach and horses, led into a central courtyard decorated with bushes and small trees, with tables for dining. We were shown into a large room with a marble floor, high ceiling, high windows with wooden shutters, and a well-equipped en suite bathroom. We arranged for a city tour for the next day.

18th November
At 9 a.m., our guide for the tour arrived—Julien, a 24-year-old woman who had just finished a degree in English at university, accompanied by a car and driver. We drove first to the Capitol, modelled on the Capitol in Washington but taller. It opened in 1929 and was used as the seat of government till 1959. Then it became a museum and government offices; it was a magnificent building dominating the area. Further south in the Vedado district, we drove past the University and stopped at the Plaza de la Revolucion. This was a huge area created for mass demonstrations and parades and dominated by a memorial to Jose Marti, a 458-foot tower with a marble statue of Marti in front. He was a hero of the Cuban war of independence from Spain from 1895 to 1898.

Government buildings, square and unattractive, surrounded the square. The front of the Ministry of the Interior was dominated by a bronze wire portrait of Che Guevara. Another building had a similar portrait of another hero of the revolution. Passing through avenues of an upper class residential district along the Calzada de Zapatawe, we skirted an immense cemetery Necropolis Colon, and drove on to the forest along the banks of the Rio Almendares, its trees burdened with creepers. Nearby, we joined the shoreline freeway, the Malecon; on the seaward side was a popular promenade. We stopped at the Hotel Nacional, built over an old fort overlooking the sea. This grand old hotel was the haunt of pre-revolutionary American Mafiosi like Meyer Lanski, film and sports personalities and heads of states. Nearby was the American embassy: facing it was a large wall decorated with revolutionary slogans.

Back in the old town, Habana Vieja, we walked through the narrow streets, beside buildings that were crumbling and those restored to their previous grandeur and colour. No structures were painted white because of the glare in sunshine. After dark, we dined at La Mina café, in Place de la Armas, with musicians playing nearby. Immense plates of food featured the most delicious lobsters. Amazingly, we found our way back to the hotel despite the dim lighting and scanty road signs to guide us.

Friday 19th November
It was obligatory to inspect a cigar factory. We walked to the Partagas factory housed in an elegant Neo-Classical 19th century building behind the Capitol, having bought entry tickets from the hotel tour agent—only to find there had been an electricity break-down and the factory was closed. We were told that it might open in half an hour and to look at the next-door exhibition of rusting train engines and buses. Back at Partagas, we joined a growing crowd, only to find that the factory was closed for the day. So we teamed up with another couple and took a taxi to a second cigar factory in the Vedado area. Its most famous cigar was Romeo y Julieta, a favourite of Sir Winston Churchill; it made 20 other brands. The factory was nationalised after the

revolution. Manufacture of Romeo y Julieta cigars continued in Puerto Rico under the USA Altaldis tobacco company.

Happily, our tickets were accepted and we joined a tour group behind an English-speaking guide. He was a young man who had recently left university with a degree in mineral engineering. He was scornful of the fact that his earnings as an engineer would have been less than what he earned in tips as a tour guide. We saw the sorting of the tobacco leaves, their wrapping into cigars and packing into boxes. The job was done by ranks of workers who were entertained by music, or story-telling broadcasts. They worked eight hours a day and had a daily quota. We took a taxi back to the hotel, had lunch, and then transferred our belongings from one large room to one even more palatial, a suite. It measured about 1,000 square yards, larger than most flats in Hong Kong.

In the afternoon, we were off again with our guide to examine the city support services, and restoration of the Habana City by the "City Historian Department". The department was funded by the government until the collapse of the Soviet Union in 1991. Since then, it had been self-financed, through restored buildings being turned into hotels which paid a percentage of their profits back to the department. We visited a women's Co-op where elderly ladies did needlework, crocheting and embroidery, dolls and shawls. Judith bought two shawls. A large convent housed an old people's day care centre, full of activity—discussion groups, dancing and physiotherapy. Other facilities were a home for abused or abandoned children, and an antenatal clinic with residential nursing. Clearly, the government was trying hard to have an inclusive system from cradle to grave, all free of charge. Tired, we dined in the hotel and were entertained by an excellent trio of a guitarist, drummer and xylophonist—a most unusual combination.

Saturday 20th November

At 10.15 a.m., Julien and her driver came to the hotel, as arranged, to take us on a castle tour. First stop was a section of the old city wall, built from 1674-1734, and the gate to the railway. Other gates at Place des Armas led to two main streets, Obispo and O'Reilly, running right through the old city to gates at what is now Central Square. We drove round the inland old city walls to the old Presidential palace, now the Museum of the Revolution; we saw beside it a tank used by Fidel Castro during the Bay of Pigs invasion in 1962.

A tunnel under the harbour entrance took us to the El Morro castle and lighthouse. The castle was captured after a 44-day siege by the British in 1762; this led to the building of an even bigger fortress, Fortaleza De San Carlos De la Cabana, the most expensive fortress in Latin America. Havana was not attacked again until the Spanish-American war in 1898. We lunched back at the hotel. In the afternoon, I walked along the waterfront from the Castillo De San Salvador at the narrow entrance to the harbour back to Plaza Des Armas. Many people were promenading; some were fishing in the dirty-looking water. A statue of Admiral Pierre D'Iberville (1661-1706) commemorated noble service for the French King Louis XIV. Children were riding small ponies round one of the parks. Rows of old cannons lined the site of the previous city wall outside the Cathedral Seminary. At the Castillo De La Real Fuerza, a draw-bridge led over the water-filled moat, with a pile of turtle shells gathered below. Waiting for rides were horse-drawn carriages, bicycle "Bitaxis", and yellow egg taxis motorised, for two passengers and a driver.

In the evening, Judith and I ventured out to try and find a Wi-Fi location for her computer. We first went along to the Florida Hotel on Calle Obispo, a highly ornate establishment fully restored to its former glory. Here a shady man led us upstairs to a shack on the roof where computers were ready for use, but not people's own ones. We were re-directed to Parque Central and the Hotel Inglaterra, and then to the Hotel Parque Central, much the most modern we had seen. Here there was secure but slow Wi-Fi in the lobby lounge; so Judith worked for an hour, while I went to sleep. It cost eight convertible pesos, known as CUC; it was one of two official currencies, along with the peso. Walking back to our hotel, we took a direct route along poorly lit, narrow back streets, frightening despite our knowledge that Cuba was a very safe place. We were glad to get back to Palacio O'Farrill. We were the only two people eating in the hotel, so had the musical trio to ourselves.

Sunday 21 November
We were up at 4.15 am, in a taxi and on our way to the airport at 5 a.m. Half of our trip along potholed roads was largely free of traffic; little groups of people waited at bus stops or for lifts. The domestic terminal was clean, with plenty of seating but basic facilities. Check-in for our flight to Santiago took an hour. Our flight on Cubana CU684 was on a Yak 420 made in Russia. The other airline flying to Santiago, Aerocaribbean, had lost a plane just two weeks before. Our 90-minute flight took us along the south coast of Cuba. The stewardess gave us a choice of coffee or soft drink or water, and a sweet to suck on descent. She was efficient but unsmiling, possibly doubling as an air marshal.

Cousin George Fleming met us at the airport. He had no car, so we took a taxi to a two-storey house; the second floor was designed and owned by Madelaine (Made). The ground floor belonged to someone else As a foreigner, George could not own a house. Cubans could only own one house. Houses in Cuba could not be bought or sold, but could be swapped between consenting owners. Cubans who chose to leave after the revolution lost their houses to the government; it handed them on to people of their choice.

Accessed by an outside staircase, the flat was comfortable; it had a living room, dining room and kitchen without intervening doors, two bedrooms, one en-suite, and a second bathroom. On the roof was a store-washroom which could double as a bedroom with bathroom, two cages with three love-birds, clothes lines and garden chairs shaded by corrugated plastic sheets on an iron support. A painter was completing the annual smartening-up traditionally done before New Year.

After settling-in, we and a neighbour, Kiki, walked round to the Melia Hotel just five minutes away, a modern glass and steel structure, where there was a taxi rank boasting a selection of ancient American cars that could comfortably take six passengers, and more modern taxis taking four. We were driven to the centre of town and Park Cespedes, to the Hotel Casa Grande, which had been frequented in the past by British author Graham Greene. We lunched at the roof-top restaurant; it was sparsely attended because the lift was out of order. For the most venerable and famous hotel in the city, the garb of the waitress was disappointing—jeans and a blouse. The scanty menu offered salad, fish and chips, chicken, ham and cheese sandwich. The food was tasty and the view was better.

I could see over the city to the harbour; immediately below us was the Park Cespedes and major buildings around it. Dominating the square was the cathedral first built in 1522 and much rebuilt since then; facing it was the city hall, Ayuntamiento, from the balcony of which Fidel Castro made a victory speech; to one side was the house of the founder of the city, Diego Velazquez, built in 1516-1530; and opposite was the Casa de la Cultura, an ornate bright pink 1919 building. We walked back to the flat. Apart from the buildings around the central square, the rest were undistinguished and dilapidated.

Monday 22 November
After breakfast, we walked round to the Melia, changed more than £500 into Cuban pesos, and hired a taxi for the day. It was a lumbering old American car built in 1952; the suspension was shot but it had a new engine, according to the driver. We had to register our stay with a local family; first, we bought the necessary stamps at a Bank on Parque Cespedes, then went down to the harbour-front Immigration office where, after a long wait and a fruitless discussion with an official, we were told we had to return the next day. Madelaine told us that it had taken her five visits to register her last guest. Our conclusion was that, in applying for a visa, it was better not to mention any personal accommodation. Many people legally ran Bed-and-Breakfast homes. They had to register, so that income can be checked, and quality of accommodation monitored.

For a good view and lunch, we drove to the top of the range of hills inland of Santiago. But the restaurant was closed on a Monday, another frustration. On the way down, we stopped at a little road-side café, Los Lapas; there we had an excellent meal of chicken, pork, plantains, tomatoes, rice, chips, beer and water for 99 pesos, equivalent to 4 CUCs. Madelaine negotiated and bought eggs from the café owner before we left—much of the economy relied on an informal and barter system.

This is how the locals can survive on their meagre salaries. Horses were the main form of transport. Back at the house, we were joined by Dr. Carlos Espinez Odio; it was through his computer that we had been communicating with Made and George. Officially, only people with business needs can use the Internet. For his help, we gave him an anti-smoking watch from COSH Hong Kong, and an anti-smoking DVD in Spanish. Carlos was about 50, talkative in good English and opinionated; he was critical of the fact that he and his wife, both doctors, earned 25 pesos — equivalent to US$25 — monthly, less than the earnings of people who catered to tourists and received tips in CUCs. He owned a bicycle and borrowed George's when he could. Cuba had two currencies. Cubans were paid in National Pesos, CUP, with which they could buy heavily subsidised food at government stores. The peso could not be exchanged for foreign money. The second currency was the convertible peso, known as CUCs, which could be exchanged. When non-Cubans arrived on the island, they changed their foreign currency into CUCs.

Later Judith and I went round to the Melia for Judith to log in on their lounge Wi-Fi. Transmission was slow because of the number of other users. A cappuccino and cup of tea cost 4CUC. Supper at home was delicious, cooked by Madelaine. Apparently, George did nothing around the house.

Tuesday 23 November
From 8-9 a.m., Judith was back at the Melia with her computer, and a faster Wi-Fi connection, as she was the only one there. Back at the Immigration office, after an appropriate wait, we were told that the papers were not yet ready and that we should wait for a phone call; but there was no problem. We all returned to the flat, dropped off Madelaine, and George continued with us to head east to Bacanoa Country Park east of Santiago. He was very keen to visit an Artist Village where he had bought pictures previously. The village was a group of government-built houses in a pleasant, wooded valley off the main road. Each artist had his or her own house. We visited three artists and one potter. Rene Lopez, bearded, rotund and a powerful personality, had painted the picture in George's sitting-room. He showed us a reclining nude that Madelaine fancied for their bedroom. George

bought a drawing from a second painter, thin, tense, and serious in contrast to Lopez. We bought an earthenware flower-pot with native Tainu decoration. There were other striking pieces but they were too heavy to take back to Hong Kong. On our way back, we passed through an area of the park, Val de la Prehistoria, which had life-sized "elephants" and "dinosaurs" roaming the hills.

A side trip took us up La Gran Piedra, a 4,048-foot mountain in the coastal range topped by an enormous rock. At the road-end, we got out of the car and climbed the 452 steps to the summit, enjoying a splendid view from the top. Training to get fit, George had often climbed the mountain on foot; he also had done long bike rides. On the way down the mountain, we stopped to buy bananas and oranges from villagers.

Back at the flat, Madelaine's mother was visiting; she was a stocky, self-confident person. That evening Carlos brought in his 11-year-old daughter, Lulu, to play for us on the violin. She played well and with aplomb. Her elder sister, aged 15, was in Havana on a scholarship at music school learning clarinet. After supper, Madelaine's brother, a hairdresser and masseur, and his son came in for a chat. Kiki was in and out, building a tree in the roof garden, mending a chandelier and doing other odd jobs for which he was paid in meals. This was one of the remarkable things about staying—friends dropped in without warning at any time.

Wednesday 24 Nov.
Breakfast prepared by Madelaine was porridge, yoghurt, green tea and fruit that Kiki helped to prepare. Kiki's habit was to go to bed early, get up at 2 a.m. and watch television. That morning he came round to our house early to have breakfast and continue with his project of making a faux tree on the roof. Madelaine had a female friend whose sister was married to a driver named

Humberto. He agreed to drive us for the next few days. This was how business was done in Cuba, through personal contacts.

That day we—George, Madelaine, Judith and I—set off with Humberto in his 4WD car to El Cobre cathedral, 20 kms west in the foothills. This was the most famous church in Cuba, visited by Pope John Paul II in 1998. It was built to house a relic, a figure of a virgin brought from Spain in 1611. The present Basilica was built in 1925. The road to the church was lined by vendors selling flowers and religious trinkets. Inside the entrance were display cases holding offerings, a bizarre collection of personal items and medals, including Hemingway's Nobel Prize for literature. Upstairs a glass case contained the tiny figure of the virgin image dressed in a yellow gown and festooned with jewels. Bouquets of flowers, mostly sunflowers, surrounded the altar. In front stood a middle-aged woman preaching a sermon to a gathering of around 30 pilgrims. The shrine was holy to Catholics and followers of the Santeria religion, an amalgam of African and Catholic practices.

Our next stop was the Castillo del Morro, an imposing castle commanding the narrow entrance to the harbour of Santiago. Built between 1638 and 1700, it was designed to keep off pirates that had already devastated the early city, founded by Velazquez in 1516. It overlooked a naval battle between USA and Spain in 1898, convincingly won by the Americans. We lunched at a restaurant just outside the castle and bought two carved wooden figurines, Giacometti-like figures. After an afternoon siesta, Judith and I went to the Melia Hotel for Wi-Fi. George joined us later; he was well known to the barman, receptionist and the taxi drivers outside. Supper with George and Madelaine was enhanced by a huge chocolate cake made by Kiki's mother.

Thursday 25th November

At 8.30 a.m., Judith, George, Madelaine and I climbed into Humberto's taxi for an overnight stay at Baracoa. It was the first point of call for Christopher Columbus in 1492; he described it in enthusiastic terms. In 1515, Velazquez founded the first Spanish settlement there. When Santiago was declared the capital of Cuba, the town of Baracoa faded in importance. It continued as a small fishing and farming community but cut off from the rest of the country by steep mountains, until a road was pushed through in the 1960s.

From Santiago, our route ran through agricultural country — sugar, vegetables, orchards and corn. The road surface was poor and traffic slow apart from the intercity buses — made in Japan — that thundered past, ignoring the potholes. We passed through Guantanamo town — close to but not to be confused with, the U.S. base of Guantanamo, permanently leased by USA from Cuba since 1903. Humberto pointed out a large lake in the valley above the American base, off limits without a permit. It was capable of flooding the base if the flood gates of the reservoir dam were opened. Our car was stopped by police who checked our driver's license — a politically sensitive area for sure. The road came down to the coast at San Antonio del Sur, running along the shore on one of a series of larva flow terraces. The country was arid, in the rain shadow of the mountains.

https://en.wikipedia.org/wiki/Guantanamo_Bay_Naval_Base

The road up over the mountains, La Farola, was paved in concrete; it wound up through increasingly thickly wooded and steep valleys. At the summit, we stopped to buy oranges from a roadside stall. We also bought Cucuchina, a sticky concoction of coconut, sugar and honey in a cone made from palm leaves. It tasted very sweet — the ultimate high-energy food. Coming down the seaward, windward side of the mountains, the greenery became lusher with many fruit trees and fields of vegetables, giving way to the considerable town of Baracoa on the coastline. The drive had taken five hours, uncomfortably for me sitting on the ridge in the centre of the back seat. George always sat in the front, because, after a knee replacement, he needed the legroom.

The town was very dilapidated, with many buildings old, unpainted and falling down. The smart ones were usually officially registered Bed and Breakfast houses, marked by a sign over the door like an anchor. The roads were full of water-filled potholes where new pipes had been laid, but no resurfacing carried out. We drove up a ridge at the back of the town to the Hotel del Castillo — as the name suggests, previously a fortress. It was comfortable, airy, with a swimming pool and spacious restaurant and the inevitable trio of guitar-playing minstrels. After a short rest, we all went out to explore the town. First objective was a Tainu (pre-Spanish), burial site. With help from villagers as to location, we found it up a path hung with washing and climbing up between little shacks. The caves were dimly lit, showing a number of Tainu artifacts, including a copy of the 3,000-year-old statue of their God of Tobacco, and a skeleton lying on its side in the foetal position in a grave.

Back in the town centre, we looked at the cathedral, ruined; walked through the art museum admiring wonderful wooden sculptures; then sat on the sea wall outside L Rusa Hotel, watching the waves pounding on the coral. The hotel was started by a Russian princess who had escaped from the revolution in Russia and lived long enough to support Fidel Castro and his revolution against Batista. We returned to the hotel to dine and an early night. The lights failed three times.

JOHN MACKAY

Friday 26th November.

At 6.30 a.m., I was up and out of the hotel, just missing the sunrise. I walked to the tip of the peninsula and inspected the Fuerte de la Punta, built by the Spaniards in 1803 to guard the entrance to the harbour. Over the years, the surrounding ground had been filled in, so that the walls were now only two feet high and the gun ports empty. Inside was a restaurant. I walked back from the peninsula and round to the old town by the sandy beach of the bay. Houses by the beach were of wood, small shacks; a slow stream spilled dirty water into the sea. Two-storey and smarter houses with intricate metal grills lined the main street; it was again a mass of holes from the work on the water mains.

I was back in time for breakfast with the others at 8 a.m. Humberto was ready to take us to see Hotel Porto Santo, which boasted a replica of the image of Black Virgin. It was on the other side of the bay, pleasantly situated above the sea, amidst palm trees. To get there, we passed a famous chocolate factory; Judith bought many bars for presents. Back at the hotel, Judith and I had a swim in the pool and chatted to an Englishman. He was spending two months exploring Cuba, travelling by bus and usually staying at B&Bs: Spanish-language skills had been a help. The others were keen to get back on the road; Madelaine had been to Baracoa several times already.

We took five hours to get back, stopping in the mountains to buy yams, plantains and oranges from Humberto's farmer friends and buy great bunches of bananas down on the plains. The back of the car was loaded by the time we had finished our purchases. The cost of the driver was 300 CUC Pesos. The intercity bus would have cost 30 pesos each for the return trip. Back in time for tea, I indulged in a large helping of chocolate cake. That evening we had Cuba's staple meal of ham and cheese sandwiches. Kiki came in carrying yet another cake made by his mother, a sponge covered in pink icing. We watched Al Jazeera TV, a documentary about Beirut during the war and the bombing of the Al Jazeera office by the Americans, killing their senior reporter.

Saturday 27th November
Judith spent the morning at the Melia Hotel on her computer. She was getting to know some of the other regulars — medical students from Barbados and Angola, with their fees and accommodation covered by the Cuban government. I helped Kiki fit an awning onto the roof laundry house, so that Madelaine would not get burnt by the morning sun. He was a great handyman. Trained as an engineer, he had to retire early with Parkinson's disease, but kept the disease under control with medication. He also may have had overexposure to lead, causing Wilson's disease.

Kiki stayed for lunch; this seemed to be the way people lived in Cuba, with payment not in money but by meals or bartered goods. Madelaine was a good cook. We ate plantain chips, tomatoes, avocados and pork. Judith insisted on washing-up. Dr Carlos cycled round at 6 p.m. for a chat and stayed till 8 p.m. and supper. A great talker, he was keen to improve his English. His wife was also a doctor, but the two could not afford a car, with monthly earning of 25 CUC Pesos each. He complained about the U.S. embargo on pharmaceuticals, many of which they now make in Cuba, and embargo on surgical instruments. Each year when Cuba asked the United Nations to vote on the U.S. embargo, it supplied a list of the names of children who had died because of a lack of surgical instruments. In 2009, only USA, Israel and Palau voted to maintain the embargo. Parcel mail was often not delivered, so philanthropists like a Mr and Mrs. Beach from England brought in computers, school books and ink.

Sunday 28th November

I slept badly being disturbed by farmyard noises next door, cocks crowing, and the cold. At 6.30 a.m., Judith and I were up for an early breakfast before being taken to the airport for Judith's departure, sadly, to attend a Bloomberg conference in New York. The taxi was an Audi, the first one I had seen in Cuba. It took only 15 minutes to get to the airport, close to the Castillo del Moro. Judith had the horrid prospect of flying to Havana, waiting seven hours for a nine-hour flight to London Gatwick; then transfer to Heathrow and a nine-hour flight to New York. It is the only time she crossed the Atlantic twice in a single day.

Washington did not allow direct flights between the U.S. and Cuba, apart from charter flights to and from the Guantanamo enclave. After the conference, Judith flew to San Francisco and finally to Hong Kong.

Back at the house, an old man with two women came to the door carrying something in a sack. I took him to be another hawker but it turned out that he was Madelaine's father bearing a gift of oranges. He had a large fruit farm near the farm of Angel Castro, the father of Fidel. Madelaine's father had two children from his first marriage—Made was one—and a daughter aged 29 from his second marriage, married to an architect and with a young son. Later Made told me that it was believed Fidel and Raul Castro had different fathers; Raul's father was a Chinese merchant. He certainly looked very different to his elder brother—smaller and slightly oriental. The mother of both had been Angel Castro's Cuban housekeeper; she was not married to him when she bore Fidel.

Kiki came in to put up the awning, so I helped him fix it in place. As usual, Madelaine was in her night dress and answering the phone in the kitchen. She and George had returned to Cuba only shortly before Judith and me, so she had a lot of catching up to do. There were three love-birds in the roof house; one escaped, but came back in again at feeding time. The cages were too small and George would have preferred to set them free.

Monday 29th November
I had a poor night's sleep, after being kept awake until after midnight by a party in the house next door. The master of ceremonies used a megaphone to guide the singers and band. After breakfast, Madelaine prepared food for us; then she departed for Holguin, where her father had a farm. At 1 p.m., Humberto arrived with his four-wheel-drive taxi for the three-hour journey to Santo Domingo, starting point for the ascent of Pico Turquino.

We set off inland on a major dual carriageway; it led through the Sierra Madre mountains and on to rolling planes further north. It was farming country — sugarcane, bananas and cattle ranches; we went through Palme Soriano, Contramaestra and on to Bayamo. This was a prosperous town with wide avenues and substantial houses, which had been founded by Diego Valezquez de Cuellar in 1516. It had been a hot bed of revolutionary activity against the Spaniards. The main roads were well maintained but the secondary roads were full of potholes and gaps between strips of tarmac. A driver had to be on the alert to avoid disaster. Turning south again, we passed through Bartolome Maso and then climbed into the hills; we came to Santo Domingo, a small village at the bottom of a steep-sided valley heavy with trees. We were welcomed by the manager of the hotel and shown to a cabin simply furnished with two beds and bathroom/toilet.

On our way to the National Park warden's office, we were conned into dining at a "paladares", a privately run restaurant presumably run by a friend of his. It was an attractive spot, with the dining area beneath a roof of flowering ipenema. The only disadvantage was the stepping stones we had to use to cross the river, about 30 yards wide, to reach the restaurant. It was all very well in daylight; but, after the meal, in the dark with only a dim light on the riverbank, it was a real trial to get across. Thank goodness I had a torch.

Tuesday 30th November

George had nearly made it to the summit a year before, climbing from the seaward side; it was a hard steep climb from sea-level to 6,578 feet. It was possible to do a one-day ascent and descent by that route, but there is no refuge to stay in overnight if caught short. From Santo Domingo, it was 13 kilometres to the summit and there is a refuge at nine kilometres, so we chose that route. During the previous year, George had been seriously ill and was not back to his usual fitness; he was undecided whether or not just to make it a day trip or to try to overnight at the refuge. In the end, he decided to come with me to the refuge. Our guide Manuele, a student of Social Sciences, spoke good English and was well informed about plants and birds. We did not see any animals, apart from small lizards.

The first step was easy, in Humberto's taxi up an extremely steep hill to Alto de Naranja at 950 metres. From then on, for the next six hours, it was a pleasant walk through a well-maintained trail along ridges and through forest, interrupted by steep ascents and steep descents. We gradually gained height and ever-closer views of the rounded tree-covered summit of the mountain. We passed by the camp where, in 1956, Fidel Castro and his 20 or so comrades hid from the forces of President Fulgencio Batista.

By the time that we reached the refuge on Pico Joachin, it was near 1 p.m. and too late to attempt the final 10-kilometer climb to the summit and back. George had struggled to keep going; he showed enormous determination. The refuge, Aguada del

Joaquin, was essentially a base for the National Park workers; it was a wooden barn containing 10 two-decker beds with mattresses for trekkers. A single bulb was controlled from the kitchen block 20 metres away; fresh water was available at a kitchen tap; a dunny was down the hill. Solar panels helped with the lighting; supplies were carried up by mules. We ate at 6 p.m. — pasta and a weak meat sauce, tea and an unpleasant tasting piece of cake. It was cold and George did not have any warm gear; I lent him a thermal vest, while I used an aluminium foil sleeping bag which unfolded from a packet about 4 x 2 x 2 inches. It was warm but there was no aeration, so it was sweaty. We were the only occupants of the barn.

Wednesday 1st December
I was glad to see the dawn at 5.45 a.m. and get up after an uncomfortable night. Breakfast was "tea", an infusion of leaves picked off a nearby citrus tree, plantain chips and the same horrid cake. George decided to return to the hotel at Santo Domingo, with a guide. It was clear to both of us that, if he went to the summit with me, we would not be able to get back to the Park entrance at Santo Domingo before dark. He turned back with regret, but happy with the hope that, before long, he would be fit enough to make the climb. Friends from Canada were coming to stay in January; he was resolved to try again then.

Miguele and I set off on the final five kilometers and 4,482 feet. The first part of the climb was the toughest — a long, steep section of natural and artificial steps leading to the top of Pico Juaquin. After that there were smaller climbs and descents, and level stretches, all through thick forest, with occasional glimpses of the ever-widening view. After just under three hours of climbing, we reached the summit, a clearing about 50 yards in diameter. In the centre was a high, stone plinth with the bronze bust of Jose Marti, considered the father of Cuba's struggle for independence from Spain. Wooden boards announced the summit height—1,974 metres. Views from the summit were blocked by the trees, but a fine viewpoint at the start of the descent allowed me to see east along the coast, and north over the Sierra Madre to the plains.

Five hours after setting out, we were back at the refuge. I was tired but otherwise in good shape. I met a large group of youngish climbers who had just walked into the refuge, all from Germany. No tourists were allowed from USA. After lunch, they were heading for the summit and returning to the camp—a long day for them. I felt for them, especially as the summit was likely to be in cloud by afternoon. After a 30-minute rest at the refuge and a plate of pasta and bottle of an energy drink, I was ready at noon for the trek back to base. We made good speed. In just over four hours, we were at the car park at Alto de Noranga, waiting for the taxi. We had stopped during the day to identify birds, spotting 14 varieties.

I lay down to rest my foot—very sore—and was intrigued to have vultures circling around. Humberto arrived after 20 minutes and took us carefully down the steep hill, strewn with boulders, to the Santo Domingo hotel, where George was waiting for me. The drive back to Santiago in the dark was memorable for the potholes, the lack of lights on bicycles and vehicles drawn by horses or oxen, the lack of signposts, and the hitchhikers by the roadside that we had to disappoint. A police traffic inspector flagged down Humberto to examine his papers, much to his annoyance.

We arrived back at Madelaine's house at 9 p.m. to find her entertaining family. I was too tired to accept any of the supper on offer. Heavy rain had fallen on Santiago in the afternoon and had begun to fall on Santo Domingo by the time we had left. We had been lucky. I thought of the trekkers at the refuge sleeping in the barn with the corrugated iron roof, full of holes. George never made the climb. Nine months later, he died of the chronic debilitating neuropathy that he had been battling for years. He was a wonderful, kind, strong character, enterprising, hardworking, and a friend to all who knew him.

Thursday 2nd December.

I slept well. I breakfasted well too, on Cuban fruit, mango, papaya, pineapple, and Malanga, a fruit only grown here; it had a hard green skin and soft orange pulp and was very tasty. All was accompanied by delicious Baracoa coffee. While Madelaine washed the clothes, I cleaned my climbing boots and sticks. Looking through my pictures, I realised with embarrassment that there were none of George. He was in bed with a bout of gastroenteritis — poor chap. For the rest of the morning, I read Cuban history from the Lonely Planet and Eyewitness Travel Guides. It was an interesting story of how the initial Spanish settlers took over the island at the expense of the Tainu and decimated them with warfare, disease, and overwork. Then the Settlers turned on Spain and fought for their own freedom. Next came the American intervention in 1898, a banana republic democracy taken advantage of by American business, and lastly the Castro revolution of 1953-58, followed by the struggle for self-sufficiency despite the American embargo.

Dr Carlos came in for lunch and to repair Madelaine's computer; he stayed on to talk about the economy. Most people were living a subsistence existence, with no bank savings. The population boom was in the 1960s and 70s with only a slight increase since then; many couples opted not to have children. The population was ageing, with 37 per cent over 60. Credit cards were not used. Unable to afford ink, Dr Carlos had his own formula for making it. Pens cost CUC 1 each. He claimed his ancestry went back to a

"Pedro" of 16th century Spain. Like him, most white Cubans had Negro blood. As a doctor, he had seen blonde, blue-eyed Cubans with sickle cell anaemia—an African disease.

Kiki came in with a ham which he cut up in the kitchen and proceeded to eat with us at supper. He had been up early to catch a bus to Bacanoa Park to go fishing; he had fished from 6 a.m. to 7 a.m. but caught nothing. As he got up to go home, he suddenly began to shake and was unable to shuffle along, a typical Parkinson sufferer. He lay down for a short while giving his pills time to act, and he was all right again. George was still suffering from enteritis. On examination, I found abdominal tenderness but no guarding, and scarring from a previous operation. I retired to bed early, and watched a film in Spanish about Che Guavera, doctor revolutionary, soldier and statesman. It ended anti-climactically in Bolivia with a failed revolution.

Friday 3rd December.
Dr. Carlos was in again, for breakfast, and to repair a puncture in the tyre of a bicycle he had borrowed from Madelaine. He was incensed by the fact that 60 Cuban doctors were the first to arrive in Haiti after its devastating earthquake. They saw 80 per cent of the patients, while the Americans arrived with their grand hospital ship and saw 15 patients per day and the US Army took over control. The Cuban effort was never publicised. George was still unwell with enteritis.

I walked into town, keen to roam around on my own and take photographs. From Calle K, I walked via Avenue Victoriano Garcon and Avenida de Los Libertadores, passing old houses most in disrepair, others smart and splendid examples of Spanish colonial architecture. There was one row of smartly maintained wooden houses close to the old Moncada Barracks, now a school. At Antiguo Cuartel, bullet holes showed where

Fidel Castro made his first attempt at revolution. At the top of the hill was the Park Historico Abel Santamaria, dominated by a tall concrete square tower with faces of revolutionary heroes embossed on the four sides. Further on were old buildings; one was a school, the others were crumbling. At the Playa de Marti, a memorial to Marti was surrounded by a pleasant tree-shaded park. The painted front of the Pateo dos los Abuelos stood out, with a restaurant and centre of music.

A band of musicians was lounging around a park bench; when they saw me with a camera, they picked up their instruments and gave me a tune. A drunken, elderly and dishevelled onion-seller jumped in front of the band and started dancing. I took photos, dropped money into their collection box and moved on. The Jose A Saco Street, a pedestrian precinct, had reputedly the best shopping in Santiago. It did not impress. A bread shop was doing good business and a single department store, the Pan American, was busy. In the rest of the little shops, nothing exciting was on show. On the left going downhill, I passed the Sala Concerto Dolores, a church converted into a concert hall. The Plaza Dolores was another pleasantly tree-shaded square with an outdoor restaurant, one part for tourists, the other for locals; both were busy. Surrounding the square were ancient two storey buildings with iron grills round their balconies.

The Museo Emilio Bacardi was housed in a splendidly restored building; formerly the headquarters of the Bacardi empire, it was abandoned after Castro took over. I was shown round its extensive collection of artifacts from the times of the first settlers, from thousands of years ago until the recent Castro revolution. Grim evidence of slavery were great iron shackles for the neck with hooks, and ankle shackles, as well as execution axe, whip and foot stocks. More unexpected items were an Egyptian Mummy, a desiccated Peruvian mummy and a shrunken head with instructions as to how to make it. Upstairs was an art exhibition. My guide was a tall, young and athletic man whose forbears had been African slaves in Haiti. He spoke excellent English and told me he also spoke Dutch, and, of course, Spanish. When I told him I had just climbed Pico Turquino, he said he was "astonished". He had climbed it when he was 13 and resolved never to do it again. I walked on down the main street Jose Maria Heredia, heavy with traffic; the pavement was lined by stalls selling wood carvings, musical instruments and leather goods. A band was playing at the Casa de la Trova. Every town had a similar place for performers. I paused to watch and listen through the barred windows to the lively music. The audience filled the available tables inside.

At the cathedral, Iglesias Catedral de la Ascension, I went into the museum. It showed portraits of all the previous Bishops, statues of holy figures, two biblical scenes made out of rice, ornate clerical robes, Jesus bleeding on a number of crosses, and a library of leather-bound books degenerating in the non-air-conditioned air. Inside, the cathedral was a gloomy place, unusual with five aisles. There was no glittering of heavy gold ornaments. Over the preceding centuries, pirates had pillaged the place several times. A block away from the cathedral, I stood on the Balcon de Valezquez looking out over the old town, the Tivoli area, towards the harbour and the mountains behind to the west. This area was more run down than the rest. Tram tracks, unused for fifty years were still embedded in some roads.

By now tired and thirsty, I returned to the Park Cespedes, the Hotel Casa Grande and the roof-top balcony restaurant. Since the lift was still not working, the restaurant was still nearly empty. A glass of lemonade tasted very good. Revived, I went across the street to listen again to the music at Casa de la Trova, then slowly walked back to Calle K. My overall impression was that the buildings of Santiago were 90 per cent decrepit, five per cent beautifully restored and five per cent ugly modern blocks of flats or offices. George was still resting. At 5.30 p.m., Judith phoned from New York to say that all was well. At 7 p.m., neighbours dropped in, as seemed to be usual there. After supper, I retired to bed and read a scary book called "American Fascists" by an American author, a diatribe against the far-right Evangelicals.

Saturday 4th December
Kiki and his mother arrived while we were eating breakfast. Kiki was celebrating his 45th birthday. He had come round to assemble and erect a new aerial for the TV. We all went out with Kiki for the 10-minute walk to his house, situated on the corner near the university in a nice residential district. It had two floors with a garage. The garage had been converted into a workshop with every kind of equipment. Everything in the living room had been made by him—table, chairs, light stand, placards on the walls, and an ingenious waterfall down one wall. The walls of the hall had been painted, as well as the dining room, colourful and inventive. When he had lost his job, he had for a while rented out rooms. But later he did not and so felt able to indulge his passion for invention.

Kiki's mother's house was in the next road, also a large two-storey structure. We sat in her living room and chatted. On the walls were two Chinese needlework pictures, wedding presents from 52 years before. Her husband was dead. There was a graduation photograph of her granddaughter in Canada, a law student doing a post-graduate degree in Halifax. Madelaine had planned for us to go to a restaurant on the island of Playa Granma, just up the channel from the Castillo el Moro. But, when we arrived at the Punta Gorda to take the ferry, we were told that it was only for foreign tour groups and that we would have to take the local ferry from a different quay. As it turned out, this was all for the best because we had an excellent meal at La Marina, on the deck above the yacht anchorage, with a view up the channel to the castle. We were entertained by a very good quartet of singers, with guitars and maracas. The bill for George, Madelaine, Kiki and I was CUC45 pesos. I paid another 14 pesos for two CDs of the band, one for Kiki and one for Madelaine

On the way home we called by to visit Dr. Carlos at his modest home in the Tivoli area. His wife and father-in-law were there. Nobody was pleased by our sudden arrival. Lulu was away being tutored by a theory professor, having spent hours already that morning in music class. We were not offered anything to eat or drink. Back at home, George and Made went for a siesta, while I went up onto the roof and sat on one of the rattan chairs with the love-birds for company, reading the introduction to Plato's "Republic." When the light failed at 5.30 p.m., I went down and joined the others for a snack of fruit and ice cream. I packed, ready for my early start tomorrow on my way back to Hong Kong. I off-loaded to George a Hong Kong Seven-A-Side Scottish rugby shirt, which he happily accepted. Kiki came round with his latest invention, a fruit or vegetable stand, the stem of bamboo, while the shelves were of discarded wire guards for fans—he was ingenious. He announced that he needed to take his pills, but needed to eat first. So Madelaine prepared a dish of ham, Zapato and salad. What a strange set up—Kiki came round with things for the house or did odd jobs and was paid with food. When Madelaine and George were away, I supposed that he lived off his mother. His own wife and child lived in Havana.

Kiki had a Spanish passport, since a grandparent had been born in Spain. So he claimed a disability allowance from Spain, and the previous year could afford a trip to see George in Canada at Hatchet Lake.

Sunday 5th December 2010

Humberto took me to the airport, where I was seen off by George — the last time I would see him. It was a long journey, a flight to Havana, a flight to Gatwick, by road to Heathrow through winter snow, finally the flight to Hong Kong. On arrival at the airport, I was greeted by a Christmas Carol, 'Jingle Bells'.

"One Country Two Systems" was alive and well.

ABU DHABI
Jebel Hafeet
Height: 1,240 metres 4,052 feet
Date: 15th March 2014

Judith and I were in Abu Dhabi to attend the World Conference on Tobacco Control. I had organised with Judith and friends to go on a tour before the conference started, to the Al Ain Oasis and to climb the country's highest mountain, Jebel Hafeet. We were driven southwest from Abu Dhabi city on an immaculate three-lane highway with a cruising speed of 120 kilometres per hour, in a Toyota four-wheel-drive seven-seat van; the driver was a Moslem from India, who had lived in the Emirates for 23 years. Thirty kilometres south of Abu Dhabi, we stopped at the Al Wathba camel racing track. It was the last day of the racing season. We saw hundreds of camels, some ridden by Arabs and some by small robot jockeys equipped with whips controlled through radio by their handlers following the race in cars.

Just before entering Al Ain, we stopped at Al Jahili fort, built for Sheik Zayed bin Sultan Al Nahayan to guard the adjacent oasis where he farmed, and for his summer retreat when the heat and humidity at the coast was intense. The fort was square, single-storey with walls 6.5 metres high and a courtyard of 1,300 square metres. It was completed in 1898, with a separate three-storey watch tower. In the 1950s, it was occupied by British forces who enlarged it with a castellated wall which incorporated the tower. The original construction was of sun-baked mud bricks with mud and straw plaster covering. Modern reconstruction included built-in plastic pipes and water cooled for air-conditioning. The exhibition of ancient artifacts in the Sheik Zayed Museum was overshadowed for me by magnificent pictures showing Wilfred Thesiger and his desert explorations with the Bedouin, which had brought him to Al Ain in the 1940s.

Al Ain was part of the slave trade route from East Africa to the Persian Gulf. Slavery was banned by the Sheik only in 1960. In Al Ain, we drove through the centre of a town with clean new buildings and a huge mosque under construction. We visited the original oasis agricultural area where there was an orchard of date palms, oranges, lemons; a man demonstrated the climbing of a date palm. We spent time in an impressive Al Ain National Museum. Judith was particularly taken with the swords. We walked through an immaculately clean and orderly market selling meat, figs and a wide array of fruit and vegetables. We bought dates and a native fruit, the size of a plum with a small stone and a crisp flesh tasting like an apple. Lunch was a splendid buffet at the Hilton Hotel, which proudly boasted that Queen Elizabeth had dined there in 1971.

Out of Al Ain, we motored round a huge government-run

market covering many acres, with covered pens holding hens, ducks, goats, cattle and many hundreds of camels. In the camel area, we saw a calf just dropped by the mother, lying motionless on the ground. Over the next half hour, it gradually struggled to its feet, encouraged by its mother and Bedouin handler. The road up Jebel Hafeet was a magnificent three-lane highway; it wound precipitously up the friable slopes of sandstone and mudstone, to nearly the top where there was a palace for the Sheik. On the ridge further over, we stopped at a car park with a café. The track leading the final last feet to the summit was closed, undergoing repairs—a big disappointment not to be able to claim another summit.

On our return journey, we stopped at the foot of the hill, at the Green Mubazarra area where hot springs gushed out of the ground and the area was green with grass and trees; smart houses of Royal family members dotted the slopes and, further down, there was a water sports complex. It was 5 p.m., so we headed back to our hotel in Abu Dhabi at top speed, getting in at 6.45 p.m.

QATAR
Qurayn Abu al Bawl
Height: 103 metres 338 feet
Date: March 2014

After the conference in Abu Dhabi, Judith and I flew to Qatar, where she had work to do with the Ministry of Health in the capital, Doha. We had one afternoon to conquer the highest natural elevation in the country; many of the hotels in Doha are higher. At 2 p.m., we were waiting in the hotel lobby when we were approached by a man immaculately dressed in Arab style. He was Indian, our driver/guide for the afternoon. We set off through heavy rush-hour traffic, until we were out of the city, when we made fast progress on good roads.

At the intersection of the main road with the road to Kharara, we were met by another guide, a Sri Lankan, also in a Toyota four-wheel-drive, who joined us in our car. The only workers in the country seemed to be non-Arab. He was equipped with an I-Pad with a map reference on it of the highest point in Qatar. We passed Kharara and continued driving along a paved road through flat desert interrupted by rare sand dunes. As indicated by the map reference, we took off over the desert stony shingle towards low ridges on the horizon. We spent the next hour driving from one ridge to another around the point marked on the Guide's I-Pad, checking altitudes on my GPS. The highest ridges were capped with limestone rock. There was no wildlife. We saw one typical Bedouin black woollen tent, and one well. We were back in our hotel at 6 p.m. — another "peak" bagged.

JORDAN
Jebel Umm Adaami
Height: 1,854 metres 29.18 North, 35.62 East
Date: June 2014

Judith and I went to Jordan at the invitation of the King
Hussein Cancer Centre, so that Judith could be a lead speaker
at a conference in Amman on tobacco. We decided that, before
the conference, we would spend a few days sightseeing, and I
would climb the highest mountain. We left Hong Kong in the
evening of June 1st, 2014. We flew Royal Jordanian Airlines to
Bangkok, a journey of two hours 20 minutes; after a 45- minute
refuelling stop, we flew a further nine hours to Amman. At 5
a.m. on June 2nd , we landed at Queen Alia Airport at the new

terminus; it had an elegant high concrete arched roof, sturdily constructed to withstand frequent earthquakes. Jordan lies along the southern edge of the African Great Rift valley. Immigration was straightforward, since we had purchased our visas in Hong Kong.

There to meet us was Joseph the driver assigned to us by Engaging Cultures, the travel agents run by Daniel Robards. Another driver was with him to take two of our pieces of baggage, containing conference clothing and 20 kilos of Tobacco Atlases, to safe keeping at Daniel's while we were touring. At 6 a.m., we set off in an eight-seater Toyota van heading west along the desert highway towards Aqaba; it was a fine carriage-way with two lanes in each direction, a good road surface with "sleeping policeman" to slow traffic at the villages and intersections. The land was dry and stony; the only remnants of the spring greenery were the sage bushes. We passed potash mines and stone quarries. Heavy goods vehicles and car transporters were coming up from Aqaba, Jordan's only port, on the Gulf of Aqaba They were heading for the population-dense areas in the north.

At 8 a.m., we stopped at a government rest house and souvenir shop, close to the turn off to Wadi Rum. We all had drinks and Joseph a cigarette, the first of many on this trip. Alcohol to a Muslim is *haram*, forbidden, because it is unlawful to harm one's own body; cigarettes are more harmful but not always *haram* – it all depends whether or not your imam is a smoker. The road to Wadi Rum had a single lane each way, running alongside the old railway; it was on flat land at the base of a series of rock buttresses of sandstone sculptured by wind and rain. The railway was the one that Lawrence of Arabia spent his time blowing up in 1918-1919 in his campaign against the Ottoman empire. On the left. "The Seven Pillars of Wisdom", a fluted buttress of rock rearing out of the sand, marked the entrance to Wadi Rum itself. On the

right reared Jebel Rum, the second highest mountain in Jordan and a favourite site for rock climbers.

At 9 a.m., we stopped at the Park entrance to register. There we met our Bedouin guide, Mosalem (Saleem), who helped us transfer our goods to the back of his beaten-up four-wheel-drive. We said farewell to Joseph and arranged to meet him at the same time the next day. He was going to drive to Aqaba to spend the day with friends. Mosalem was about 45, bearded and wearing the traditional long white robe, *thaub*, and the red and white headdress, *mendeel*, with black cords to hold it on the head, *mirreers*. Later we discovered that his father had been the Bedouin who, with British adventurers like Tony Howard, promoted the establishment of the Wadi Rum National Park. Mosalem had two wives and eight children. Education in Jordan was free.

The short track of asphalt road lasted only until the end of Wadi Rum village. We drove cross country on the largely flat, firm desert with brown remnants of the spring grass and green sage bushes. A few camels were grazing on the meagre fodder.

We stopped in a patch of shade behind a rock buttress for Mosalem to say his morning prayers, replace a van fuse, and have a smoke. Another Bedouin, a friend of his, drove up in another four-wheel-drive; he was searching for his herd of camels that had strayed from Saudi Arabia across the border a few miles away. At 9.50 a.m., we arrived at the foot of Jebel Umm Adaami, the highest mountain in Jordan at 1,860 metres; it is 500 metres higher than Ben Nevis, the highest mountain in the British Isles. However, the vertical climb difference from the base was only 364 metres. Two climbers and their guide finished their descent as we arrived, young Chinese men from Hong Kong—what a small world. They were the only other party we saw all day.

At 10.20 a.m., Mosalem and I started climbing; we left Judith behind at her request. She judged that her knees would not do well on the steep rocky terrain. The first part was a scramble, edging up slabs of sandstone; one third of the way up, there was a more level sandy area with hardy flowers in bloom, thistles even. Further up, the vague, rocky track wound up a shoulder of the mountain to the summit ridge, a jumble of hard rock boulders, difficult to walk over. The hardness of the rocks was the reason the mountain had not been worn away like other mountains composed of sandstone.

The summit view was worth it—miles of desert in every direction, studded with rock outcrops rising to slightly less than Jebel Umm Adaami's height. We could see over the border to Saudi Arabia. We paused at the summit for some time for me to take pictures, and for Mosalem to enjoy the experience. We shared food, a couple of oranges and energy bars. The orange peel, Mosalem advised, would be appreciated by the mice living below in the rock crevasses. I photographed one lizard about a foot long that did not stir at my approach; it was belly-bloated from a recent very large meal. By the end of our 24 hours together,

I was convinced that Mosalem had a profound love of his land and was happy to share it with others. I rejoiced that I had scaled another summit to add to my collection.

Conscious that I had estimated to Judith three hours for the total climb, we started down the mountain, reaching "base camp" exactly on time. The climb had taken 27 hours of non-stop travel, calculated from the time I left the house in Hong Kong. I had found the climb not at all difficult, having prepared myself by hiking on the hills in Sai Kung in temperatures up to 35C. I had read that summer temperatures in Jordan went up to 40C; but, on the day, I climbed the temperature was a delightful 25C.

Back in the four-wheel-drive, Mosalem took us in a different direction from our approach route, past more fantastic rock formations, to a shaded area where he stopped to make lunch. He laid out rattan mats on which we could recline; but, to start with, we were more interested in photographing the curious rock sculptures and in gathering the dried-out sage bush roots for his fire. He made two fires, one that burnt over foil-wrapped sweet potatoes and a second one on which he placed a blackened teapot to provide welcome cups of hot sweet tea. He cut up nuts and tomatoes into a saucepan, and added a can of some kind of bean. Together with loaves of Jordanian flat-bread, this made for a wonderfully tasty meal.

Then it was time for us to have a siesta and for Mosalem to say his prayers. Later, driving on slowly, we stopped at a sand-dune, wind-blown ripples on it unbroken until we arrived. Later we stopped at another spot where I amused myself by trying to identify the animal tracks in the sand. Most numerous were the lizard tracks, each bush having a large hole under it—a lizard den. A walking lizard leaves a sinuous trail from its tail dragging on the sand; the running lizard has its tail way off the ground so there are only widely spaced footprints. Other prints Saleem helped me to identify were those of jerboa or Jerbil jumping mice, of a fox and cub, a hedgehog, and crows. At night, the desert was clearly a hive of activity.

At sunset, we paused at a good viewing point; there was not a cloud in the sky, so the sun sank behind a ridge with only a brief golden glow. We did not have to go much further to reach our Bedouin camp, consisting of two rows of square tents, black and grey from the goat and sheep wool from which they were made. The tent floors were raised off the sand and there were proper metal frame beds and heavy blankets. One larger tent was the dining and socialising area, with carpets on the floor and benches round the sides; a shisha or hubble-bubble smoking apparatus was available. Tanks of water were wedged onto the cliff wall nearby supplying water to two toilets cum showers. Electric lighting appeared very briefly, so we had to make use of our torches. Dinner was a large dish of rice with beans, olives, chicken and lamb, flat bread, with spoons provided.

Traditionally, you used your right hand to eat the food and accepted the compliment of the goat's eye when offered. I was happy to use the spoon provided and select my own meat. We were in bed by 9 p.m. — a long day.

In North Africa, I enjoyed the totally different Arabic communities, Berber hospitality, the rocky climbs in Morocco and Jordan and the contrast of motorised trips in the Gulf States. I saw the dramatic difference that oil wealth has made to formerly desert states.

EPILOGUE

Since the Jordan expedition in 2014, I had done a lot of travelling with the family but attempted no new country peaks. My climb again on Ma On Shan in January 2019 was made to assess my fitness for further climbs having had a transient ischaemic attack (TIA) four years earlier which had left me with some unsteadiness; and I was still having episodes of atrial fibrillation.

Ma On Shan
Height: 702 m 2,303 ft
Date: January 2019

This peak is one of the 15 mountains over 2,000 feet in Hong Kong. Tai Mo Shan at 957 metres and Sunset Peak on Lantau Island at 869 metres are the only two over 3,000 feet. I have climbed Ma On Shan a number of times. Usually, I walked from the road end at the abandoned village of Wong Chuk Yeung; once, starting from the south coast of Sai Kung peninsula at Sha Ha Beach.

When I first visited Wong Chuk Yeung 40 years before, it was inhabited, an active farming community since 1660 in a valley hidden in the mountains, far from marauding pirates. It had its own school and well-water and concrete trails financed by

the Kadoorie Agricultural Association. In later years, the last, elderly villagers had left. The fields were barricaded off by a developer who had bought the land, a recurring pattern in the New Territories.

The trail to the summit skirted the old village, joined the Maclehose trail and climbed up the side of the mountain through forests. It emerged to traverse a narrow ridge, then rose steeply up to the shoulder of the mountain, at 1,800 feet. At this point, the Maclehose Trail continued west along the ridge leading to Buffalo Hill. The summit route was marked by a notice warning of danger ahead. There I rested, ate and drank.

The last part of the climb required scrambling over steep rocky terrain. The narrow path led over a ridge, with cliffs falling away on either side. The summit was rounded, marked by a Trig Point. The views made the climb worth-while, to the south over Sai Kung Peninsula, and north over the valley containing abandoned iron mines, and further north and east over Shatin Valley. An overgrown trail led north to The Hunch

Back mountains, overlooking Shatin Valley.

On the way down to Wong Chuk Yuen on very tired legs, I walked slowly and carefully to avoid a fall, and was hugely relieved to reach my car. It was great to achieve the summit, but the effort involved had taken away the pleasure. This may have been the last time I do this climb.

Now aged 87, I can look back on 30 years during which I have enjoyed all that I accomplished in mountain trekking, experienced the delights of many countries, and met wonderful people. The memories will live on. If these accounts inspire others to take to the hills, I will be delighted.

A LOVE OF MOUNTAINS

About The Author

Dr. John Mackay was born in Scotland, the second son of his father, an officer in the Indian army, and his mother, both from Moray in Scotland. During World War II he and the family were in India. Ever since he has loved to travel. Back in Scotland after the war he went to a public school, did National Service in the RAF, and entered Edinburgh University qualifying as a doctor in 1961. During University years, his thirst for adventure took him on hitch-hiking trips in Europe and across North America. As a doctor, he chose to do two years of further training in Nassau in the Bahamas and in Britain, before settling in Hong Kong, for the first thirty years with a private group practice. He married Judith, a newly qualified doctor in 1967; they have two sons and three grandchildren. Judith has built an international career as an advocate for a tobacco-free world. In the last thirty years, he has travelled extensively with the goal of climbing the highest point in each country visited.